Economy and settlement
in Neolithic and Early Bronze Age
Britain and Europe

Economy and settlement in Neolithic and Early Bronze Age Britain and Europe

Papers delivered at a Conference held in
the University of Leicester, December 1969
edited by D. D. A. SIMPSON

Leicester University Press   1971

First published in 1971 by Leicester University Press
Distributed in North America by Humanities Press Inc., New York

Copyright © Leicester University Press, 1971

Designed by Arthur Lockwood

Set in Monotype Plantin 110
Printed in Great Britain by Western Printing Services Ltd, Bristol

ISBN 0 7185 1094 1

301.294 SIM

Contents

6   List of line illustrations

8   List of plates

9   Abbreviations

11   Notes on the environment of early farming communities in Britain
J. G. EVANS

27   Habitat change on the calcareous soils of Britain:
the impact of Neolithic man
J. G. EVANS

75   Diet, economy and biosocial change in late prehistoric Europe
DON BROTHWELL

89   Causewayed enclosures
I. F. SMITH

113   Settlements in later Neolithic Britain
I. J. McINNES

131   Beaker houses and settlements in Britain
D. D. A. SIMPSON

153   Early prehistoric agriculture in Western Europe:
some archaeological evidence
P. J. FOWLER

183   Index

Line illustrations

1. Section of a tufa deposit at Cherhill, Wiltshire 14
2. Distribution of Neolithic barrows in Yorkshire 21
3. Location map 28–9
4. Ascott-under-Wychwood: buried subsoil 30
5. Ascott-under-Wychwood: snail histogram 32–3
6. Ascott-under-Wychwood: subsoil hollow, plan 36
7. Ascott-under-Wychwood: subsoil hollow, section 37
8. South Street: sections 42
9. South Street: snail histogram 44–5
10. South Street: plough marks 47
11. Northton: land-snail histogram 54–5
12. Northton: relative abundance of marine molluscs 60–1
13. Distribution map of excavated causewayed enclosures 91
14. Hembury: plan 93
15. Hembury: sections 99
16. Principal sites referred to in the text 114
17. Plans of houses at Mount Pleasant and Ronaldsway 116
18. Plans of houses at Skara Brae and Ness of Gruting 117
19. Plans of settlements at Honington and Playden 121
20. Plans of Streatley 125
21. Plans of enclosures at Fengate and Sonning 127
22. Principal sites referred to in the text 133
23. Plans of houses at Lough Gur, Downpatrick, Gwithian and Beacon Hill 134
24. Plans of houses at Belle Tout, Northton and Woodhead 137
25. Plans of settlements at Swarkeston and Easton Down 139
26. Plans of house at Rinyo and the 'Benie Hoose' 142
27. Plans of Neolithic hut at Waulud's Bank and mortuary houses, Beaulieu 144
28. Plan and elevation of beehive hut, Harris, and plan of black house, Skye 146–7
29. Plans and reconstruction of houses on the Goldberg 149

30. Plans of structures at Penha Verde and Oltingen   150
31. Intensity of agriculture in Europe   155
32. Rock engravings from Val Camonica and South Sweden   156
33. Reconstruction of crook-ard with stone share   161
34. Map of criss-cross plough-marks in England   164
35. Plans of barrows and Celtic field lynchets   172
36. Theoretical method of Celtic field system layout   176
37. Elementary analysis of Celtic field systems to show block layout   177

Plates

between pp. 104–5

1.   Buried soil at Chinnor
2a.   Ascott-under-Wychwood: buried soil
2b.   South Street: buried soil
3a.   Beckhampton Road: section
3b.   Kilham: buried soil
4.   Northton: section
5a–d.   Low and high power views of a cinder (?burnt bread) and control sample
6.   Aerial photograph: Windmill Hill
7.   Aerial photograph: Hambledon Hill
8.   Aerial photograph: Ogbourne Maizey

Abbreviations

Ant. J.	*Antiquaries Journal*
Arch.	*Archaeologia*
Arch. J.	*Archaeological Journal*
Procs Camb. Ant. Soc.	*Proceedings of the Cambridge Antiquarian Society*
Procs Hants. Field Club	*Proceedings of the Hampshire Field Club*
P.P.S.	*Proceedings of the Prehistoric Society*
P.R.I.A.	*Proceedings of the Royal Irish Academy*
P.S.A.S.	*Proceedings of the Society of Antiquaries of Scotland*
Révue Arch.	*Révue Archaeologique*
S.A.C.	*Surrey Archaeological Collections*
Trans. Bristol & Glos. Arch. Soc.	*Transactions of the Bristol & Gloucestershire Archaeological Society*
W.A.M.	*Wiltshire Archaeological Magazine*
Y.A.J.	*Yorkshire Archaeological Journal*

Notes and references are printed at the end of each article. The pages on which the notes appear are given, in diamond brackets, on the headline to each text page.

Notes on the environment of early farming communities in Britain

J. G. EVANS

These notes are offered as a series of ideas – nothing more – about the environment of Britain in the third and fourth millennia B.C. Certain aspects of the environment which may have been of interest to early farming communities, particularly pioneer groups, where they settled and what they did with the land, are discussed. Pollen analysis has yielded much valuable information about vegetational changes which preceded and accompanied settlement. But there is still a big gap in our knowledge regarding the effect of Neolithic man on the forest, the size of his clearances and the methods employed by him to grow cereal crops. A possible and certainly interesting approach to these problems is the study of buried soils and their contained biological indicators.

The level of the sea and the littoral habitat

The level of the sea governs the distribution of land, the form of the coast-line (harbours, strands, etc.), the existence of islands and land bridges and the strength of currents and tides.[1] The main Post-glacial rise of the sea-level terminated around 4500 B.C., and when the first groups of farmers began to colonize Britain there is little question of there being a land bridge with the Continent, or between Great Britain and Ireland. Reservations have been expressed about this,[2] and Corcoran has stressed the possibility of a marshland link with the Continent across the southern part of the North Sea during the third millennium. Even if this were so, however, "a narrower channel or large areas of marshy foreshore do not presuppose easier passages; they may have involved furious tidal races and fickle landings."[3]

During the rise of sea-level (*c.* 6000 to 4000 B.C.) the sea penetrated inland in many low-lying areas depositing thick beds of clay; for instance in the East Anglian fens, the Somerset Levels,[4] Morecambe Bay and the Firth of Forth

(Carse Clay). Subsequent emergence resulted in the formation of extensive reed swamps in these areas,[5] which may have attracted man by their abundance of grasses at a time before forest clearance and the development of terrestrial grass-lands had got under way (reed thatch anyway is more durable than straw thatch), and by their wealth of game. The formation of drowned river-valleys took place at about the same time, creating natural harbours and navigable routes inland.

Later marine transgression resulted in the submergence of Neolithic land-surfaces. The unlocated source of Group I axes in Cornwall[6] and presumed sites along the Continental littoral and immediate hinterland from which early Neo-lithic farmers set sail for Britain[7] are thought to have been lost in this way. Other sites were buried beneath thick deposits of clay, for instance at Peacock's Farm in the Cambridgeshire Fens (Buttery Clay),[8] and the Lyonesse surface in Essex at Clacton and Walton-on-the-Naze (*Scrobicularia* Clay).[9] Along rivers, the rising water-table converted well-drained arable into damp pasture and swamp; and occupation sites were buried beneath layers of alluvium and peat as happened at Ebbsfleet in Kent.[10]

Godwin[11] and Jelgersma[12] have discussed the interpretation of coastal sedi-ments of Post-glacial age. Alternating beds of peat and marine clay reflect respectively marine regressions and transgressions though such changes could reflect local changes in the form of the coast-line rather than absolute changes of sea-level. Smith has suggested on archaeological grounds that the deposition of the Fen Clay in East Anglia was not synchronous with the submergence of the Lyonesse surface in Essex.[13]

In northern Britain, in the area of isostatic recovery, raised beaches of Late- and Post-glacial age are a characteristic feature of the coastal fringe. The '25-foot beach' is classically associated with Neolithic settlement and its value as a tract of fertile land is discussed below. Donner[14] has urged that the term '25-foot beach' be replaced by the term 'Main Post-glacial Shoreline' because "this shoreline may be found at heights of over forty feet in the zone of maximum isostatic recovery and below sea-level elsewhere. In addition there is probably more than one beach in this height range."[15] The age of the transgression which formed the beach, and during which the carse clays were deposited, is determined to 6000 – 4000 B.C.;[16] its emergence took place between 5000 and 3000 B.C.

Thus the time interval between the emergence of the shoreline and its settle-ment by farming communities could be more than 2,000 years but in some inst-ances may have been much less. For instance Scott, with reference to the west coast of Kintyre, suggests that the extensive 25-foot raised beach did not exist for the earliest Neolithic colonists.[17] The development of a soil sufficiently mature to support cultivation or grazing would depend on local circumstances such as time of emergence and constitution of the beach material; Dimbleby[18] suggests a period of 2000 to 4000 years for the maturation of a brown-earth soil. Nor is it certain what kind of vegetation would have been growing on ancient beach deposits. The investigation of buried soils and radiocarbon dates from these are needed from Neolithic sites on the Main Post-glacial Shoreline. Each site must clearly be treated on its own merits and generalizations about soil types and their fertility, and the prevailing vegetation cover, cannot be made without critical individual investigations.

The importance of the littoral habitat to primitive man has frequently been discussed[19] and the idea that a strand-looping existence may be adopted as an easy alternative by people forced for one reason or another to abandon their normal way of life is well known. For instance, Clark[20] suggests that "a diet in which shell-fish are a mainstay is normally associated with a low level of culture". To early farmers settling in a forested land, an economy based partly on shell-fish may have been attractive, at least for a few seasons while the better potentialities of their new environment were being learnt, and clearings made. The coastal fringe can be visualized as a ribbon of open land with an abundant food supply in the form of a variety of shell-fish, and with ancient beaches left high and dry by the retreating sea; of the latter, the younger might have carried a vegetation cover of open woodland, scrub or even grassland depending on how long they had been uplifted from the sea, while the older beaches probably supported mature and fertile soils and a vegetation of high forest. Such a variety of habitats of different ages each providing a different variety of exploitable food or raw material may have been particularly appealing to pioneer farming communities.

The fertile machair, calcareous blown sand, of the Outer Hebrides may have been an added inducement to littoral settlement in those islands, though in at least one case, Northton in South Harris, the earliest settlement was prior to the onset of machair formation,[21] and as pointed out in the section on soils (see p. 22), settlement in the Outer Hebrides in the Neolithic period may have been geared to pastoral rather than arable farming. In view of this and of what has been said above about settlement in relationship to raised beaches, we must be wary in suggesting a positive relationship between a particular deposit of drift or soil and a farming community simply because the two may occur in close proximity. Actual use of a particular soil type or a significant correlation between settlement and soil type must be demonstrated.

Climate

The Neolithic and Early Bronze Age periods fall in the later part of the Climatic Optimum when the mean annual temperature of Britain was 2 to 3°C higher than today. The evidence for the Climatic Optimum is largely biological, depending on the northward spread beyond their present-day limits of certain cold-susceptible plant and animal species.[22]

During the Boreal and Atlantic periods short episodes of forest recession occurred, some of which may be of climatic origin.[23] One, the Piora Oscillation, comes at the end of the Atlantic period (*c.* 3400 to 3000 B.C.), and although not yet recognized in Britain, certainly warrants consideration in view of its co-incidence with the arrival of farming communities. Forest recession, recognized in Yorkshire during the Atlantic period, has been attributed to climate by Walker.[24] Other workers, notably Dimbleby,[25] are in favour of an anthropogenic origin for such episodes (see p. 17).

The Atlantic period is characterized by an increased wetness following a dry phase at the end of the Boreal. There was a rise of lake levels, renewed and wide-spread growth of blanket bog and a sharp rise, in the pollen diagrams, of alder.[26] In calcareous regions, as a result of the rising water table, extensive deposits of tufa formed. Where artifacts are stratified beneath or within tufa these are of Meso-lithic type,[27] and faunal evidence suggests an Atlantic age for the main period of tufa formation.[28] At Blashenwell in Dorset there is a radiocarbon date of 4490 ± 150 B.C. from near the middle of the tufa deposit[29] and at Cherhill, Wilts., one of 5280 ± 140 B.C. for a charcoal lens at the base of the tufa (fig. 1).[30] Deposits of tufa today frequently comprise slight terraces above the flood-plains of rivers and streams. They are no longer actively accumulating and at Cherhill a radiocarbon date from a Neolithic ditch cut into the tufa deposit of *c.* 2700 B.C. suggests that tufa formation may be confined to the Atlantic period as Kerney suggests (fig. 1).

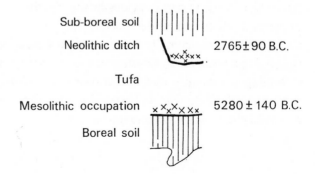

Figure 1. Section of a tufa
deposit at Cherhill, Wiltshire.

Tufa probably provides good agricultural land, since it is generally friable, lime-rich and close to water but at the same time above the level of the active flood-plain. Thus by *c.* 2000 B.C. the surface of the tufa at Cherhill had become sufficiently dry to be cultivated, as was attested by the presence there of a late Neolithic cultivation soil, in the upper levels of a ditch.

So much then for the Atlantic period. Its characterization by Blytt and Sernander as an episode of warm wet climate seems to have stood the test of time, even though we may have to accept a series of small-scale climatic oscillations within that period, some of which anyway may eventually prove to be anthropogenic. But what of the Sub-boreal? There is no clear evidence in peat-bog stratigraphy or in the pollen record for a xerothermic period, corresponding to the Sub-boreal, in Britain,[31] though a case may still be made for a trend towards continentality in the first half of the Sub-boreal in Europe as a whole. The marked change to open vegetation around 3000 B.C. and particularly during the Bronze Age[32] is generally felt to be a reflection of forest clearance by farming communities for the purpose of creating agricultural land or pasture. The same applies to changes in the land-snail fauna and perhaps to certain pedological changes too.

For instance, the silty texture of certain Bronze Age soils and deposits, allegedly wind-sorted, e.g. in the Y-holes of Stonehenge and the ditch of the Nutbane long barrow, has given rise to the idea of a phase of dry climate at some time during the Bronze Age,[33] the argument being briefly as follows. "For wind to be an important agency in filling artificial pits and ditches requires a climate at least seasonally dry and a cover of only sparse vegetation, so that bare soil is exposed to wind-erosion. These conditions do not ever obtain at the present day, but it appears as if they did so during at least part of the Bronze Age." However, the destruction of the ground-layer vegetation and exposure of the soil to the elements could have been caused by over-grazing or by cultivation and is unlikely to have been caused by a climatic shift to drier conditions alone. Furthermore, it has recently been shown in Yorkshire that, given suitable meteorological conditions, massive wind erosion and deposition of sediments can take place today in a few months of one year;[34] in this particular case the conditions were a below-average rainfall, an above-average temperature and a very high frequency of gale-force winds. The East Anglian fens are also an area susceptible to massive wind erosion as was demonstrated in the Spring of 1968.[35]

Molluscan evidence from the Nutbane silt[36] points to a moist and shaded micro-habitat, not one markedly dry and open. Cornwall[37] suggests therefore that the silt component of the deposit may be of Cretaceous origin, being the insoluble residue of the Chalk, incorporated into the Chalk in Cretaceous times. Perrin however[38] has shown that the silty fraction of chalk soils is probably drift-derived, and the recognition of superficial features of periglacial origin filled with material of silty texture and preserved beneath Neolithic and Bronze Age soils[39] seems to support this conclusion.

A great deal more work needs to be done on these silty deposits before their true origin is ascertained. One is all the more wary of interpreting them in terms of a dry climate when neither the pollen record nor peat-bog stratigraphy give any clear indication that such conditions existed.

The climatic deterioration is thought to have taken place over a long period of time in a series of stages rather than as a single, sudden worsening. This at any rate is the impression obtained from the study of recurrence horizons in raised bogs. One of the earliest of these was at *c.* 3400 B.C. with others, of perhaps increasing intensity, at 2300, 1200 and 600 B.C., the latter marking the zone VIIb/VIII boundary.[40] Prehistoric wooden trackways in the Somerset Levels were built at various stages since 3000 B.C. in an attempt to keep open communications in a low-lying area subjected, in the face of a deteriorating climate, to successive phases of renewed growth of blanket bog.[41] But it is well to remember that climatic changes reflected in bog stratigraphy need not be reflected, nor indeed manifested, in downland areas as well. There is, for instance, no clear evidence that during the Sub-boreal period the water-table was higher on the Chalk than today, or that springs emerged higher up valleys; in fact there is positive evidence that this was not the case.[42]

Seddon[43] has emphasized the cyclical nature of Post-glacial climate as a whole, suggesting a periodicity of between 500 and 1000 years; "periodic climate change on this scale can now be recognized as one of the constant features of the environment common to both prehistoric and historic periods." This is a clear warning against the indiscriminate application of rigid climatic values appreciable only in the course of ages.

Vegetation

The dominant vegetation type in Britain during the Atlantic period was forest. Oak, elm, lime, alder, hazel and birch were the main tree species, with birch more common in the north and west and pine an important element in the eastern Scottish highlands. In Ireland and much of Scotland there was no lime. Alder grew predominantly, though not exclusively, in wet places.[44]

Chalk and limestone downland areas and other extensive tracts of countryside now characteristically treeless, such as moors and heaths, were once forested.

This has been shown by pollen analysis of buried soils[45] and peat and lake sediments[46] in acid areas and by land-snail analysis of the calcareous soils of chalk, limestone and wind-blown shell sand.[47] On the Chalk, where the evidence of former forest is largely indirect, we can only guess at the character of the natural vegetation. Elm and lime, generally found on base-rich soils, are likely to have been common; and birch, ash, yew and juniper probably flourished locally. Oak and hawthorn-type charcoals are frequent on Neolithic sites and pollen analysis of chalk soils[48] and of organic deposits adjacent to the Chalk escarpment in Kent[49] have shown all the major forest trees to have been present, with hazel particularly abundant. Beech, though present in the third millennium, did not become widespread until the Iron Age.

During the Atlantic period, tree belts were some hundreds of feet higher in the mountains of Europe than now, and also extended further north and east.[50] The loess lands of Central Europe were forested – the "steppenheide" theory has long been discarded – and the now-bare limestone regions of the Mediterranean possibly also. Open vegetation was restricted to montane regions – in Britain above c. 2,500ft – and to areas too unstable or otherwise unsuitable for the growth of trees, such as cliffs, active screes, reed swamps, growing bogs, river flood-plains and gravel banks and a variety of littoral habitats – shingle bars, sand-dunes and so on. Grassland, so familiar a part of the British scene today, probably did not exist, apart from the high-montane type.[51]

Forest recession during the Atlantic period

Variation of the vegetation with time during the Atlantic period is more widely recognized now than formerly.[52] No doubt, as has been discussed above, a part of this variation is due to climatic changes. Thus soil horizons, indicating a temporary drying out of the environment and unlikely to have been caused by man, occur in deposits of tufa. Dimbleby[53] suggested that pre-agricultural communities may have been responsible for episodes of forest recession at Oakhanger in Hampshire and at sites in the North York Moors. Fire was suggested as the main agent in the destruction of the forest, which in some cases was followed by leaching and loss of soil structure, preventing regeneration of the climax forest. Mesolithic forest clearance on Dartmoor has been suggested by Simmons[54] and the evidence from Britain as a whole has been discussed by Simmons[55] and Smith.[56] Two types of effect have been suggested, one in which fire is used and where birch is a conspicuous member of the regenerating forest, the other where trees are felled individually with axes and in which the regenerating forest shows little or no difference from its original state. The former generally takes place in upland situations, while the latter seems more characteristic of lowlying places.

No examples are known from chalk or limestone sites with the possible exception of Ascott-under-Wychwood discussed in this volume.[57] A number of Neolithic sites are known however from which Mesolithic artifacts have been recovered and this may not be without significance here.

Harris[58] has discussed "marginal transition zones or ecotones between major ecosystems, especially forest- and woodland-edge situations" as providing suitable environments for the invention of agriculture, and in the same way, ecotones may have been favoured by early agricultural settlers in Britain in providing "optimum access to the most assured and variable supply of wild plants and animals", an important consideration in the first few seasons of settlement. The littoral environment has been suggested as meeting a need of this kind (see p. 20) and the same applies to the forest-river ecotone. Nor should the communicational and possible defensive attributes of such situations be overlooked. To early farmers, open land was at a premium, and may have been settled in the short-term despite such disadvantages as poor soils, exposure and distance from water, prior to permanent settlement in areas more suitable to their economy and way of life. For instance the establishment of a cereal crop in the very first season of settlement, if only to provide seed-corn, would be essential, unless of course a community were entirely dependent on stock-raising. Thus in studying the settlement pattern of these early communities it is areas which were open country in the fourth millennium which should perhaps be examined, particularly when the presence of former hunter-gatherer communities is suspected. For the activities of these savages may have brought about the irreversible destruction of small and large areas of forest, and, as a side effect set in motion the processes which led to the degradation of our heathland soils.[59] There may have been no cultural link between the two kinds of community, but an environmental link cannot always be excluded.

A note on the interpretation of the vegetational changes
at the Atlantic – Sub-boreal transition

The causes of the vegetational changes which took place around 3000 B.C. are not clear.[60] The cause of the *elm decline* for instance has not been satisfactorily explained, and the evidence for its being anthropogenic, while suggestive, is not totally conclusive. The difficulty is in distinguishing between climatic, natural-environmental and anthropogenic influences. The same applies to the causes of forest clearance. Waateringe[61] has warned against the use of "cultural pollen grains" as evidence of cultivation or any form of human interference with the environment. "The appearance of pollen grains of *Plantago maior* and *P. lanceolata* before and contemporary with the elm decline is, unless accompanied by pollen of Cerialia and archaeological material, not necessarily an indication of the presence of Neolithic man".

This is of some importance in view of what has been said above about the environment of ecotones. Waateringe states that "these contact zones (ecotones), were the natural pastures of wild grazing animals . . . available only along the seacoast and in river valleys, where the development of forest was hindered by unstable milieu factors"; "The same sort of milieu and a closely related vegetation can appear from natural causes as from trampling and grazing by man and his livestock." As we have suggested that it is in such zones that the earliest traces of farming communities may be found, the need for caution in interpreting the evidence is considerable. This is perhaps a suitable point at which to stress once again the need for the study of habitation sites and buried soil profiles.

Soils

In the past, as today, soil type was a major factor in determining the pattern and intensity of human settlement and the kind of land-use practised: "there is no doubt that the earliest farmers preferred the more pervious soils",[62] and in Central Europe there is close correspondence between the areas of Danubian settlement and loess soils.[63] In Britain, Neolithic man tended to settle the lighter soils such as those of the Chalk, the Oolite and Carboniferous limestones, glacio-fluvial gravels, river-terraces, ancient sea-beaches and blown sand. Smith[64] has suggested that settlement on the lighter soils in the south and east of Britain during the third millennium was geared to arable farming as shown by the distribution of grain-storage pits. Elsewhere soils are heavier or otherwise unsuitable for arable farming and the climate, particularly in the west, generally damper; in these areas storage pits are rare, though not entirely absent. Corcoran[65] in discussing the siting of Cotswold-Severn tombs suggests "a preference on the part of their builders for light, easily drained soils which, under natural conditions, would have supported woodland and undergrowth capable of clearance by Neolithic tools and techniques."

At Pitnacree in Perthshire a Neolithic soil beneath a round barrow is thought to have been cultivated prior to 2800 B.C.[66] A series of barrows along the Tay valley of possibly equivalent age are sited at low levels, on the lower terraces of the river, and may reflect the establishment there of agricultural settlers early in the third millennium.

The raised beaches around the northern coasts of Britain provide fertile and easily tillable soils in areas otherwise capped by boulder clay. "Such alluvial stretches, though doubtless far from treeless, would be at least lighter and on the whole better drained and hence more amenable to cultivation than the boulder clays and disintegration products capping the old metamorphic and eruptive rocks of the west."[67] Of Kintyre, Scott writes: "fertile soils suitable for arable cultivation are confined to alluvial gravels in the glens and to raised beaches . . . It appears likely that such raised beaches, in a landscape not otherwise responsive to primitive methods of tillage, proved attractive to Neolithic colonists".[68] Henshall, on the other hand, has suggested that in north-east Scotland of the lighter soils, the more fertile would be chosen, and raised beach deposits were thus avoided when suitable and more fertile alternatives were available.[69]

In east Yorkshire, Neolithic burial mounds and storage pits are, with one or two exceptions, restricted to the base-rich soils of the Wolds, on the south side of the Vale of Pickering and the Corallian limestone to the north (fig. 2). The pattern of Beaker settlement, if that is what burial mounds reflect, is much the same. There is an interesting extension of this pattern in two directions, one into the Vale of Pickering, where there are several finds of stone axes, perhaps associated with tree-felling and woodworking activities, the other on to the generally acidic soils of the moors beyond the Corallian belt, where numerous arrowheads have been found suggesting that here were the hunting grounds of these early agricultural communities. It was not until the Bronze Age that farming took place on the moors.[70]

As Clark pointed out in 1952, the preference of Neolithic man for light soils relates to properties of the soils themselves such as their ease of tillage or suitability for pasture, rather than to characteristics of their natural vegetation. (This applies to the structure of the vegetation, not its detailed species composition, for it should not be forgotten that lime and elm, both trees possibly used preferentially by Neolithic man, are characteristic species of base-rich soils.) "The idea that soils like the loess of Central Europe or the 'Breckland' of East Anglia were occupied by neolithic man because they were 'open' or free from forest can no longer be entertained in view of what pollen analysts have been able to learn about the former vegetation of these and similar territories. The all pervasiveness of the post-glacial forest in temperate Europe has already been sufficiently stressed."[71]

The avoidance of acidic sandy soils such as those of the Yorkshire Moors and the Weald of Kent and Surrey may thus relate to their poor base status, low fertility and high susceptibility to erosion through leaching and loss of structure

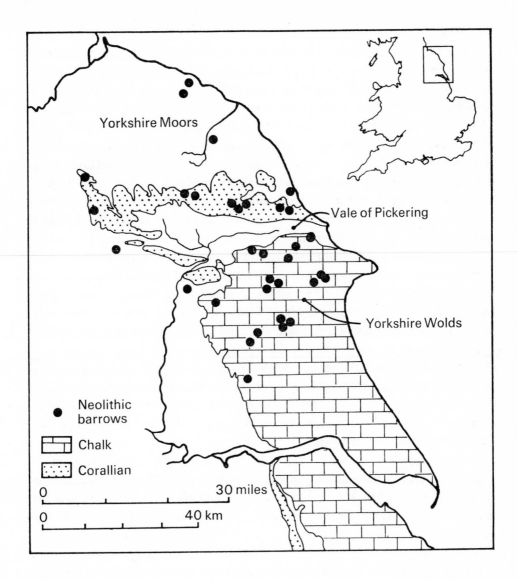

Figure 2. Distribution map of Neolithic barrows in east Yorkshire in relation to soil type. Compiled from various sources.

once cleared of forest and then cultivated or grazed. On level ground human interference might precipitate the formation of bog. Similarly, Henshall has indicated that early farmers avoided beach deposits, when more fertile but equally light soils were available. Such selection implies that Neolithic man had a considerable knowledge of his environment for while today podsolic, these soils may, prior to forest clearance and cultivation, have been less base-deficient and of brown-earth type.[72] When it is remembered too that some areas of the York-shire Wolds may also have supported brown-earth soils,[73] the selection of the latter is even more remarkable. Selection was perhaps made on the species composition of the forest rather than through a direct examination of the soil, though so sensitive to soil types does Neolithic man appear to have been that he may well have dug the occasional pit to examine the soil profile. Corcoran's explanation of the avoidance of the Mendips by Cotswold-Severn tomb builders implies similar acute powers of observation of vegetation or soil types.[74]

Tomb distribution in parts of Scotland indicates avoidance of the richer, heavier soils, cairns being sited often close to the upper limit of present-day arable, a preference being shown for upland, less fertile and even marginal land.[75] The distribution is said to relate to the type of vegetation supported by the soil, as much as to the soil type *per se*, the heavier more fertile soils supporting denser and less-easily cleared forest. The evidence for a difference in forest type between that of the heavier and that of the lighter soils is not however clear, either in this case or elsewhere in Britain where such differences have been invoked to explain presence or absence of settlement.

In contrast, some Neolithic sites are on heavy soils or soils with impeded drainage, as Grimes pointed out in the case of Anglesey.[76] The earliest occupation horizon at the machair site of Northton in the Outer Hebrides is on boulder clay. None of the large collection of sherds from the occupation horizons of this site, contemporary with the deposition of wind-blown sand or on boulder clay, and associated with a phase of forest clearance, had a single grain impression. Clearance was evidently for pasture, not arable and it has been pointed out to me[77] how the distribution of Neolithic cairns in the Hebrides is in pasture land, not on the fertile machair. Even on the lighter soils, clearance may have been for pasture as suggested by Corcoran in the case of the Cotswold-Severn tomb builders on the Oolite soils of the Cotswolds.[78]

Wooldridge and Linton[79] drew attention to the existence of a group of soils in south-east England intermediate between heavy clay soils and porous soils and which were of largely loessic origin. These they suggested were ideally suited to early settlement, being neither too porous nor of impeded drainage and thus giving optimum conditions for agriculture or pasturage. The loessic element too would provide a richer suite of weatherable minerals than found in a purer geological substratum. The recognition that tracts of chalk soils comprise a similar element is of significance here.[80] Grimes, writing of Anglesey, concludes that "the influence of these light-medium soils in early settlement has at all times been dominant and continuous".

Changes of soil type

Since the beginnings of agriculture in Britain there have been several changes of soil type caused by man; some may be of even greater antiquity, reflecting the activities of hunter-gatherer communities. Yet others are due to natural phenomena. The question of soil development and change during the Post-glacial has been discussed by Dimbleby[81] with particular reference to the relative contributions of man and nature.

Mackereth[82] has suggested a period of soil erosion in several valleys of the Lake District around 3000 B.C., a possible result of Neolithic forest clearance. Dimbleby[83] has shown that clearance of forest in certain areas which are now heathland was associated in some cases with the onset of leaching in brown earths and their degradation to soils of podsol type. And in Holland it is generally the case that soils beneath Neolithic barrows are brown earths, while those under Bronze Age mounds on the same subsoil type are podsols.

The various changes which took place in calcareous soils have been discussed in the second paper of this volume. Thus Kerney[84] has demonstrated a phase of Neolithic forest clearance at Brook in Kent which caused erosion of a rendsina soil down the slopes of a dry valley and its accumulation as hillwash in the valley bottom. Generally such deposits are of later origin; they are almost ubiquitous in scarp valleys of the Chalk, sometimes up to 3m thick (see plate 1), and where present have resulted in the burial of Neolithic and Bronze Age settlement sites, for instance at Durrington Walls in Wiltshire.[85]

Finally the extensive growth and spread of blanket peat, particularly after *c.* 600 B.C., has both buried and preserved former Neolithic and Bronze Age land surfaces as at Ballynagilly in Co. Tyrone.[86] "Beneath the dreary blanket bog is preserved the untouched landscape of Bronze Age and Neolithic times". It has also converted vast areas of what was once good upland pasture into worthless land.

Notes

1. I. W. Cornwall, *The World of Ancient Man* (1964), pp. 113–24.
2. T. G. E. Powell, J. X. W. P. Corcoran, F. Lynch and J. G. Scott, *Megalithic Enquiries in the West of Britain: a Liverpool Symposium* (1969), p. 79.
3. *Antiquity*, XLIII (1969), 176–86.
4. *P.P.S.*, XXVI (1960), 1–36; 33.
5. W. Pennington, *The History of British Vegetation* (1969), p. 57.
6. *P.P.S.*, XXVIII (1962), 211.
7. *Antiquity*, XLIII (1969), 176–86.
8. *P.P.S.*, XXI (1955), 5.
9. F. E. Zeuner, *Dating the Past: An Introduction to Geomorphology* (1958), p. 97. *Annual Report of the University of London Institute of Archaeology*, XI (1955), 29–42.
10. *Ant. J.*, XLX (1939), 405–20.
11. *Journal of Ecology*, XXXI (1943), 199–247.
12. *World Climate from 8000 to 0 B.C.* (Royal Meteorological Society, 1966), pp. 54–71.
13. *Annual Report of the University of London Institute of Archaeology*, XI (1955), 29–42.
14. D. Walker and R. G. West (eds.), *Studies in the Vegetational History of the British Isles* (1970), pp. 23–39.
15. *Transactions of the Institute of British Geographers*, no. 39 (1966), 1–8.
16. Walker and West, *op. cit.*, p. 34.
17. Powell, Corcoran, Lynch and Scott, *op. cit.*, p. 225.
18. *Proceedings of the Royal Society*, B, CLXI (1965), 355–62.
19. P. J. Ucko and G. W. Dimbleby (eds.), *The Domestication and Exploitation of Plants and Animals* (1969), pp. 477–84; Cornwall, *op. cit.*, p. 113.
20. J. G. D. Clark, *Prehistoric Europe: The Economic Basis* (1952), p. 52.
21. J. G. Evans, 'Habitat change on the calcareous soils of Britain: the impact of Neolithic man', in this volume.
22. *Geologiska Föreningens i Stockholm Förhandlingar*, LXVI (1944), 463–83. H. Godwin, *The History of the British Flora* (1956), figs 12 and 13. Botanical evidence: *World Climate from 8000 to 0 B.C.* (Royal Meteorological Society, 1966), pp. 99–123.
23. *idem.*
24. *P.P.S.*, XXII (1956), 23–8.
25. G. W. Dimbleby, *The Development of the British Heathlands and their Soils*, Oxford Forestry Memoir, no. 23 (1962).
26. *World Climate from 8000 to 0 B.C.* (Royal Meteorological Society, 1966), pp. 3–14.
27. *P.P.S.*, IV (1938), 330–4.
28. *Philosophical Transactions of the Royal Society*, B, CCXLVIII (1964), 135–204.
29. *Radiocarbon*, III (1961), 39–45.
30. *Archaeological Review*, no. 2 (1967), 8–9.
31. Pennington, *op. cit.*, and *World Climate from 8000 to 0 B.C.* (Royal Meteorological Society, 1966).
32. Walker and West, *op. cit.*, pp. 97–116.
33. *P.P.S.*, XIX (1953), 138.
34. *Nature*, CCXVI (1967), 20–2.
35. *Farmers Weekly*, LXVIII (22 March 1968), 52.
36. private communication from M. P. Kerney.
37. D. Brothwell and E. Higgs (eds.), *Science in Archaeology*, London (1969), p. 130.

38. *Nature*, CLXXVIII (1956), 31–2.
39. *W.A.M.*, XLIII (1968), 12–26.
40. J. A. Taylor (ed.), *Weather and Agriculture* (1967), pp. 173–85.
41. *P.P.S.*, XXXIV (1968), 238–58; XXVI (1960), 1–36.
42. *Bulletin of the Institute of Archaeology, University of London*, VIII–IX (1970), 109–16; *Philosophical Transactions of the Royal Society*, B, CCXLVIII (1964), 135–204.
43. Taylor, *op. cit.*
44. Pennington, *op. cit.*, pp. 55–61.
45. Dimbleby, *op. cit.*
46. *Nature*, CLIV (1944), 6.
47. J. G. Evans, 'Habitat change on the calcareous soils of Britain: the impact of Neolithic man', in this volume.
48. private communication from G. W. Dimbleby.
49. *Veröffentlichingen Geobotanische Institut Rübel, Zurich*, XXXVII (1962), 83–99.
50. Godwin, *op. cit.*
51. Pennington, *op. cit.*
52. Walker and West, *op. cit.*, pp. 81–96; *World Climate from 8000 to 0 B.C.* (Royal Meteorological Society, 1966).
53. *P.P.S.*, XXVI (1960), 246–62.
54. *ibid.*, XXXV (1960), 203–19.
55. Ucko and Dimbleby, *op. cit.*, pp. 110–19.
56. Walker and West, *op. cit.*
57. J. G. Evans, 'Habitat change on the calcareous soils of Britain: the impact of Neolithic man', in this volume.
58. Ucko and Dimbleby, *op. cit.*, pp. 3–15.
59. Dimbleby, *op. cit.*
60. *World Climate from 8000 to 0 B.C.* (Royal Meteorological Society, 1966); Walker and West, *op. cit.*
61. *Vegetatio*, XV (1968), 292–6.
62. Clark, *op. cit.*, p. 91.
63. *ibid.*, fig. 45.
64. *P.P.S.*, XXX (1964), 352–81.
65. Powell, Corcoran, Lynch and Scott, *op. cit.*, pp. 39–40.
66. *P.P.S.*, XXXI (1965), 34–57.
67. *Scottish Geographical Magazine*, L (1934), 18–25.
68. *P.P.S.*, XXX (1964), 134–58.
69. A. S. Henshall, *The Chambered Tombs of Scotland*, vol. I (1963).
70. F. Elgee, *Early Man in North-East Yorkshire* (1930); Dimbleby, *op. cit.*
71. Clark, *op. cit.*, p. 91.
72. Dimbleby, *op. cit.*
73. J. G. Evans, 'Habitat change on the calcareous soils of Britain: the impact of Neolithic man', in this volume.
74. Powell, Corcoran, Lynch and Scott, *op. cit.*, p. 27.
75. Henshall, *op. cit.*; Dimbleby, *op. cit.*
76. *Antiquity*, XIX (1945), 169–74.
77. private communication from D. D. A. Simpson.
78. Powell, Corcoran, Lynch and Scott, *op. cit.*
79. *Antiquity*, VII (1933), 297–310.

80. *Nature*, CLXXVIII (1956), 31–2; *W.A.M.*, XLIII (1968), 12–26.
81. *Proceedings of the Royal Society*, B, CLXI (1965), 355–62.
82. *ibid.*, pp. 295–309.
83. Dimbleby, *op. cit.*
84. *Philosophical Transactions of the Royal Society*, B, CCXLVIII (1964), 135–204.
85. *Antiquity*, XLII (1968), 20–6.
86. *Current Archaeology*, no. 24 (1971), 11–13.

Habitat change
on the calcareous soils of Britain:
the impact of Neolithic man

J. G. EVANS

The fact of forest clearance in much of Britain by Neolithic man has been established through pollen analysis of peat bogs and lake sediments; and various forms of subsequent land use have been attested.[1] Where the subsoil is lime-rich however, there is little information due to the ill-preservation of pollen in calcareous deposits. This is particularly unfortunate since some of these areas, for instance the south and east of England, were among the most heavily settled by Neolithic man; and although it has generally been assumed on ecological grounds that the Chalk once supported forest, little is known of its structure or composition. Nor is it known when clearance took place, what techniques were used in this process, or what forms of land use were employed subsequently.

There are only two recorded instances of forest clearance on the Chalk in prehistoric times. Pollen analysis by Godwin of organic sediments, close to the North Downs in east Kent at Wingham, showed that at least one area had been largely deforested towards the end of the Neolithic period (c. 1700 B.C.).[2] And Kerney, Brown and Chandler have demonstrated a phase of forest clearance not far away at Brook on the scarp of the North Downs, using the technique of land-snail analysis. Clearance was dated to c. 2600 B.C. by radiocarbon assay.

Although considered as a possibility by Pitt-Rivers, and used by Kennard for almost 50 years, the technique of snail analysis in reconstructing environments of the past was not put on a sound quantitative basis until the mid-1950s.[3] Since then, largely due to the work of B. W. Sparks and M. P. Kerney, the analysis of land and freshwater Mollusca has become established as a valuable technique of Quaternary research (see Appendix B).

In this paper three Neolithic sites are examined through a combination of snail analysis and soil studies. The first comprises an ancient soil profile on limestone, buried beneath a Neolithic long barrow at Ascott-under-Wychwood in the

Figure 3. Location of sites.
1. Ascott-under-Wychwood
2. South Street
3. Northton
4. Wayland's Smithy
5. Avebury
6. West Kennet Long Barrow
7. Horslip
8. Windmill Hill
9. Silbury Hill
10. Beckhampton Road
11. Knap Hill
12. Marden
13. Durrington Walls
14. Brook
15. Julliberrie's Grave
16. Thickthorn Down
17. Kilham
18. Willerby Wold
19. Arreton Down
20. Earl's Farm Down
(Amesbury, G. 71)

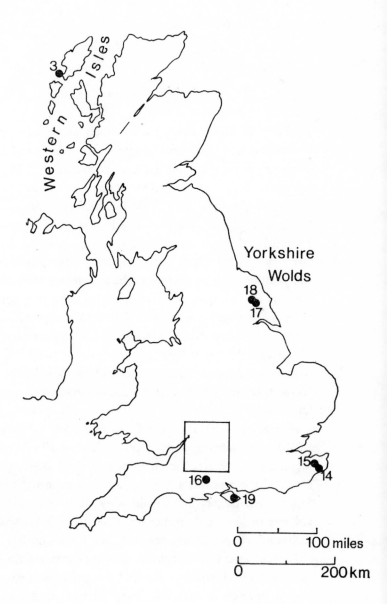

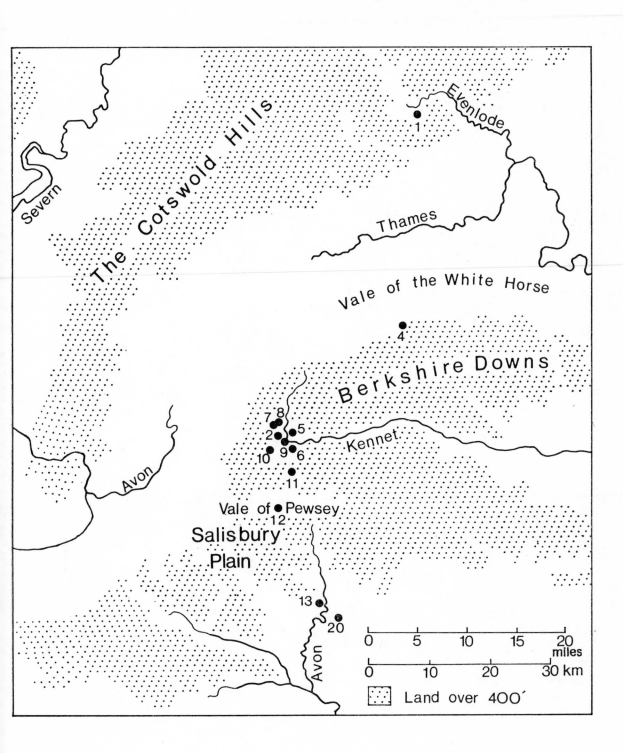

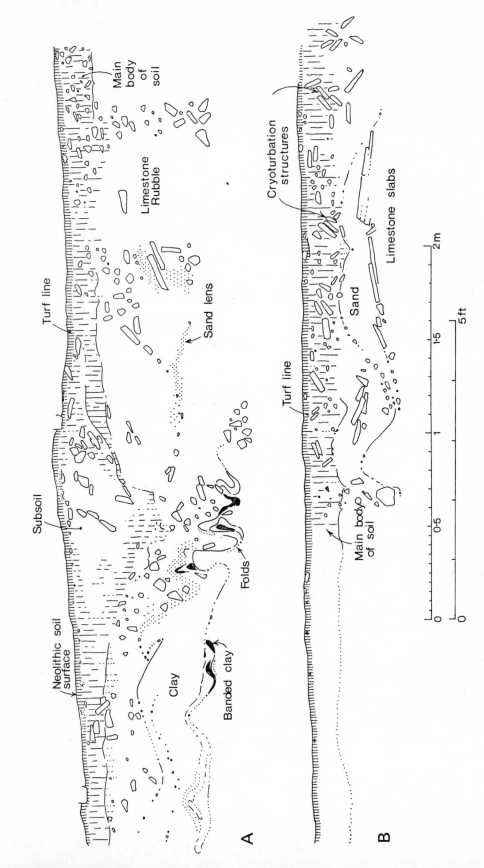

Figure 4. Ascott-under-Wychwood. (A) Buried soil and (B) subsoil.

Oxfordshire Cotswolds. The second, at South Street in north Wiltshire, is a similar site but on the Chalk. The third comprises a series of Neolithic and Beaker occupation horizons at Northton in the Outer Hebrides, stratified in a deposit of calcareous shell sand.

Ascott-under-Wychwood

The Ascott-under-Wychwood long barrow is situated in the Oxfordshire Cotswolds at *c.* 400ft O.D. on the side of a tributary valley of the River Evenlode, one mile due south of the village of Ascott-under-Wychwood (fig. 3).[4] The subsoil is Oolite limestone with areas of clay and has been strongly disturbed by periglacial action.

The pre-barrow soil profile stood out as a dark humic horizon, averaging about 20 to 25cm thick (fig. 4; plate 2a). It showed considerable lateral variation and it will be convenient first therefore to describe a generalized profile where the subsoil is limestone rubble (figs. 4 and 5A).

Depth below buried
soil surface (cm)

0–5	*Turf-line.* Relatively stone-free calcareous loam; dark-grey/brown, rich in humus; with a blocky structure when dry.
5–*c.* 25	*Main body of the soil.* Dark-brown calcareous loam with numerous limestone fragments.
c. 25–*c.* 50	*Subsoil hollows.* Localized penetrations into the subsoil of humic material. Possibly the casts of decayed tree-roots.
c. 25/*c.* 50+	*Subsoil.* Shattered limestone rubble and finer debris.

This profile is classed as a rendsina, that is, a soil comprising a calcareous A-horizon (0–*c.* 25cm) developed on lime-rich parent material, the C-horizon (*c.* 25/*c.* 50+ cm). From the historical point of view however it is preferable to consider the A-horizon as comprising two distinct horizons, the turf-line and the main body of the soil.

A series of samples from this profile was analysed for land snails (table 1 on p. 41; fig. 5A), and the results plotted as a histogram of relative abundance. The fauna from the subsoil hollow suggests an environment of light or slightly open woodland (26–46). Shade-loving species, such as *Discus rotundatus, Carychium tridentatum* and various Zonitidae predominate, and with the exception of *Vallonia costata,* open-country species are absent. The latter, while generally favouring open habitats, often occurring in enormous numbers, may also live at a low level of abundance in more shaded places. Its presence here at 6 per cent abundance may be taken to indicate some slight openness in an otherwise forested landscape; but whether implying a local clearing or reflecting the general condition of the forest is not certain.

In the main body of the profile (fig. 5A, 6–26) the fauna is similar to that below, but differs in the higher absolute number of shells, and the fall to *c.* 1 per cent, of *Vallonia costata*. These differences suggest the development of an almost totally

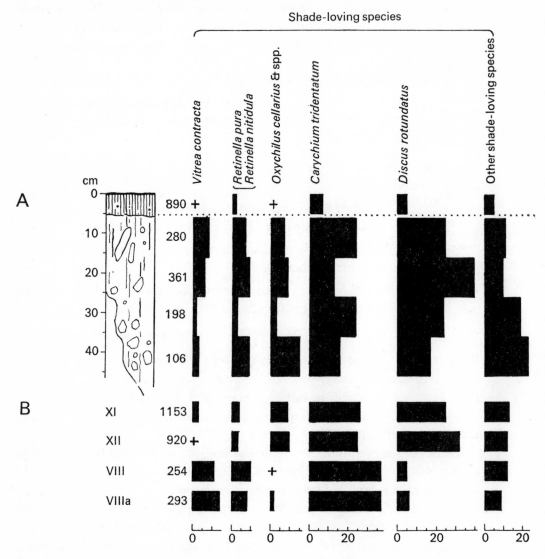

Figure 5. Ascott-under-Wychwood. Land-snail diagram. (A) Buried soil; (B) subsoil hollow.

shaded environment. The presence of three species conservative in their requirements for undisturbed habitats – *Acicula fusca*, *Vertigo pusilla* and *Vertigo
alpestris* – the richness of the fauna in species and its closed woodland character
all point to an environment free from human disturbance; one can well envisage
a thick carpet of leaf litter, a tangled mass of fallen trunks and branches and,
above, the unbroken arboreal canopy.

Within the main body of the soil are small groups of steeply pitched stones

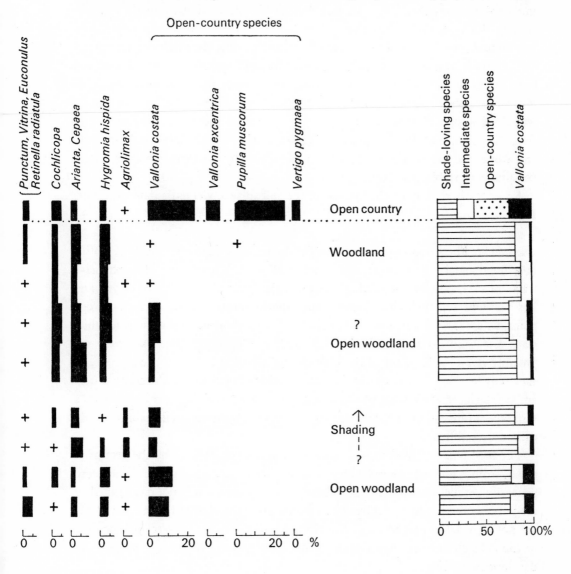

(fig. 4), structures which are probably the product of frost heaving under peri-glacial conditions at a time prior to the formation of the Post-glacial soil. Their preservation supports rather neatly the evidence of the land-snail fauna in indicating the soil profile to be undisturbed. For had disturbance taken place to any depth, for instance by ploughing, these structures would have been destroyed.

In contrast, the turf-line (0–5) contains an open-country fauna, strongly suggesting clearance of the forest cover at this level and the creation of an open grassland environment. Four species typical of open habitats, namely *Vallonia costata*, *Vallonia excentrica*, *Pupilla muscorum* and *Vertigo pygmaea*, are well represented, constituting 61 per cent of the fauna, while the shade-loving species decline from 82 per cent to 20 per cent. The large quantity of pot sherds and flint-knapping debris, spreads of charcoal and several pits associated with this horizon suggest that the change in the land-snail fauna from one of closed woodland to one of open country reflects the artificial destruction of an area of forest by man. The formation of the turf-line with a well-developed structure and stone-free nature was probably brought about by earthworm-sorting under conditions of stable grassland.

A radiocarbon assay of charcoal from the soil surface yielded a date of *c.* 2800 B.C.

The subsoil. The subsoil over a large area of the site was shattered limestone rubble in a finer matrix, with occasional patches of sand. There were also extensive tracts of clay, possibly of solifual origin, which gave rise to a more clayey and less pervious soil than that derived from the limestone rubble (fig. 4). At one point, where the subsoil consisted of alternating bands of green, brown and white clays and sands, a series of folds was strikingly apparent (fig. 4). These are possibly due to solifluxion of the clay during a period of sub-arctic climate, or they may be related to involutions (cryoturbation structures) produced by differ-ential freezing and thawing of the ground. In places, the clay was overlain by a thin layer of limestone rubble, a redistribution of subsoil material again probably caused by solifluxion.

The final phase of frost weathering on the site is represented by the groups of small, steeply-pitched stones alluded to above, which in plan constitute linear and generally parallel features (fig. 4). Their mode of formation is not clear but they are possibly the product of differential freezing and thawing of the ground. They are not artificial in origin – e.g. ploughmarks – as they are too securely bonded to the subsoil; nor are they related to the solid geology of the site as they are developed in drift.

In spite of abundant evidence indicative of sub-arctic climatic conditions at Ascott-under-Wychwood (solifluxion and frost-heaving) prior to the development of the Post-glacial soil, and in spite of extensive sampling of the finer elements of the subsoil at various places on the site, no snail fauna which could be related to this period was located.

Subsoil hollows. Extending below the base of the main body of the soil, but in some cases originating from within the profile itself, was a number of hollows of a variety of shapes and containing a variety of deposits. Some of these were simple depressions, either steep-sided or bowl-shaped. Others were more complex consisting of obliquely-set wedge-shaped cavities which commonly occurred in pairs so arranged as to undercut and virtually isolate a block of subsoil (fig. 4). Small cavities were also present either as separate entities or associated with larger hollows. The origin of these features is not clear. Some may be the casts of tree-roots long since decayed, and in view of the molluscan evidence for the former presence of forest this would seem a reasonable hypothesis. Others are perhaps of periglacial origin being filled-in hollows left at the close of the Late-glacial period.

The molluscan fauna from one of these hollows has been discussed above where it was suggested that it might reflect a woodland environment, slightly open (fig. 5A, 26–46). Another, more complex hollow was investigated in some detail (figs. 6 and 7). In plan (fig. 6) it consisted of a sub-rectangular area about 3m by 2m, around the periphery of which were six subsidiary hollows. These were quite distinct from the several archaeological pits in the area characterized by their regularity and clearly-defined limits. A part of the main hollow was cut off by an obliquely set wedge of subsoil, thought to be *in situ* material and not part of the fill due to its secure bonding to the surrounding rock.

The fill of the smaller section of the subsoil hollow thus isolated (fig. 7, section ZY) was a compact pale-grey/brown (humic) loam with an abundance of fine gritty limestone rubble. Two samples of this were analysed for land snails (fig. 5B, VIII and VIIIa; table 1). The fauna suggests an open woodland environment being dominated by woodland species, but with *Vallonia costata* at values of 12 per cent and 10 per cent abundance. It was also curiously restricted in certain aspects, for instance in the low values for *Oxychilus cellarius* and *Discus rotundatus* and the high value of *Vitrea contracta*.

In contrast, the fill of the main part of the hollow was more humic, comprising a dark-brown/orange mottled loam again with masses of small limestone fragments suggesting physical weathering to have been an important process in the filling of the hollow (fig. 7, section ZY).

Two samples of this material (fig. 5B, XI and XII; table 1) yielded a fauna which showed some interesting differences from that of VIII and VIIIa, differences which suggested some closing over of the arboreal canopy and an environment more shaded than before. Thus *Vallonia costata* has fallen to not more than 6 per cent abundance, *Vitrea contracta* has become less important while *Oxychilus cellarius* and *Discus rotundatus* have attained a more usual level of abundance for woodland faunas. The relict woodland species *Acanthinula lamellata* was also present. Another noticeable feature was the large number of snails in the samples,

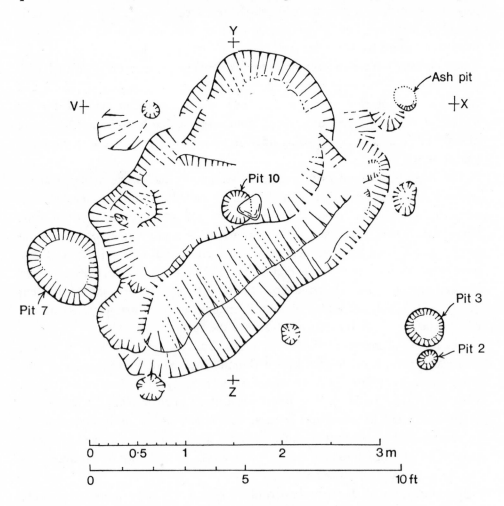

Figure 6. Ascott-under-Wychwood. Plan of subsoil hollow and adjacent pits.

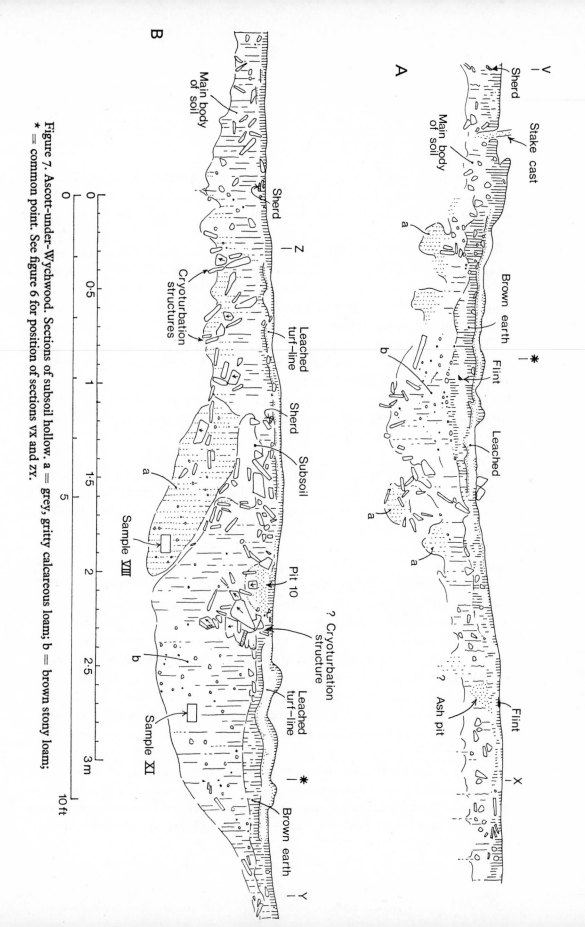

Figure 7. Ascott-under-Wychwood. Sections of subsoil hollow. a = grey, gritty calcareous loam; b = brown stony loam; * = common point. See figure 6 for position of sections vx and zy.

an indication of highly suitable environmental conditions, and suggesting the infilling of the hollow to have been a gradual process.

Above this material was a layer of dark-brown/orange mottled stone-free loam which was decalcified and thus devoid of shells (fig. 7, brown earth). This is probably the B-horizon of a brown-earth soil which developed from the underlying rendsiniform material in a fully forested environment undisturbed by man. This type of profile was present in other parts of the site, only where there was an absence of Neolithic occupation debris; its preservation in the subsoil hollow is due to its protected situation in the upper levels of the fill. In some places, a brown earth does not appear to have formed at all, for instance in the first profile described above (fig. 5A). It is not quite clear why this should be but it may relate to variations in the carbonate content of the subsoil.

The stratigraphical relationship between the two profiles described, from which land-snail faunas have been obtained (figs. 5A and B), is not at all clear. But in both cases we seem to be dealing with a forested environment, initially open but later becoming increasingly shaded, and in one case this vegetational change is accompanied by a change in soil type from a rendsina to a brown earth.

There are two possible explanations for these habitat changes. The first is that we are dealing with an episode in the natural development of the Post-glacial forest, the faunas with a high percentage of *Vallonia costata* (VIII and VIIIa) reflecting an early stage, perhaps in the Boreal period, and the faunas with a low percentage of *V. costata* representing a stage in the Atlantic period when the closed structure of the climax forest had been attained. This is perhaps the most reasonable hypothesis; certainly the restricted nature of the fauna of samples VIII and VIIIa and particularly the very low values for *Discus rotundatus*, a species which does not appear in Britain until towards the end of the Boreal period, taken with its spectacular increase later on, are suggestive of an early Post-glacial date.

The second possible explanation is that there was a local opening of the forest canopy caused by natural or artificial factors of the environment. And here we must consider briefly the stratigraphical context of human artifacts in relation to the soil profiles. Neolithic material occurs only in the turf-line, and unless in pits, does not occur below this level. It is thus unlikely that this early phase of open forest is connected with Neolithic activity. Mesolithic artifacts however are not thus restricted, a number of microliths having been found in the calcareous fill of the main part of the subsoil hollow described above (i.e. from the position of samples XI and XII, fig. 5B), and separated from overlying Neolithic occupation debris by a brown-earth soil, sterile of both Neolithic and Mesolithic artifacts. With the Mesolithic material in the subsoil hollow were charred fragments of hazel-nut shells and fragments of burnt bone. It was noticed that neither the snail shells nor the occasional small mammal bones from this situation were burnt. A large quantity of Mesolithic material has been found elsewhere on the site, indicating the presence of a band of hunter-gatherers, at least some of whom were present at a time well previous to the Neolithic occupation. It is unlikely that Mesolithic man was directly responsible for opening the forest canopy, but it is difficult to avoid the inference that there is a connexion of some sort between the phase of open woodland and the contemporary occupation of the site by Mesolithic man.

The turf-line. The upper 3 to 5cm of the soil profile generally comprise a well-defined horizon which is strongly humic, calcareous and stone-free, with a blocky structure when dry. Its snail fauna suggests an environment of grassland contemporary with its formation.

Where associated with a concentration of Neolithic occupation debris, the turf-line frequently shows signs of leaching. The dark coloration is lost and the soil assumes a pale-blue tint. This is presumably due to the removal of iron and humus, which are reprecipitated as narrow bands above and below the leached zone (fig. 7), first the iron and then the humus. This process probably takes place after burial of the soil, for in some instances humus and iron have been reprecipitated in mound material just above the old soil surface.

It is not clear why iron and humus move in this way as such processes are usually confined to conditions of low pH, not occurring in lime-rich soils. The association of leached areas with occupation debris may be of some significance. For instance when the soil is buried the oxidation of organic matter perhaps results temporarily in a reducing atmosphere due to the uptake of oxygen during the processes of microbial decay. Ferric iron would then become reduced to ferrous iron which, being soluble, would move easily through the soil, only being precipitated when reconverted to ferric iron once an oxidizing atmosphere were reached. Thus although the actual leaching process takes place after burial, the areas of the turf which show this phenomenon may have differed in some way prior to burial from those which do not.

In certain areas no turf-line is present, particularly where there is a brown-earth profile, suggesting that the presence of a turf-line is associated with human activity of some sort, for example in the creation of a grassland environment.

There are two phases of Neolithic occupation. The earliest comprises pits dug into the soil profile and underlying subsoil sealed by the turf-line. The second comprises occupation debris – pot sherds, flints and bone – on and within the turf-line. Radiocarbon dates for the two phases are as follows:

Pit 7, charcoal. (BM–491b) 2943 ± 70 B.C.
Charcoal on the old
soil surface. (BM–492) 2785 ± 70 B.C.

The reason for the marked unevenness of the soil profile overlying the subsoil hollow (fig. 7) is unknown. Ants, moles or Neolithic man may have been responsible.

The sequence of events at Ascott-under-Wychwood can now be summarized as follows. First there was a phase of periglacial weathering when sheets of clay and limestone rubble were laid down over the site by solifluxion. This was followed by a period of milder frost weathering resulting in the formation of cryoturbation structures – lines of pitched stones at the subsoil surface. Later, in the Post-glacial, the site was clothed with light woodland, and for a time occupied by a group of Mesolithic people. Then the woodland became dense and shaded as the arboreal canopy closed over. A decalcified soil of brown-earth type formed, in places sealing the underlying Mesolithic occupation debris – burnt bone, charred hazelnut shells and microliths. Finally the site was reoccupied, this time by Neolithic people who cleared the forest over part of the site. They did not, however, disturb the soil apart from digging pits and disrupting the surface; if they tilled the soil, this was confined to the surface. There were two episodes at least of Neolithic activity, the latest of which is dated to *c.* 2800 B.C.

South Street

The South Street Long Barrow lies at the foot of a low hill at *c.* 540ft O.D. on Middle Chalk,[5] situated about three-quarters of a mile west of Avebury in north Wiltshire (fig. 3).

Weathering phenomena of the pre-barrow environment fall into three categories (fig. 8; plate 2b) as follows: (i) the buried soil profile beneath the barrow; (ii) pockets of humic, fine chalky rubble extending from the base of the soil profile to depths of 60cm into the subsoil (subsoil hollows); (iii) the parent material (C-horizon) of the Post-glacial soil. These will be described in chronological order.

The parent material of the Post-glacial soil (fig. 8A) comprises a series of pockets or involutions up to 70cm deep, filled with a fine buff-colored chalky deposit, in a matrix of coombe rock.[6] They are the product of differential freezing and thawing of the ground during a period of sub-arctic climate and contain a snail fauna

	Subsoil hollow				Buried soil				
sample/cm	VIIIa	VIII	XII	XI	36 – 46	26 – 36	16 – 26	6 – 16	0 – 5
dry weight of sample (kg)	2.0	2.0	2.0	2.0	1.33	1.25	1.32	1.30	1.23
Acicula fusca (Montagu)	—	—	1	1	1	—	6	9	2
Carychium tridentatum (Risso)	109	92	227	305	16	48	45	66	66
Cochlicopa lubrica (Müller)	—	—	—	cf. 1	—	—	—	2	5
Cochlicopa lubricella (Porro)	—	—	—	—	—	+	—	—	5
Cochlicopa spp.	6	7	12	19	4	10	9	6	40
Columella edentula (Draparnaud)	2	2	3	12	—	—	3	2	—
Vertigo pusilla Müller	4	2	8	19	1	—	—	—	—
Vertigo pygmaea (Draparnaud)	—	—	—	—	—	—	—	—	41
Vertigo alpestris Alder	—	—	1	—	—	—	—	1	—
Pupilla muscorum (Linné)	—	—	—	—	—	—	—	1	239
Lauria cylindracea (da Costa)	—	—	5	3	—	1	—	—	—
Acanthinula aculeata (Müller)	17	19	13	34	2	11	10	12	14
Acanthinula lamellata (Jeffreys)	—	—	2	10	—	—	—	—	—
Vallonia costata (Müller)	29	29	36	74	3	13	2	4	219
Vallonia excentrica Sterki	—	—	—	—	—	—	—	—	65
Ena montana (Draparnaud)	—	—	2	3	1	4	2	2	5
Ena obscura (Müller)	—	—	—	3	—	2	2	—	4
Marpessa laminata (Montagu)	—	1	6	7	2	4	3	1	1
Clausilia bidentata (Ström)	3	6	62	51	15	15	8	9	17
Helicigona lapicida (Linné)	—	—	3	1	1	—	—	—	—
Arianta arbustorum (Linné)	—	—	—	+	—	—	—	—	—
Helix (Cepaea) hortensis Müller	+	—	—	+	—	—	—	+	+
Helix (Cepaea) nemoralis Linné	+	—	—	2	+	+	+	+	+
Arianta, Helix (Cepaea) spp.	9	6	56	48	8	10	10	14	24
Hygromia striolata (C. Pfeiffer)	—	—	—	6	—	—	—	—	—
Hygromia hispida (Linné)	11	13	20	14	3	12	15	14	28
Punctum pygmaeum (Draparnaud)	10	5	9	17	—	—	—	—	—
Discus rotundatus (Müller)	19	12	290	302	17	48	142	71	42
Euconulus fulvus (Müller)	?+	1	1	—	—	—	2	1	—
Vitrea crystallina (Müller)	—	—	—	—	—	—	1	—	—
Vitrea contracta (Westerlund)	41	28	11	39	3	5	22	22	7
Oxychilus cellarius (Müller)	4	1	81	105	16	7	34	19	11
Oxychilus alliarius (Miller)	cf. 1	cf. 1	cf. 6	cf. 2	—	—	cf. 2	cf. 2	—
Retinella radiatula (Alder)	2	—	3	1	1	1	—	3	11
Retinella pura (Alder)	10	8	25	40	7	4	19	10	7
Retinella nitidula (Draparnaud)	15	18	5	9	2	3	14	8	13
Vitrina pellucida (Müller)	?+	—	1	—	—	—	—	1	19
Limax, Agriolimax spp.	4	3	31	25	—	—	2	—	5

Table 1. Ascott-under-Wychwood

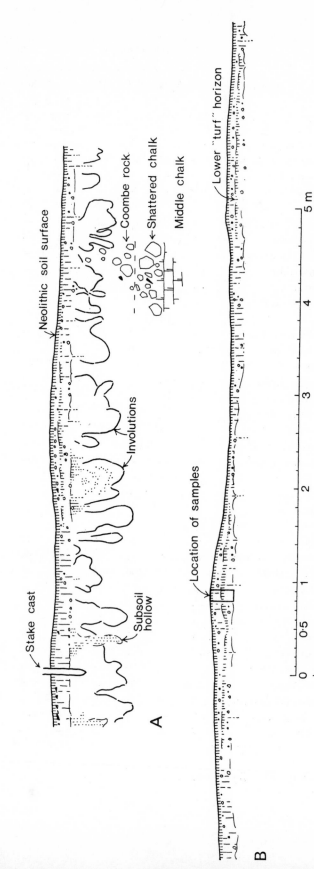

Figure 8. South Street. Sections of buried soil and subsoil.

characteristic of the Late-Weichselian period in southern England. Samples of two involutions were analysed (fig. 9C, I and II; table 2), and the faunas from both correspond closely, being dominated by *Pupilla muscorum*, with other typical Late-glacial species, notably *Helicella itala* and *Abida secale*, present as well. An open-country, probably tundra, environment is indicated.

The subsoil hollows occurred at irregular intervals over the entire site, an area of about 600 sq m. They were of a variety of shapes and sizes, some being slight depressions, not more than 5cm deep, others being of much greater depth penetrating the subsoil up to 60cm below the base of the soil (fig. 8A). Yet others branched and undercut the coombe rock in irregular tunnels and clefts. All appeared of later origin than the involutions, which they cut through or overlay. Their mode of origin is uncertain and possibly various; they may be casts of former tree-roots, they may be solution hollows, or they may be of periglacial origin. Their fill is humic and compact and characterized by its large quantity of chalky debris (fig. 9B), suggesting physical weathering of the subsoil to have been an important factor in their formation.

Analysis of the snail fauna from a vertical series of five samples taken from one of these hollows (fig. 9B; table 2 on pp. 50–1) yielded a fully temperate assemblage dominated by shade-loving species, though with a substantial open-country element as well. As at Ascott-under-Wychwood, it is possible that this fauna reflects a period early on in the Post-glacial before a full forest cover had developed. Thus it is known from other sites in the area, and in similar topographical positions (see Appendix A), that a land-snail fauna of *totally* shade-loving facies existed on the Chalk during the Atlantic period, and there is no reason why this should not have been the case at South Street. Secondly, the fauna cannot be linked with a phase of human activity so its composition is probably a reflection of the natural environment. Thirdly, the fauna is virtually devoid of *Pomatias elegans*, a snail which arrived in Britain relatively late in the Post-glacial, perhaps between 6000 and 5000 B.C. And finally, pollen analysis of the material showed it to be devoid of lime (*Tilia*) suggesting a Boreal age, that is, somewhere in the period 7000 to 5000 B.C.[7] Thus the open character of this fauna probably reflects an early stage in the development of the Post-glacial forest when this was still relatively open.

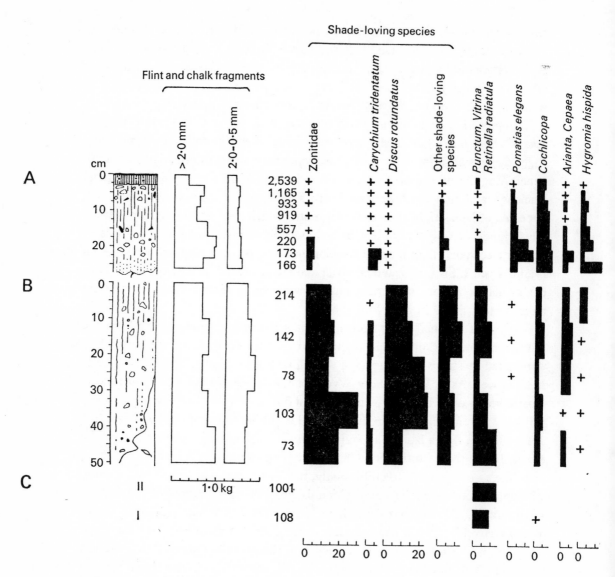

Figure 9. South Street. Land-snail diagram. (A) Buried soil; (B) subsoil hollow; (C) involutions.

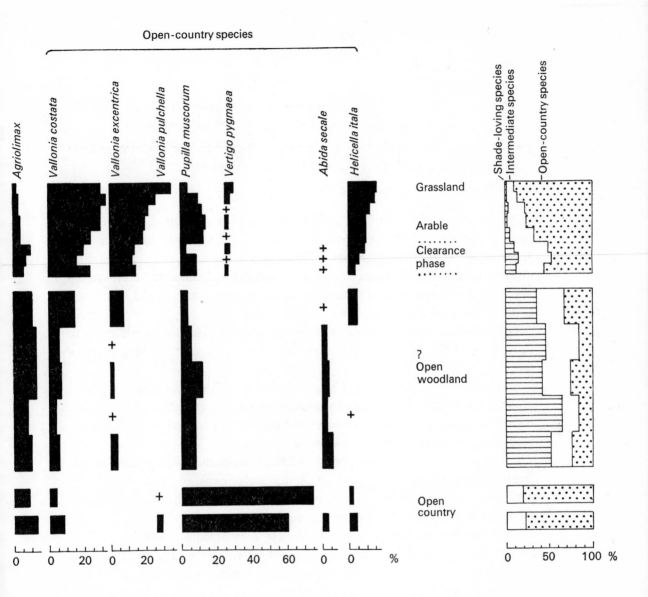

The profile of the buried soil was as follows (figs. 8 and 9A):

Depth below buried
soil surface (cm)

0–3	*Turf-line.* Dark-grey to black calcareous loam; virtually stone-free, and with a blocky structure when dry.
3–*c.* 27	*Main body of the soil.* Dark-grey to black calcareous loam with numerous small chalk fragments.
c. 27+	*Parent material.*

As at Ascott-under-Wychwood, this soil is a rendsina and superficially the two profiles are similar. But on close examination, fundamental differences are apparent all of which suggest that at South Street the soil has been vigorously disturbed to its base. This is in complete contrast to the situation at Ascott-under-Wychwood where, it will be remembered, disturbance was confined to the soil surface. These differences can now be enumerated:

1. Neither the involutions nor the subsoil hollows extend upwards into the main body of the soil. At Ascott they did, in places almost reaching the surface.

2. At the base of the profile, scored into the subsoil surface, are two sets of grooves, filled with humic material and running roughly at right-angles (fig. 10). These have been discussed elsewhere[8] and are thought to have been caused by ploughing. At Ascott no such marks were present.

3. The surface of the soil was gently undulating while the base was more or less level, so that the profile was of uneven depth, varying between 5 and 30cm (fig. 8; plate 2b). At Ascott, variations in depth were due largely to humic penetrations into the subsoil rather than to surface irregularities.

4. Within the thicker parts of the profile a rudimentary layering can be recognized, with a relatively stone-free zone (fig. 9A, 9–17cm; fig. 8) intercalated in the main body of the soil. No corresponding horizon was present at Ascott.

5. Finally, the land-snail fauna throughout the profile is one of open-country type (see p. 49). At Ascott, with the exception of the turf-line, the fauna was one of forest.

First of all then, there was a phase of ploughing which disturbed the soil to its base. The significance of this phase is not clear. That a pattern of plough-marks has been preserved at all suggests the process to have been short-lived, though within the main pattern there are several subsidiary directions perhaps indicating more than one phase.

Figure 10. South Street. Plan of Neolithic plough-marks beneath the long barrow mound.

The uneven thickness of the soil and the layering in the deeper parts is unusual in chalk soils; it is reminiscent of the structure of Celtic field lynchets where the profile is the product of accretion to the surface. Thus the lower stony zone (fig. 9A, *c.* 15–25cm) may be the vestiges of the natural soil disturbed by ploughing; the relatively stone-free zone (*c.* 10–*c.* 15) the product of worm-sorting during a period of surface stability, and the upper stony zone (3–*c.* 10cm) the product of renewed disturbance, lateral transport and deposition. The material comprising the latter presumably derives from, and resulted in, the ambient areas of thin soil. The form of the surface undulations of the soil in plan was unclear; they were however not linear features. The nature of the process which caused them can only be speculative, as is the case also with the plough-marks. It is however an obvious inference to regard the latter as the result of deep ploughing in order to break up the soil preparatory to the formation of a seed bed, and the former as the result of some sort of less vigorous tillage.

The final stage in the history of the soil at South Street, prior to its burial, was the formation of a thin turf-line, probably brought about by earthworm sorting in a grassland environment (fig. 9A, 0–3cm). As at Ascott-under-Wychwood, this is a continuous layer, a kind of skin to the soil, pierced solely by archaeological features such as the casts of decayed stakes.

Charcoal from the soil surface yielded a radiocarbon date of (BM–356) 2810 ± 130 B.C.

The land-snail fauna throughout the profile (fig. 9A) is of open-country type. When looked at in detail three distinct assemblages can be recognized which confirm and amplify the land-use sequence suggested above through a considera-tion of the soil profile.

In the lower stony horizon (*c.* 17–26cm) the fauna contains a shade-loving element and is richer in species than the layers above. This is possibly the vestiges of the forest fauna of the Atlantic period, largely destroyed by ploughing, and mixed with later open-country elements. It is distinct from the fauna in the subsoil hollow, suggested as being of Boreal age though some of the differences may be of local environmental rather than of chronological significance. The increase of *Pomatias elegans* is noteworthy and as suggested above may be of chronological significance.

If then we are right in claiming a pure woodland fauna once to have existed at South Street, the following conclusions can be made. First, the shade-loving component of the fauna could not have lived under conditions of continuous ploughing nor could dead shells have remained intact for long, thus supporting the idea reached independently on morphological grounds that the phase of ploughing was short-lived. And second, if the fauna at this level is an artificial hybrid resulting from the mixing of an open-country fauna and a woodland fauna by plough action, then the phase of forest clearance and introduction of an open-country fauna on the one hand and the phase of ploughing on the other must be seen as two separate events.

Above *c.* 17cm the shade-loving component of the fauna falls to insignificant levels and an open-country fauna prevails. *Vallonia costata, V. excentrica, Helicella itala* and *Pupilla muscorum* are the main elements, with a few others such as *Cochlicopa, Hygromia hispida* and *Vertigo pygmaea* often found in open grassland situations, present as well. The high abundance of *Pupilla muscorum* between 3 and 17cm suggests an unstable soil surface, as this species prefers a broken substratum with patches of loose rubbly soil rather than a continuous grass sward, supporting the suggestion that cultivation was taking place intermittently in this horizon.

The fauna in the turf-line (0–3cm) suggests an environment of dry, short-turfed grassland. The two species of *Vallonia* and *Helicella itala* predominate, and the marked decline of *Pupilla muscorum* confirms in a particularly convincing manner the interpretation of this horizon as the product of a non-arable, stable grassland environment.

As at Ascott-under-Wychwood, the succession of events at South Street suggests that we are dealing with a phase of forest clearance probably brought about by Neolithic farming communities early in the third millennium B.C. How this process took place is unclear but it has been suggested above that it preceded the phase of ploughing. In contrast to Ascott-under-Wychwood, the soil at South Street contained little evidence of Neolithic man, though sufficient to demonstrate his presence on the site prior to the construction of the barrow. There were three sherds of undecorated Neolithic pottery and a quantity of prehistoric flint-flakes, cores and scrapers; a sickle flint with a high gloss along one edge and made from a flake struck from a polished flint axe was also recovered – an amusing though possibly fortuitous testimony of the environmental history of the site. Bone fragments of domesticated animals – sheep/goat, cattle and pig were also present.

At the base of the turf-line (i.e. at 3cm below the soil surface) in two places were found concentrations of flint flakes and cores, probably knapping debris *in situ,* though moved down from the surface by worm-action. On the soil surface itself were two concentrations of charcoal fragments. These instances lend support to the other evidence which indicates the final phase of land-use at South Street to have been non-arable.

sample/cm	Involutions		Subsoil hollow				
	I	II	40 – 50	30 – 40	20 – 30	10 – 20	0 – 10
dry weight of sample (kg)	2.0	2.0	2.0	2.0	2.0	2.0	2.0
Pomatias elegans (Müller)	—	—	—	—	+	+	3
Carychium tridentatum (Risso)	—	—	2	2	2	5	1
Cochlicopa lubricella (Porro)	—	—	—	—	—	—	—
Cochlicopa spp.	+	—	2	4	2	7	6
Vertigo pusilla Müller	—	—	—	—	—	—	—
Vertigo pygmaea (Draparnaud)	—	—	—	—	—	—	—
Pupilla muscorum (Linné)	65	740	6	8	10	9	8
Abida secale (Draparnaud)	3	—	6	3	4	5	2
Acanthinula aculeata (Müller)	—	—	2	7	1	6	9
Vallonia costata (Müller)	9	37	5	4	6	9	32
Vallonia pulchella (Müller)	cf. 3	5	—	—	—	—	—
Vallonia excentrica Sterki	—	—	3	1	2	1	18
Ena montana (Draparnaud)	—	—	—	—	—	1	—
Ena obscura (Müller)	—	—	—	—	—	—	1
Marpessa laminata (Montagu)	—	—	—	—	—	—	1
Clausilia bidentata (Ström)	—	—	3	1	4	11	10
Balea perversa (Linné)	—	—	—	cf. 1	—	—	—
Helicigona lapicida (Linné)	—	—	—	—	—	—	—
Arianta arbustorum (Linné)	—	—	—	+	+	—	—
Helix (Cepaea) hortensis Müller	—	—	—	—	1	2	+
Helix (Cepaea) nemoralis Linné	—	—	+	+	—	+	+
Arianta, Helix (Cepaea) spp.	—	—	2	—	3	8	8
Hygromia hispida (Linné)	—	—	1	1	1	2	9
Helicella itala (Linné)	4	19	—	cf. 1	—	—	10
Punctum pygmaeum (Draparnaud)	3	49	5	3	1	8	8
Discus rotundatus (Müller)	—	—	8	24	18	22	27
Euconulus fulvus (Müller)	1	1	1	—	—	—	—
Vitrea contracta (Westerlund)	—	—	8	12	7	18	8
Oxychilus cellarius (Müller)	—	—	—	—	—	—	—
Oxychilus alliarius (Miller)	—	—	—	5	2	—	4
Retinella radiatula (Alder)	—	—	2	4	2	6	3
Retinella pura (Alder)	—	—	2	9	—	2	6
Retinella nitidula (Draparnaud)	—	—	5	4	1	2	12
Vitrina pellucida (Müller)	6	71	2	1	—	1	3
Limax, Agriolimax spp.	14	79	8	8	10	17	25

Table 2. South Street

			Buried soil				
23 – 26 2.0	20 – 23 2.0	17 – 20 2.0	13 – 17 2.0	9 – 13 2.0	6 – 9 2.0	3 – 6 2.0	0 – 3 2.0
6	22	22	25	30	32	21	15
8	13	2	9	5	6	2	2
1	1	1	2	6	6	5	23
13	15	16	32	62	46	44	94
—	1	—	—	—	—	—	—
4	2	7	8	18	10	31	118
14	16	7	75	127	118	113	113
+	+	+	—	—	—	—	—
1	1	1	1	1	1	—	—
39	27	44	144	277	280	385	755
—	—	—	—	—	—	—	—
24	22	31	111	185	209	302	866
—	—	—	—	—	—	—	2
—	—	—	—	—	—	—	—
—	—	—	—	2	2	—	—
4	3	10	8	16	12	6	5
—	—	—	—	—	—	—	—
—	—	—	cf. 1	+	—	—	—
—	—	—	—	—	—	—	—
—	+	+	+	+	+	+	—
—	—	+	+	+	+	+	+
4	11	4	14	14	18	11	9
20	4	15	27	32	39	20	27
6	11	20	61	89	114	172	408
3	1	2	1	3	2	8	16
1	1	—	4	1	2	1	—
—	—	1	—	1	—	—	—
2	2	2	2	—	2	—	3
2	1	4	2	6	3	2	—
—	—	—	—	—	—	—	—
1	2	2	2	5	2	3	24
1	1	1	1	—	1	—	—
1	3	1	2	—	2	4	4
2	1	3	1	2	—	1	12
9	12	23	24	37	26	34	43

One final point of interest perhaps bearing on the clearance phase itself is that numerous natural flint fragments from the soil profile examined by Dr Isobel Smith were found to be crackled or reddened *on one surface only* as if by fire. Firing of the vegetation on the site is suggested by this observation, at a time previous to the formation of the turf-line. This may have taken place between the first phase of stability and the final phase of cultivation (i.e. at the *c.* 10cm level), or during the initial clearance phase.

We can now briefly summarize the succession of events at South Street prior to the construction of the barrow. First of all, towards the end of the Last Glaciation, there was a phase of sub-arctic climate and an environment of tundra at which time frost structures (involutions) formed and a characteristic Late-Weichselian snail fauna was present. Then, during the Boreal period there is evidence for a phase of light woodland, probably followed in the Atlantic period by an environment of high forest. This forest was cleared totally by Neolithic man early in the third millennium and was succeeded by an elaborate series of land-use changes. An episode of deep ploughing seems to have been among the earliest of these. Then followed a phase of surface stability reflected by the formation of a relatively stone-free horizon in the soil, which was succeeded by a phase of instability during which the creation of a hummocky soil profile took place. Finally before the construction of the barrow there was an episode of surface stability with an environment of dry, short-turfed grassland. Charcoal from the soil surface was dated by radiocarbon assay to *c.* 2800 B.C.

Northton

The machair site at Northton is situated in the south-west extremity of the Isle of Harris, Inverness-shire (fig. 3). The site comprises a series of Neolithic, Beaker and Iron Age occupation horizons stratified within about five metres of wind-lain calcareous shell-sand (see plate 4) derived largely from beach deposits. The subsoil is non-calcareous boulder clay. Today, the base of the deposit is just above high-tide level and the exposed section is being eroded, probably by storm action.

A section through the deposits showed the following stratigraphy (fig. 11; plate 4):

Depth below
surface (cm)

0–12.5	Modern turf. Dark-grey loamy sand, strongly humic.
12.5–20	Blown sand. Light-brownish-grey; humic.
20–30	Buried turf. Dark-grey loamy sand, strongly humic.

30–65	Iron Age II occupation horizon. Shell midden consisting largely of cockles, *Cardium (Cerastoderma) edule.*
65–*c.* 97	Clean wind-blown sand.
c. 97–175	Pale-brown (humic) wind-blown sand.
175–195	Iron Age I occupation horizon. Brown sand, stained with organic matter and containing charcoal fragments.
195–265	Pale-brown (humic) wind-blown sand.
265–295	Beaker II occupation horizon. Brown sand, stained with organic matter and containing charcoal fragments. Intercalated lenses of clean wind-blown sand.
295–325	Clean wind-blown sand.
325–355	Beaker I occupation horizon. Brown sand, stained with organic matter and containing charcoal fragments.
355–375	Clean wind-blown sand. A thin layer of comminuted marine shell occurs at the base of this layer.
375–407.5	Neolithic II occupation horizon.

	375–382.5	Black sandy clay with charcoal fragments.
	382.5–392.5	Grey sand.
	392.5–402.5	Dark-grey sand with charcoal fragments.
	402.5–407.5	Black sandy clay with charcoal fragments.

407.5–480	Clean wind-blown sand.
480–520	Non-calcareous sand, mottled green.
520–545	Neolithic I occupation horizon. Black clay loam with intercalated layers of charcoal and quartz sand.
545 +	Non-calcareous boulder clay.

Although the deposits showed a certain amount of lateral variation, mainly in the thickness of the individual layers, this section is fairly representative of the site as a whole. Between 44 and 115cm a short section of sediment, laterally displaced from the main section where it was not represented, has been inserted. The critical layer is the horizon of clean wind-blown sand between 65 and *c.* 97cm in which *Helicella itala*, probably introduced on to the site by man, appears for the first time.

A series of samples was taken through this section and analysed for land snails (fig. 11; table 3 opposite p. 62). The weights of the samples varied so the actual numbers extracted from each and on which the percentages are based have been listed, as usual, on the right of the stratigraphical column while a more realistic representation of the variation in abundance through the deposit has been

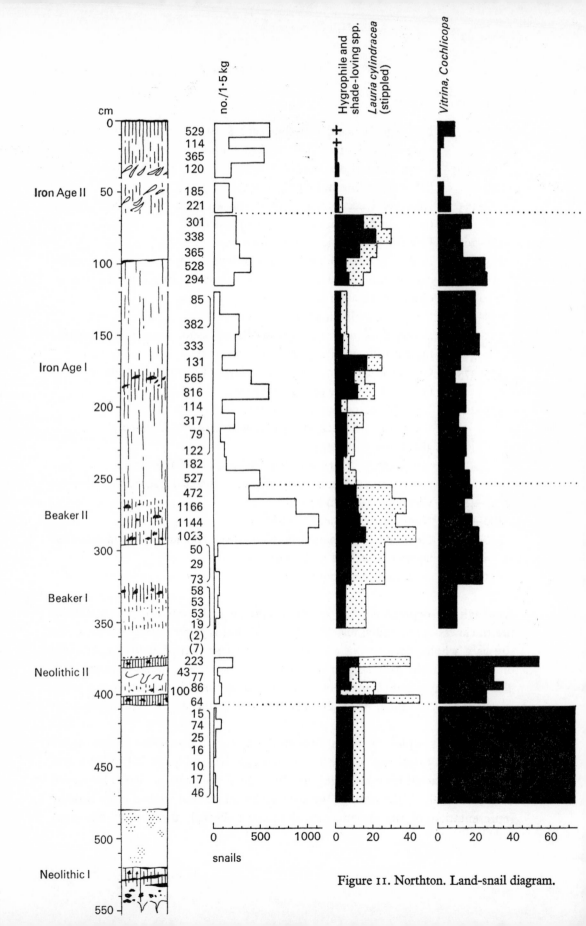

Figure 11. Northton. Land-snail diagram.

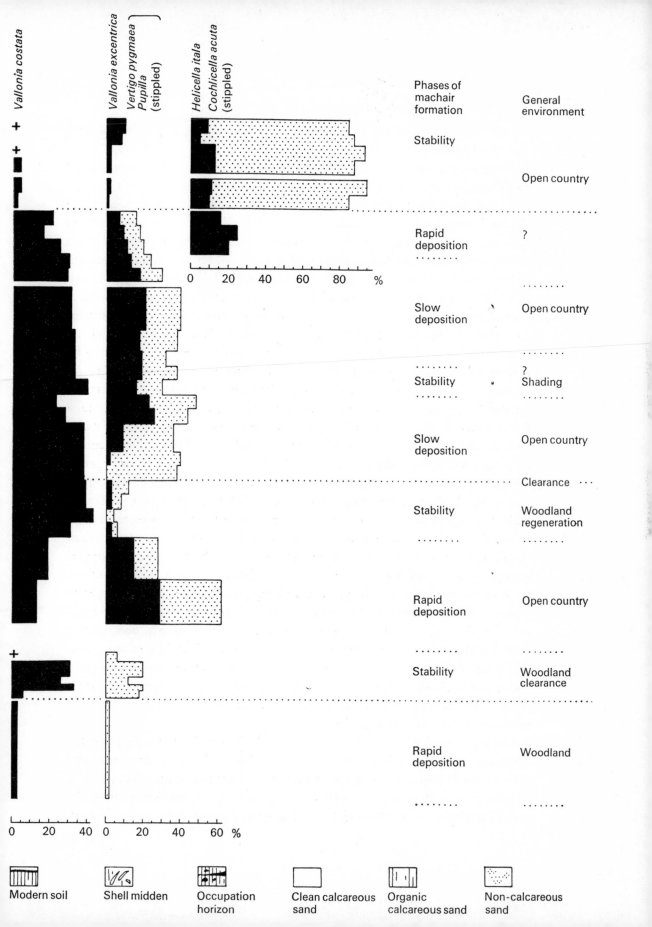

Vallonia costata

Vallonia excentrica
Vertigo pygmaea
Pupilla (stippled)

Helicella itala
Cochlicella acuta (stippled)

Phases of machair formation

General environment

Stability

Open country

Rapid deposition   ?

Slow deposition   Open country

Stability   ? Shading

Slow deposition   Open country

Clearance

Stability   Woodland regeneration

Rapid deposition   Open country

Stability   Woodland clearance

Rapid deposition   Woodland

0   20   40   60   80   %

0   20   40   0   20   40   60   %

Modern soil   Shell midden   Occupation horizon   Clean calcareous sand   Organic calcareous sand   Non-calcareous sand obtained by calculating the numbers per 1.5kg of sample (air dry) and plotting these as an open histogram.

Twenty-nine species of land snail were extracted and these have been plotted as a graph of relative abundance in five ecological groups as follows: (a) Hygrophile and shade-loving species. There were 20 species in this group, of which *Lauria cylindracea* was the most abundant. They range from those such as *Lymnaea truncatula* and *Carychium minimum* which are true hygrophiles living close to water on reeds or even, in the case of *Lymnaea*, actually in water, through others such as *Oxychilus alliarius* and *Carychium tridentatum* which favour relatively undisturbed, moist or shaded places, to those such as *Clausilia bidentata*, *Vertigo substriata* and *Lauria cylindracea* which are essentially rupestral species occurring on stone walls or under logs and stones. The abundance of individual species was, apart from *Lauria cylindracea*, too low for separate graphs to be meaningful. (b) The second group comprises three species, *Vitrina pellucida*, *Cochlicopa lubrica* and *C. lubricella*. As can be seen these are very abundant in the deposit but are unfortunately of uncertain ecological significance. *Vitrina* is found today in South Harris in hollows between sand-dunes amongst damp herbage and less frequently on the dunes themselves on blades of marram. It certainly tends towards the more open habitats. *Cochlicopa* comprises two species whose habitats are slightly different, *C. lubricella* tending to favour more open places than *C. lubrica*. Unfortunately all but the adults of these two species are difficult to distinguish and no attempt has been made therefore to separate them in the diagram. (c) *Vallonia costata*. Not a lot is known about this common species apart from the fact that it generally lives in grassland, is fond of rupestral habitats such as stone walls, and may occur in closed woodland in low numbers. (d) *Vallonia excentrica*, *Vertigo pygmaea* and *Pupilla muscorum*. These are species of open-country, never found in shaded places and generally living in dry habitats. Today, only *Vallonia excentrica* is common in South Harris, occurring in grazed fields on the stable machair surface. (e) *Helicella itala* and *Cochlicella acuta*. These are two xerophile species which have been introduced in recent times into South Harris, probably through the activities of man. They are found abundantly in the driest habitats, amongst the marram grass of the active dunes, where they predominate over all other species.

The interpretation of the diagram (fig. 11) is difficult due to the fact that the origin of the shells is various. It is frequently not clear whether shells were blown with the sand or were living on the surface on which the sand was accumulating. In some cases both processes may have been operating. In addition, some shells, particularly those in the Neolithic II occupation horizon, have probably been transported on to the site by man. It is likely, for instance, that during phases of rapid deposition of sand (fig. 11) shells were incorporated by wind-transport and so may derive from a variety of habitats. During phases of slow deposition or stability an assemblage is more likely to represent the true composition of a living, *in situ* population, except of course when brought in with occupation debris or turves by man.

The Neolithic I occupation horizon rests on boulder clay and is devoid of shells. The overlying layer of non-calcareous sand is sterile of artifacts and also devoid of shells.

Shells first appear in the layer of clean calcareous sand (407.5–480cm) but are sparse, and the five samples have therefore been amalgamated to calculate the percentage values. A spot sample from the layer as a whole was also taken and the shells from this have been included with those from the five standard samples to give the following list:

Hygrophile and shade-loving species (21 per cent)

Carychium tridentatum	11
Lymnaea truncatula	1
Vertigo pusilla	2
Vertigo substriata	3
Helix hortensis	1
Punctum pygmaeum	1
Euconulus fulvus	4
Vitrea contracta	1
Oxychilus alliarius	15
Retinella nitidula	2
Lauria cylindracea	16

Vitrina, Cochlicopa (75 per cent)

Vitrina pellucida	38
Cochlicopa	165

Vallonia costata (3 per cent)   8

Vallonia excentrica, Vertigo pygmaea, Pupilla (1 per cent)

Vertigo pygmaea	3
Pupilla muscorum	1

This fauna is clearly dominated by two groups, the hygrophile and shade-loving group and the *Vitrina, Cochlicopa* group. Open-country species, *Vertigo pygmaea* and *Pupilla*, comprise 1 per cent of the fauna and *Vallonia costata* 3 per cent. The fauna thus reflects a shaded environment, with the low abundance of *V. pygmaea*, *Pupilla* and *V. costata* implying a small amount of open ground. A forested environment would seem most likely though it must be borne in mind that the virtual absence of open-country species may be as much a function of the lime-poor nature of the boulder-clay land surface from which these shells probably derive, as of the absence of open ground.

In the Neolithic II horizon, the fauna shows a marked rise in the open-country element, *Vallonia costata* attaining about 30 per cent and *Vertigo pygmaea* and *Pupilla* together *c.* 20 per cent. If our original inference as to the wooded nature of the environment is correct then we would seem here to be dealing with a phase of forest recession, probably brought about by Neolithic man.

The make-up of the Neolithic II occupation horizon is complex, comprising two layers of sandy clay, one at the base and one at the top with a central section of grey sand. The former are probably turfs stripped from adjacent areas while the latter probably represents a slight blow of sand during the occupation period. *Vallonia costata* and *Pupilla muscorum* are abundant in the blown sand, suggesting a dry, open habitat, while hygrophiles and shade-loving species dominate the fauna in the sandy-clay layers.

Above the Neolithic II occupation horizon, rapid deposition of clean sand once more resumes, continuing more or less unchecked to 295cm. But the fauna, unlike that in the layer below the Neolithic II horizon, is dominated by open-country species with *Vallonia excentrica* appearing for the first time. An open landscape is to be envisaged at this stage.

The Beaker I occupation horizon appears to have had little effect in stabilizing the machair surface which is interesting in view of the enormous quantity of pottery it produced and the presence of two stone-built houses at this stage.

At the beginning of the Beaker II horizon conditions in the machair change dramatically. The deposits lose their former clean appearance and become stained with organic matter, perhaps implying the sand to be derived not from the beach but from a secondary source such as an eroding section of the machair. This condition persists up to *c.* 97cm. There is also an enormous rise in the number of shells of about 20-fold, suggesting a decrease in the rate of accumulation. Weathering and incipient humification of the deposits may now be taking place concurrent with accumulation. In the Beaker II occupation horizon itself there is an increase in the numbers of hygrophile and shade-loving species and a fall in the numbers of *Vallonia excentrica*, *Vertigo pygmaea* and *Pupilla*, the former becoming almost entirely absent at times. These faunal changes, which were foreshadowed in the underlying layer of blown sand, imply a period of machair stabilization and a shading over of the environment possibly with the regeneration of forest. It is fairly certain that this period of stabilization is not due to the Beaker II occupation, for there was far less pottery in it than in the Beaker I horizon and as was mentioned there was no evidence for a period of stabilization during this earlier Beaker phase.

Sand accumulation resumes at *c.* 265cm but more slowly than before. Open-country species again become important, first *Vertigo pygmaea* and *Pupilla* then *Vallonia excentrica*, the order in which, it is to be noticed, they first appeared in the sequence. Hygrophiles and shade-loving species decline. A second phase of woodland clearance is indicated.

Up to *c.* 97cm there are few further changes of note. Apart from a slight indication of a period of machair stability corresponding to the Iron Age I horizon when some shading-over of the environment may have occurred, the snail fauna remains constant.

Subsequent changes do not really concern the present discussion. Above *c.* 97cm rapid deposition of clean sand (as occurred below the Beaker II horizon) takes place once more and the two xerophile species most characteristic of the present-day fauna, *Helicella itala* and *Cochlicella acuta*, successively appear. Hygrophile and shade-loving species are finally reduced to less than 1 per cent, a reflection of the very open conditions which now exist.

There is thus evidence at Northton for a phase of prehistoric forest clearance. which may have been initiated during the Neolithic I phase and is at any rate securely associated with the Neolithic II and Beaker I occupation levels. This was followed by a phase of woodland regeneration during the Beaker II occupation which in its turn was succeeded by a second phase of clearance. In both cases, clearance was probably for pasture as none of the sherds from the occupation horizons bore grain impressions nor were there found querns, sickles or other trappings of an arable farming community.

Today, the Outer Hebrides are among the most treeless areas of Britain but, in addition to the land-snail evidence just put forward for former woodland, information from a variety of other sources points to the same conclusions. Not least is the fact that trees do grow in the Outer Hebrides today, albeit in sheltered places. Birch wood is recorded on the slopes of the Allt Volagir, South Uist, and at several places stunted sycamore, hawthorn and ash may be seen. Remains of birch and pine stumps are of common occurrence at the base of, and within the lower layers of, the blanket peat. "Even St. Kilda is likely to have had birch-hazel scrub at one time and pollen from its peat indicates that pine, alder, elm and oak were probably widespread in the Outer Hebrides, their pollen having reached St. Kilda in the aerial plankton."[9] And there are several submerged or intertidal forests along the western shores of the islands. Wood from one of these at Borve, Benbecula, has yielded a radiocarbon date of 3750 ± 170 B.C.[10]

The cause of the onset of sand deposition and the mechanism of machair build-up are uncertain. The deposition of blown sand in the first instance may have been brought about by a fall of sea-level, leaving exposed banks of dry shell sand. It may be that man had no part in causing the initial deposition, for instance by clearance or cultivation of machair already established elsewhere, as the sand seems too clean to be derived from a source other than the beach. Ritchie has suggested that at Borve in Benbecula, the onset of sand deposition was around 3750 B.C., on the basis of the radiocarbon assay of intertidal wood peat (quoted above) associated with interstratified sand which he considers to be of aeolian

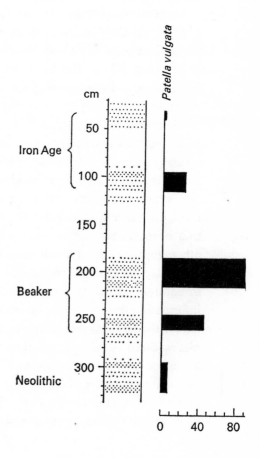

Figure 12. Changes in the composition of the shell-fish assemblage and suggested marine and terrestrial environments in a prehistoric midden at Northton, Isle of Harris.
Patella = limpet
Cardium = cockle
Nucella = dog whelk
Littorina = winkle
Mytilus = mussel
Pecten = scallop
Ostrea = oyster
M. margaritifera = fresh-water mussel
Helix hortensis = land-snail

origin. One may also wonder whether clearance was not an altogether natural process brought about by the overwhelming of the forest by wind-blown sand.

An insight into some of the environmental changes which took place during the formation of the machair can be obtained by looking at the food-shell debris, mostly marine, in the various occupation horizons of the site (fig. 12). For apart from perhaps reflecting the preferences of prehistoric man for particular kinds of shell-fish, these changes may also relate to the availability of various species as determined by the presence of suitable habitats, in turn a function of the level of the sea. Thus in the Neolithic II horizon a variety of species was eaten, particularly the edible cockle, *Cardium (Cerastoderma) edule*, suggesting the presence of extensive tracts of intertidal sand in which this animal lives. The virtual absence of *Cardium* from the Beaker occupation levels, and the dependence of man on rocky shore species alone, suggest that a rise of sea-level took

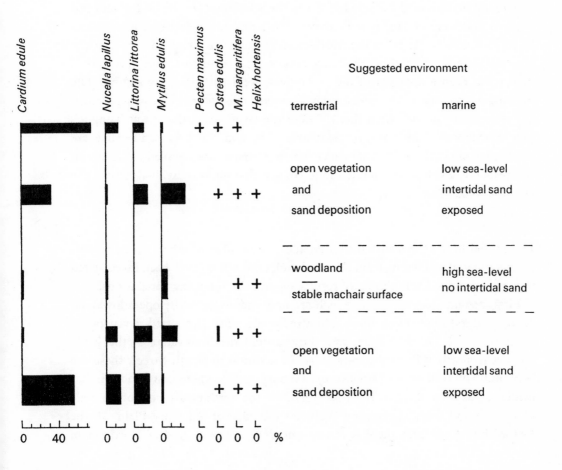

place at this time, causing the destruction of the habitat of the cockle. Then in the Iron Age these changes are reversed and, particularly in Iron Age II, the cockle becomes once again a species of importance in the shell-fish diet of man, suggesting that a fall of sea-level had taken place.

This hypothesis of a period of high sea-level during the Beaker occupation of the site and periods of low sea-level during the previous Neolithic I and later Iron Age periods would go some way to explaining the observed changes in machair stratigraphy. Thus the two periods of low sea-level may be associated with the two corresponding periods when rapid build-up of the machair took place, perhaps by the sub-aerial erosion of ridges of marine sand left high and dry above high-water-mark by the receding sea. The intervening period of high sea-level may have submerged this source of sand, preventing further build-up of the machair and thus ensuring its stabilization during the Beaker II occupation.

The importance of the cockle harvest to the inhabitants of the Outer Isles and western shores of Scotland is well conveyed by a mid-nineteenth-century account of P. H. Gosse.[11] "It is on the north-western coasts of Scotland . . . that the greatest abundance of these mollusca occurs, and there they may form not a luxury but even a necessity of life to the poor semi-barbarous population. The inhabitants of those rocky regions enjoy an unenviable notoriety for being habitually dependent on this mean diet. 'Where the river meets the sea at Tongue', says Macculloch, 'there is a considerable ebb, and the long sand-banks are productive of cockles in an abundance which is almost unexampled . . . Without this resource, I believe it is not too much to say, that many individuals must have died for want.'"

Discussion

In addition to the three sites discussed above, a number of others on calcareous parent material and dating from the third millennium B.C. have been investigated (fig. 3; Appendix A). Preliminary results suggest the following conclusions.

First, certain areas of Britain which are now characteristically open downland or agricultural land, often bleak and windswept, once supported a vegetation cover of forest. On the Chalk, four sites around the headwaters of the River Kennet in north Wiltshire suggest this. In addition to South Street, these are Windmill Hill (causewayed enclosure), Avebury and Beckhampton Road. Similar evidence has been obtained from Knap Hill on the north escarpment of the Vale of Pewsey and from Durrington Walls on the edge of Salisbury Plain. In the Oxfordshire Cotswolds there is Ascott-under-Wychwood. And at Northton in the Outer Hebrides land-snails from the basal layers of the machair similarly suggest a once-forested land.

It has generally been assumed on ecological grounds that these areas once supported forest and the demonstration by molluscan analysis that this was indeed the case comes as little surprise. More important is the fact that forest clearance in these areas took place early in the third millennium B.C. as dated by radio-carbon; at some sites a fourth millennium date is possible. Although the evidence is circumstantial it is likely that forest clearance was an artificial process brought about by early farming communities.

In addition to this evidence there are two pollen diagrams, one from Wingham and the other from Frogholt in Kent, close to the North Downs, which show that forest clearance on the Chalk had been achieved by 1700 and 1000 B.C. respectively.[12] And Kerney has demonstrated a phase of forest clearance on the North Downs escarpment at Brook, dated to c. 2600 B.C. by radiocarbon.

Following clearance, two kinds of land-use or treatment of the soil can be recognized, one in which disturbance is confined to the soil surface, the other involving total disturbance of the profile. Ascott-under-Wychwood is an example of the former; others are Beckhampton Road (plate 3a) near Avebury in N. Wilt-shire and Kilham (plate 3b) in the Yorkshire Wolds. The latter is a non-calcareous brown-earth soil at the base of which is a strongly developed clay-illuviation (Bt) horizon. The soils at South Street, Wayland's Smithy, Horslip and Silbury Hill (turf-stack) are examples of profiles which have been deeply disturbed.

What these two kinds of land-use imply, if anything, is at the moment totally speculative. Perhaps they reflect a distinction between pastoral and arable farm-ing. Or we may be dealing with different forms of cultivation, on the one hand by a slash-and-burn technique, on the other by more vigorous tillage of the soil. Alternatively they may simply reflect differences of technique dictated by soil type or other local environmental or social factors.

Avebury and Durrington Walls are somewhat intermediate in type between South Street and Ascott-under-Wychwood, there being some disturbance of the soil below the turf-line but not sufficient to destroy the character of the woodland fauna.

At Brook in Kent an episode of forest clearance on the sides of a scarp-face coombe known as the Devil's Kneadingtrough resulted in the accumulation of a deposit 70cm thick in the coombe bottom. This process, if not altogether associated with the steep profile of the coombe, may be the result of deep dis-turbance of the soil as occurred at South Street.

At a number of sites the type of land-use is not clear, but an open-country snail fauna is present, characterized by an abundance of *Vallonia costata* and *V. excentrica* with other grassland species in varying numbers. At these sites it can be safely assumed that forest clearance has taken place. The sites are Julliberrie's Grave, Kent, Thickthorn Down, Dorset, the West Kennet Long Barrow near Avebury, north Wiltshire, Arreton Down on the Isle of Wight and Earl's Farm Down near Durrington Walls in the valley of the Wiltshire Avon. Ploughmarks were recorded at the latter.

The faunas from Knap Hill and Windmill Hill causewayed enclosures are dominated by woodland species, the open-country element being minimal. These are the only sites at which clearance has not been demonstrated.

At two sites, Marden in the Vale of Pewsey and Kilham in the Yorkshire Wolds (plate 3b), the buried soil is a decalcified brown earth with a pronounced horizon of illuviated clay at the base (*sol lessivé*). At Marden there was a period of Neolithic occupation prior to the burial of the soil and it is possible that the onset of illuviation was associated in some way with forest clearance, in the same way as is podsolization.[13] This would be an interesting topic for future research.

The buried soil at Willerby Wold and parts of the profile at Ascott-under-Wychwood were of brown-earth type.

A final point of considerable interest is that with the exception of Brook where regeneration took place, and the two causewayed enclosures, Knap Hill and Windmill Hill, where clearance was not demonstrated, the environment, immediately prior to burial of the soil profile, was one of stable and dry short-turfed grassland in all the sites studied. This strongly suggests that the regeneration of scrub or woodland was prevented by grazing, which at Marden, Durrington Walls and Beckhampton Road may have continued for many centuries.

Appendix A: sites mentioned in the text

Except where stated to the contrary, the sites comprise ancient soils buried beneath Neolithic earthworks of the third millennium B.C. The number of each site is that shown on fig. 3.

1. *Ascott-under-Wychwood* (SP 299175).[14] Neolithic long barrow excavated by D. Benson for M.P.B.W. and Oxford City and County Museum, 1966–9. Land-snail fauna from the buried soil suggests open woodland with associated Mesolithic occupation, followed by a phase of closed woodland. Neolithic forest clearance then took place with subsequent disturbance of the soil surface. Radiocarbon assay of charcoal from soil surface gave a date of (BM–492) 2785 ± 70 B.C. and from a Neolithic pit a date of (BM–491b) 2943 ± 70 B.C.

2. *South Street* (SU 090693).[15] Neolithic long barrow. Snail fauna from subsoil hollow beneath the mound suggests a former environment of open woodland. A closed woodland environment during the Atlantic period probably followed. An episode of forest clearance, probably Neolithic, then took place. The buried soil was disturbed by cultivation through its entire depth and plough-marks were present on the subsoil surface. Land-snails from the buried soil indicate an open-country environment. Charcoal from the soil surface gave a C-14 date of (BM-356) 2810 ± 130 B.C.[16]

3. *Northton* (NF 975913).[17] A series of Neolithic and Beaker occupation horizons in a deposit of calcareous wind-blown sand. Land-snail faunas indicate a former woodland environment, then a phase of woodland clearance during Neolithic and Beaker occupation followed by a phase of woodland regeneration.

4. *Wayland's Smithy II* (SU 281854).[18] Neolithic chambered tomb. Buried soil below mound thought to have been disturbed by cultivation. Land-snail fauna examined by M. P. Kerney and found to be of open-country type, dominated by *Vallonia costata* and *V. excentrica*.[19] Charcoal from surface of buried soil gave a C-14 date of 2820 ± 130 B.C.

5. *Avebury* (SU 101698). Rescue excavation of part of the henge bank by Mrs F. de M. Vatcher for M.P.B.W., 1969. Land-snail fauna of the buried soil indicates a phase of open woodland, probably early Post-glacial in age, followed by a phase of closed woodland. There was then an episode of

forest clearance, probably of Neolithic origin; possible ploughmarks were
present at the surface of the subsoil. Date of burial of the soil *c.* 2000 B.C.

6. *West Kennet Long Barrow* (SU 105677).[20] Neolithic chambered tomb, thought
to have been constructed in the first half of the third millennium. Soil pit
1.2m square dug into mound at 33m west of façade and 6m north of long
axis, by permission of M.P.B.W. Land-snail fauna from buried soil dominated by *Vallonia costata* and *V. excentrica* indicating an open, grassland
landscape. Soil appeared little disturbed, and may not have been cultivated.[21]

7. *Horslip* (SU 086705).[22] Neolithic long barrow. Monolith of buried soil
provided by Dr I. F. Smith. Soil possibly cultivated. Land-snail fauna of
open-country type dominated by *Vallonia costata*, *V. excentrica* and *Helicella
itala*. Radiocarbon assay of antler from the bottom of the ditch gave a date
of (BM–180) 3240 ± 150 B.C.[23] which is probably the date of burial of the
soil.

8. *Windmill Hill* (SU 087715).[24] Neolithic causewayed enclosure. Soil pit dug
by permission of National Trust and M.P.B.W. 1.2m sq. in Outer Bank V,
10m north of south end of bank. Buried soil extremely stony and appeared
to lack a turf-line; much occupation debris recorded from previous excavations. Land-snail fauna[25] dominated by woodland species. This is curious in
view of the time interval (200–400 years) between occupation of the site
(BM–73 2950 ± 150 B.C. from charcoal in soil) and construction of the
enclosure bank (BM–74 2570 ± 150 B.C. from charcoal in primary fill of
ditch). It is possible that the turf was stripped from the soil prior to construction as suggested by Dimbleby.[26]

9. *Silbury Hill* (SU 100685).[27] Neolithic mound. Buried soil non-calcareous
on Clay-with-flints. Turfs of turf-stack of rendsina type comprising a turf-
line *c.* 2.0cm thick and an underlying stony horizon suggesting cultivation
as at Wayland's Smithy. Land-snail fauna of open-country type, largely
Vallonia excentrica, *V. costata*, *Helicella itala* and *Vertigo pygmaea*. C–14
assay of unburnt vegetation from surface of turfs yielded a date of (I–4136)
2145 ± 95 B.C.[28]

10. *Beckhampton Road* (SU 066677).[29] Neolithic long barrow. Soil profile comprises a thin turf-line and an undisturbed layer below (plate 3a), as at
Ascott-under-Wychwood. The land-snail fauna from the lower part of the
soil is a woodland one; that from the turf-line, open-country.[30] C–14 assay
of charcoal from the turf-line gave a date of (NPL–138) 3250 ± 160 B.C.
C–14 assay of antler from the mound (probably the date of burial of the soil)
gave a date of (BM–506b) 2517 ± 90 B.C.[31]

11. *Knap Hill* (SU 121636).[32] Neolithic causewayed enclosure. Land-snail fauna from buried soil, examined by B. W. Sparks, is similar to that from Windmill Hill in being dominated by woodland species. C–14 assay of antler from the primary rubble of the ditch gave a date of (BM–205) 2760 ± 115 B.C., probably dating the burial of the soil.[33]

12. *Marden* (SU 091584).[34] A Neolithic henge dated by C–14 assay of charcoal from the bottom of the ditch to (BM–557) 1989 ± 50 B.C.[35] The buried soil beneath the bank was a non-calcareous *sol lessivé* developed on calcareous drift. A C–14 assay of charcoal associated with Middle Neolithic pottery in a layer about 7cm below the buried soil surface yielded a date of (BM–560) 2653 ± 60 B.C. There is thus a time span of *c.* 700 years between occupation and the construction of the henge; during this time the clay illuviation horizon at the base of the profile may have formed, perhaps due to the effects of forest clearance. No such horizon formed at Durrington Walls where a similar time interval was involved.

13. *Durrington Walls* (SU 153435).[36] A Neolithic henge monument. The buried soil beneath the henge bank comprised a turf-line and an underlying stony horizon. The former contained a land-snail fauna of open-country type indicative of a stable grassland environment; in the latter was a mixed fauna of open-country and shade-loving species suggesting a certain amount of disturbance but not to the extent of that at South Street. A fauna from a subsoil hollow below this layer indicated an environment of open woodland. Forest clearance and possibly cultivation may have taken place and may be associated with Middle Neolithic occupation debris sealed beneath the bank. C–14 assay of charcoal from the latter gave a date of (NPL–191) 2450 ± 150 B.C. The date of the henge itself and thus of the burial of the soil is dated by C–14 assay of material from the ditch bottom to *c.* 2000 B.C.[37] As at Marden and Beckhampton Road there is thus a time lapse of several hundred years between the initial forest clearance and land-use phase on the one hand and the burial of the soil on the other, during which time there was an environment of stable short-turfed grassland.

14. *Brook* (TR 077453).[38] Chalky hillwash (70cm thick) in the bottom of a coombe; snail fauna suggests partial forest clearance. Overlain by a soil with a fauna indicating regeneration of woodland. Charcoal from the soil gave a C–14 date of (BM–245) 2590 ± 105 B.C.[39] associated with Neolithic pottery. Soil buried by a further hillwash deposit of Iron Age origin.

15. *Julliberrie's Grave* (TR 078532).[40] Neolithic long barrow. Fauna from the buried soil, examined by A. S. Kennard, indicates an open environment,

Pupilla muscorum, Vallonia costata and *V. excentrica* being abundant. However, *Pomatias elegans, Carychium tridentatum* and various Zonitidae are also common, suggesting either some influence of scrub or that two distinct faunas were present which were not separated in the sampling.

16. *Thickthorn Down* (ST 971123).[41] Neolithic long barrow. In the buried soil (turf-line) beneath the mound was a land-snail fauna (examined by A. S. Kennard) of completely open-country type; *Vallonia costata* and *Vallonia excentrica* were the only species present in abundance.

17. *Kilham* (TA 056674).[42] Neolithic long barrow. Buried soil a non-calcareous *sol lessivé* with a pronounced clay illuviation horizon at the base (plate 3b). The long barrow was dated by radiocarbon assay of burnt structural elements to (BM–293) 2880 ± 125 B.C. Prior to the construction of the long barrow, the site had been occupied by Mesolithic man.

18. *Willerby Wold* (TA 029761).[43] Neolithic long barrow. The buried soil, examined by I. W. Cornwall, was barely calcareous and of mature brownearth type. Mollusca were absent. The construction of the barrow was dated by C–14 assay of charred structural elements to *c.* 3000 B.C.[44]

19. *Arreton Down* (SZ 536874).[45] Early Bronze Age round barrow. Buried soil comprises a stone-free turf-line *c.* 5cm thick and an underlying stony horizon *c.* 15cm thick, which appears much disturbed, possibly by cultivation. Late-Neolithic occupation debris (Mortlake pottery) present in the soil. Land-snail fauna (examined by B. W. Sparks) dominated by *Vallonia costata* and *V. excentrica* with *Helicella itala* and *Pupilla muscorum* in lesser abundance indicating a totally open landscape.

20. *Earl's Farm Down* (*Amesbury, G.* 71) (SU 184419).[46] Beaker barrow dated by C–14 to *c.* 2000 B.C. Buried soil a rendsina with a thin turf-line. At the base of the soil, scored into the subsoil surface, was a series of one-way ploughmarks indicating possible cultivation of the soil at some time prior to the construction of the barrow. Land-snail fauna examined by M. P. Kerney who concluded that the environment indicated was dry and completely open short-turfed grassland.

Appendix B: analysis of land snails from archaeological deposits

Preparation of the section

The section to be sampled is thoroughly cleaned by scraping with a pointing trowel, and made as near vertical as its height will allow. It is then photographed, and a scale drawing made of a representative part.

Sampling

Samples are cut as blocks of earth from the section, starting at the base and working upwards. About 1 to 2 kg is usually sufficient to provide the requisite number of shells for counting. The samples are placed in polythene bags (20 × 30 cm is a convenient size), labelled, and air-dried as soon as possible. The sample interval may be varied from as little as 1.0cm to as much as 20cm and depends on factors such as the consistency of the deposits and the rate of faunal change which is suspected within them.

Analysis

The air-dried samples are weighed, then placed in a bowl of water and allowed to collapse; the process can be speeded up by gentle stirring. A large number of shells generally float to the surface and can be poured off into a sieve, mesh size 0.5mm. The sludge is then passed through a series of sieves, smallest mesh 0.5mm, thoroughly washed and then oven-dried. Resistant soil crumbs can be easily removed by treatment with 100 vol. hydrogen peroxide. All shells are then extracted from the residue.

The contents of the entire sample are counted. Identification is done with a low-power binocular microscope (*c.* × 10 and × 20 serve for most purposes); only apices are counted to avoid including the same individual more than once.

There are a number of difficulties of identification which need not be discussed here in detail. For instance no attempt has been made to separate the various species of limacid slugs (fam. Limacidae). The two species of *Cochlicopa, C. lubrica* and *C. lubricella,* are difficult to separate as small juveniles; and the same applies to the two species of *Cepaea, C. hortensis* and *C. nemoralis,* and *Arianta arbustorum.* Shell fragments of the latter however can be distinguished from those of *Cepaea* spp. and where present are indicated in the tables as a plus sign.

Presentation of results

The results of analysis are presented as a histogram of relative abundance; percentages, unless specifically stated, are of the total fauna.

On the left of the diagram is placed the stratigraphical column with the depth below a convenient datum (e.g. ancient or modern soil surface) in cm. On the immediate right of this are listed the numbers of shells in each sample on which the percentages are based. The snail species or groups of species occupy the main part of the diagram, generally with shade-loving species on the left, intermediate species in the centre and open-country species on the right. On the far right an interpretation of the results may be suggested, with a composite histogram of the three main ecological groups.

Interpretation of the assemblages

The detailed interpretation of molluscan assemblages has been discussed on several occasions by B. W. Sparks and M. P. Kerney.[47]

In the case of soil profiles which have developed *in situ*, which applies to most of the sites discussed in this paper, one of the main problems is in estimating the area of environment represented by a particular fauna. Detailed stratigraphical studies of a single horizon would help to resolve this problem. Another difficulty is that snail faunas are only an indirect reflection of the vegetation and other aspects of a habitat. Inferences about past environments made from subfossil assemblages are based largely on the present-day ecology of species,[48] and these may have changed considerably over the past 6000 years.

Four broad ecological groups of land snails may be recognized, namely marsh species, shade-loving species, intermediate species and open-country species.

Marsh species include *Lymnaea truncatula*, *Carychium minimum*, *Succinea* spp., *Vertigo antivertigo* (Draparnaud), *V. angustior* and *Zonitoides nitidus*. All are rare on terrestrial sites on chalk and limestone though may occasionally occur in low-lying situations. In the present study they were found only at Northton.

The shade-loving species are those which thrive best in damp, shaded and undisturbed places, though some are not restricted to specifically shaded habitats, and a few may sometimes be found in quite open and exposed situations. The family Zonitidae including the genera *Euconulus*, *Vitrea*, *Oxychilus* and *Retinella*, may be conveniently plotted as a single unit, though in some cases, as at Ascott-under-Wychwood, it is useful to consider each separately. *Carychium tridentatum* and *Discus rotundatus* usually occur in sufficient abundance for separate graphs to be plotted. The "Other shade-loving species" include the Clausiliidae, *Ena* spp., *Acanthinula*, *Helicigona*, and *Vitrina* and several others generally occurring in relatively low numbers and for which individual plots would be meaningless; many in this group are to be found under logs and stones, on walls and even on the trunks of trees.

It is occasionally convenient to separate from the shade-loving species a small group which appear to be particularly tolerant of more open habitats than the rest. These are *Punctum pygmaeum, Euconulus fulvus, Retinella radiatula* and *Vitrina pellucida*. This has been done at both South Street and Ascott-under-Wychwood.

The intermediate species comprise *Pomatias elegans, Cochlicopa* spp., *Cepaea* spp. and *Arianta arbustorum, Hygromia hispida* and the Limacidae. With the exception of *Pomatias elegans*, these species are either difficult to identify as is the case with the Limacidae, or their ecological implications are uncertain. *Pomatias elegans* is particularly fond of scrub or habitats where the soil surface is bare of vegetation and loose and rubbly.

Of the open-country species, none but *Vallonia costata* ever occur in shaded habitats, and most are found in dry, open situations being particularly fond of grassland. They are *Pupilla muscorum, Vertigo pygmaea, Abida secale, Vallonia costata, Vallonia excentrica, Helicella itala* and *Cochlicella acuta*. Their presence in a fauna is thus a good indication of open ground. *Vallonia costata*, as has already been discussed, can occur in woodland habitats in low numbers.

Truncatellina cylindrica (Férussac) is another species in the open-country group, but is extremely rare. It was present for instance in the turf-line at Durrington Walls.

Acknowledgments

I would particularly like to thank Isobel Smith, Michael Kerney and Don Benson for their help, encouragement and critical discussion during the course of this work. My grateful thanks also to the archaeologists who, in allowing me to work on their sites, have made possible this study of buried soils.

The field-work and laboratory analyses were done in the Department of Human Environment, Institute of Archaeology, London University, during the tenure of a N.E.R.C. research grant.

Notes

1. H. Godwin, *The History of the British Flora* (1956); A. G. Smith, in D. Walker and R. G. West (eds), *Studies in the Vegetational History of the British Isles* (1970), pp. 81–96.
2. *Veröffentlichingen Geobotanische Institut Rübel, Zurich*, XXXVII (1962), 83–99.
3. *Proceedings of the Malacological Society*, XV (1923), 241–59.
4. For details of the location and excavation of this and other sites mentioned in the text, see Appendix A and fig. 3. Unless otherwise stated sites comprise buried soils beneath Neolithic earthworks.
5. Lower Turonian and not Lower Chalk as marked on the 1″ Geological Survey map. Kindly determined by D. J. Carter, Department of Geology, Imperial College.
6. *W.A.M.*, LXIII (1968), 12–26.
7. private communication from G. W. Dimbleby.
8. *Antiquity*, LXI (1967), 289–301.
9. F. F. Darling and J. M. Boyd, *The Highlands and Islands* (1964), p. 50.
10. *Transactions of the Institute of British Geographers*, XXXIX (1966), 79–86.
11. P. H. Gosse, *A Year at the Shore* (1865).
12. *Veröffentlichingen Geobotanische Institut Rübel, Zurich*, XXXVII (1962), 83–99.
13. G. W. Dimbleby, *The Development of the British Heathlands and their Soils* (1962), Oxford Forestry Memoir, no. 23.
14. *Current Archaeology*, no. 24 (1971), 7–10.
15. *Antiquity*, XLII (1968), 138–42.
16. *ibid.*, XLIII (1969), 144–5.
17. *ibid.*, XL (1966), 137–9.
18. *ibid.*, XXXIX (1965), 126–33.
19. private communication from M. P. Kerney.
20. S. Piggott, *The West Kennet Long Barrow. Excavations 1955–56* (1962).
21. *Symposium of the Zoological Society of London*, no. 22 (1968), 293–317.
22. *Antiquity*, XXXIV (1960), 297–9.
23. *ibid.*, XL (1966), 299.
24. I. F. Smith, *Windmill Hill and Avebury: Excavations by Alexander Keiller, 1925–1939* (1965).
25. *W.A.M.*, LXI (1966), 91–2.
26. Smith, *op. cit.*
27. *Antiquity*, XLIV (1970), 313–14.
28. *ibid.*, XLIII (1969), 216.
29. *ibid.*, XLII (1968), 138–42.
30. *Symposium of the Zoological Society of London*, no. 22 (1968), 293–317.
31. private communication from I. F. Smith.
32. *W.A.M.*, LX (1965), 1–23.
33. *Antiquity*, XLIII (1969), 304–5.
34. *ibid.*, XLIV (1970), 56–7.
35. private communication from G. J. Wainwright.
36. *Ant. J.*, XLVII (1967), 166–84; *Antiquity*, XLII (1968), 20–6.
37. G. J. Wainwright, *Durrington Walls* (forthcoming).
38. *Philosophical Transactions of the Royal Society*, B, CCXLVIII (1964), 135–204.
39. private communication from M. P. Kerney; *Radiocarbon*, XIII no. 2 (1971) (forthcoming).
40. *Ant. J.*, XIX (1939), 260–81.

41. *P.P.S.*, II (1936), 77–96.
42. *Antiquity*, XLV (1971), 50–53.
43. *P.P.S.*, XXIX (1963), 173–205.
44. *Antiquity*, XLI (1967), 306–7.
45. *P.P.S.*, XXVI (1960), 263–302.
46. *ibid.*, XXXIII (1967), 336–66.
47. *Philosophical Transactions of the Royal Society*, B, CCXLVI (1963), 203–54; *ibid.*, B, CCXLVIII (1964), 135–204; *Proceedings of the Linnaean Society of London*, CLXXII (1961), 71–80; *Journal of Animal Ecology*, XXXIII (1964), 87–98.
48. *Journal of Ecology*, XXII (1934), 1–38.

Diet, economy and biosocial change in late prehistoric Europe

DON BROTHWELL

During the past two decades, archaeology has become more and more concerned with ecological variation in relation to the evolution of earlier cultures, and with the need of earlier peoples to adapt to, pursue, and evolve different economies. Whatever cultural elaborations or eccentricities a community might display, it had to bow to the primary dictates of providing sufficient food to maintain health and provide sufficient energy for day-to-day labours. During the two million years or so of our evolution, the quest for food has thus been a primary life force, with most other human activities being very secondary to it.

However, the intensive work of recent years has been concerned not only with determining broad economic change in earlier communities, but also with detailing the actual foods eaten.[1] One can of course consider general differences in overall economy without reference to nutritional aspects in detail, but there is no doubt that the more fully the nutritional status can be worked out, the more the economic basis of human cultural evolution can be seen in all its complexity. My contribution here is at least to outline the range of culturally meaningful information we now have on diet in prehistoric Europe and to consider some of the biosocial repercussions of economic and dietary change.

Perhaps I should also say at this point what is meant here by 'biosocial change', and why I use this term. It is probably not an expression yet to be heard behind the sombre portals of the Society of Antiquaries, but I would like to suggest that in the new 'Sciencemanship' of archaeology it is a term which certainly has meaning and use. For many decades there was a symbiotic, but rather apartheid, relationship between archaeology and human biological studies. Material or information moved in one or other direction, but the complex interrelations between biological and cultural man were somewhat underrated. In actual fact, the distinctiveness of human evolution, in contrast to that of other mammals, has depended upon the genetic and adaptive potentialities of earlier populations influencing the cultural environment which man gradually built up around himself, and this in turn has acted as a selective pressure which caused further progressive biological change; what our American colleagues would call 'feedback reciprocal interaction'. Those wishing to pursue this concept a little further might begin with the recent collection of essays edited by Ashley Montagu (1968) and called *Culture, Man's Adaptive Dimension*. This biosocial mesh is in operation today just as it was in Neolithic or early Pleistocene times, only the variables having to some extent changed.

So, what I wish to accomplish is this: first, I want to discuss the assessment of diet in late prehistoric Europe, review the sort of information which can be collected, and comment on the problem of getting a truly representative picture of the nutrition of earlier groups. To some extent, it will be worthwhile playing devil's advocate here. Secondly, my concern will be with the possible biosocial changes which took place when the agricultural revolution was well established.

In a recent published symposium called *Man the Hunter*, edited by Richard Lee and Irven De Vore,[2] various contributors emphasize the long time-span of hominid evolution during which only hunting and collecting economies were operating. There seems little doubt that the food quest was a powerful selective force influencing evolving behaviour patterns as well as biological micro-evolution. Looking at modern civilized populations, we see economies and an attitude to food which are very different. Many are now chronically over-fed, and many abuse themselves with food biasses which are injurious to health. Between these two dietary extremes come the early agriculturalists. The current view is that these revolutionary changes in economy were initiated in south-west Asia, and with missionary zeal – or at least with the slow determination of the Salvation Army – influenced a gradual wave of change north-westwards through Europe. This shows up in the C-14 dates now associated with the onset of Neolithic economies in parts of Europe.[3] Some developmental trend of this sort certainly took place, but I think at this stage we must be careful not to accept a picture of economic evolution which is too tidy and text-bookish.

Can we, for instance, really put all the blame on the Mesopotamians of some ten millennia ago? Because archaeological evidence indicates that in this region profound economic changes were beginning, are we justified in also concluding that this was the only region of the Old World where man began very early to exert control over wild plant and animal populations? I must confess that I still suspect that the advanced Upper Palaeolithic Societies of Europe, who must have had a wide knowledge of the world around them, may have at times resorted to animal capture and thence breeding, or the intentional planting of wild food plants. In other words, the change-over to a predominantly farming economy marked the crossing of a cultural threshold which may first have been reached in Asia, but this need not mean that Late Palaeolithic societies in Europe were not versatile enough to have experimented with some farming techniques. Higgs and Jarman, in a recent critical assessment of our knowledge of the origins of agriculture, remark: "The economies of Palaeolithic peoples remain unstudied, largely because of the unwarranted assumption that all men were then hunter/ gatherers. On this assumption rests the hypothesis that the Near East was an innovating centre where the innovations necessary for a beginning of domestication first occurred. It seems more likely that it was an area where the techniques and symbiases of the inhabitants of colder regions were adjacent to temperate and sub-tropical areas, in each of which different forms of symbiosis had long existed. Collected together and integrated they formed complex, powerful and expanding economies".[4]

But we have not finished with the problems of studying biological data which may be relevant to the history of agriculture and dietary change. Are we yet even in a position to tell from excavated food debris and such evidence that an earlier community was keeping or growing and selectively breeding domesticable stocks? In the London conference which took place in 1968 on the domestication and exploitation of plants and animals[5] there were clearly varying views and degrees of confidence on this point. The most critical comment was by Dr R. J. Berry, who considers that: "it is not possible to recognize any traits which inevitably accompany domestication, and, even worse, most of the criteria by which domestication has been claimed to be recognizable, may occur as a result of processes which have nothing to do with domestication".[6]

Thus, what I think must be concluded from my comments so far is that although we see a very different form of food-producing economy extending from the Neolithic we are really quite uncertain as to the antiquity of what might be called the 'agricultural outlook'. Moreover, we are not yet able to say with any confidence when domesticable stocks showed changes which were certainly indicative of human control and selective breeding.

During the fifth to the second millennia B.C. in Europe, vast changes in food-use took place. Probably of special importance was the cultivation and increased consumption of cereals. In table 1, assembled by Mrs Jane Renfrew, the earliest examples of European crops are given, together with data from Near Eastern sites. The pulses, which are also listed, are probably not of domestic varieties. Even from this limited evidence it is clear that there was a wide variety of early

Sites	Dates—B.C.	Wild Einkorn	Einkorn	Wild Emmer	Emmer	Bread wheat	Wild 2-row barley	Hulled 2-row barley	Hulled 6-row barley	Naked 2-row barley	Naked 6-row barley	Oat	Millet	Pea	Lentil	Vetch	Flax
Ali Kosh (B.M.)	7500–6750	x	x	–	x	–	x	–	x?	–	–	–	–	–	–	–	–
Ali Kosh (A.K.)	6750–6000	–	–	–	x	–	–	x	–	x	–	Wd	–	–	–	–	–
Ali Kosh (M.J.)	6000–5600	–	–	–	x	–	–	x	–	–	–	Wd	–	–	–	x	–
Tepe Sabz (Sabz)	5500–5000	–	–	–	–	x	–	x	–	x	–	–	–	–	x	x	x
Tepe Guran	6200–5500	–	–	–	–	–	x	x	–	–	–	–	–	–	–	–	–
Tell es-Sawwan	5800–5600	–	x	–	x	x	–	x	–	x	x	–	–	–	–	–	x
Tell Mureybat	8050–7542	x	–	–	–	–	x	–	–	–	–	–	–	–	–	x	x
Tell Ramad	c. 7000	–	x	–	x	C	–	x	–	–	–	–	–	–	x	–	–
Jericho, P.P. Neo.	c. 7000	–	x	–	x	–	–	x	–	–	–	–	–	x	x	x	–
Beidha, P.P. Neo. B.	c. 7000	–	–	–	x	–	x	–	x?	–	–	Wd	–	–	–	x	–
Jarmo	c. 6750	x	x	x	x	–	x	–	–	–	–	–	–	x	x	x	–
Matarrah	c. 5500	–	–	–	x	–	–	x	–	–	–	–	–	–	–	–	–
‘Amuq A.	c. 5750	–	–	–	x	–	–	B	–	–	–	Wd	–	–	–	–	–
Mersin, E. Neo.	c. 5750	–	–	–	–	–	–	–	x	–	–	–	–	–	–	–	–
Catal Hüyük, VI-II	5850–5600	–	x	–	x	x	x	–	–	–	x	–	–	x	–	x	–
Aceramic Hacilar	c. 7000	x	–	–	x	–	–	–	–	–	x	–	–	x	x	x	–
Ceramic Hacilar	5800–5000	–	x	–	x	x	–	x	x	–	x	–	–	–	x	–	–
Can Hasan, L. Neo.	c. 5250	–	–	–	W	–	–	–	–	x	–	–	–	x	–	–	–
Knossos, Stratum X	c. 6100	–	–	–	x	x	–	B	–	–	–	–	–	–	–	–	–
Aceramic Ghediki	c. 6–5000	–	x	–	x	–	–	x	x	–	–	–	–	x	x	x	–
Aceramic Sesklo	c. 6–5000	–	–	–	x	–	–	x	–	–	–	–	–	x	–	–	–
Aceramic Argissa	c. 6–5000	–	x	–	x	–	–	–	–	x	–	–	x	–	x	–	–
Aceramic Achilleion	c. 6–5000	–	–	–	x	–	–	–	–	–	–	x	–	–	–	–	–
Nea Nikomedeia	c. 6200	–	–	–	W	–	–	B	–	–	–	–	–	–	x	–	–
Karanovo I	c. 5000	–	x	–	x	–	–	–	–	–	–	–	–	–	x	–	–
Azmaska Moghila, E. Neo.	c. 5000	–	x	–	x	–	–	–	–	–	–	–	–	–	x	–	–

W = Wheat unspecified   B = Barley unspecified   Wd = Wild form   C = Club wheat

Table 1

cereal crops, and such variation continues into later prehistoric times. Various combinations of factors must have gone into producing these variations in cereal preference including differences in the natural environment and cultural whims and biasses. To give an example of the sequences of cereal cultivation in a restricted area, one might select the British Isles. This area has been reviewed by Godwin,[7] who gives the proportional frequencies of wheat, barley, oats and rye for the major cultural phases from the Neolithic to Anglo-Saxon times, and shows that there was much variation in the temporally fluctuating pattern.

As regards the varieties of wheats in early Europe generally, Einkorn and Emmer were established early, but there appears to have been a climatic differential with the result that, in England for example, Einkorn may not have become established. Club wheat also occurs in the third millennium B.C. in Europe, and appears to have adapted to a wide range of environments. Finally, spelt extends back in Europe at least until the second millennium B.C. Generally in Europe, barley took second place in importance to the wheats, with the other cereal plants having lower ratings.

Incidentally, much of the evidence for these cereals is in the form of carbonized grain or cereal impressions on pottery, bricks and other such materials. Sometimes this type of evidence can be all too easily lost unless the most careful excavating methods are employed. I recall that some time ago I was sent carbonized grain from an Iron Age site in Bedfordshire, and the material was so covered in a sticky chalk matrix that it might easily have been missed had the excavator not exerted great care. As well as these well established lines of food plant data, it is still possible that new techniques may eventually permit a wider range of data retrieval. As far as my own limited experience goes, I have been interested in the black carbonized material known as 'clinker'. This material could appear in ash or refuse deposits and is sometimes associated with cremated bone. Starting with an easier example, I recently submitted a fragment of what was already suspected of being a lump of burnt English Iron Age bread to examination by the scanning electron microscope. This coke-like substance was compared with experimentally burnt unleavened bread, and at various magnifications the similarities in structure were very encouraging (plate 5).

But to return to Neolithic/Bronze Age food plants, what other evidence is so far available? Pulses have already been mentioned as possibly having considerable antiquity as food. In Europe, there is certain Swiss evidence of the pea and blue vetchling during the third millennium B.C., and at a similar time the horse bean was being used in the Mediterranean area, arriving in the northern parts of Europe about the first millennium B.C. As yet it is not possible to be sure whether flax was first cultivated for its linseed oil or for the fibres, but meanwhile it is worth noting that we have evidence of the spread of the domestic form at least into Switzerland, Spain, Holland and Britain during the Neolithic phase. To continue our shopping list of plants which were probably cultivated in at least some parts of Europe, olives were established in Crete by the third millennium B.C., and figs in Greece and Crete. Onions were possibly being planted in the gardens of the Bronze Age Greeks. In the case of a number of food plants, there is still uncertainty as to the nature of the finds, that is, whether they are truly wild or to some extent domesticated. In this group are to be included apples, almonds and grapes. It might be mentioned here that of course some food plants were unlikely to have aroused attention from the point of view of selective planting: for example, the sloe which is known from the Swiss Neolithic; also the walnut, acorns and hazelnut, which have been identified from a few sites of so-called Neolithic and Bronze Age date. In contrast to this brief list of late prehistoric food plants it should be mentioned that a large number of foods were then unknown in Europe, including potatoes, carrots, swedes, maize, tomatoes, peppers, sunflower seeds, bananas, citrus fruits, groundnuts and peaches. Plant sugars, so important today, were also not being used. Such 'for and against' listing is still a very rough-and-ready procedure, and it is important to realize that chance sampling and preservation differentials are unlikely to result in unbiased data. In many respects cereals must have offered maximum opportunities for preservation, either as charred grain or imprints, whereas fungi for instance – which I believe could have been an important wild harvest, as it still is in parts of Europe today – could only be expected to survive as food evidence in very exceptional circumstances. Gabel[8] has recently emphasized the point that the number of preserved plant remains may usually represent only a portion of the species considered economically important by an early population, giving New World evidence to support this.

One final comment on plant foods; these late prehistoric cultures might be regarded as in a special phase of nutritional experimentation. Inheriting a considerable knowledge of natural history from their Palaeolithic forefathers, they were placed in the exciting and powerful position of being able to mould plant development to their needs. In this situation, one would expect them to have experimented with a variety of plants, some of which were later abandoned as cultivable forms. For example, gold of pleasure (*Camelina sativa*) has had a very chequered career, probably being regarded as a weed more often than not. However, we have evidence at least as early as Iron Age times in Denmark that it was grown with flax as an oil-yielding plant. Food plants are by no means the most hardy of species and the early farmers, of necessity, were moving and planting in a wide variety of soils and climates. Wild seed plants must at times have been an important dietary stand-by when crops failed, and the food yields from these sources could have been considerable.

Recent observations in the Near East show that in some areas families might collect as much as 40 kilograms of wild grain in a day.[9] At least by the first century B.C. the water darnel, a weed especially tolerant to drought and flood, was being grown in China as an insurance policy in case of other crop failure. One wonders whether this was a habit which other early cultivators had evolved. For instance, two forms of couch grass have roots of nutritive value. There are historical references to *Agropyron repens* showing that it has been used as a cattle feed and for human use. Carbonized tubers of the onion couch (*Arrhenatherum tuberosum*) have been found with six-row barley at a Bronze Age site in Wiltshire, and one is tempted to ask whether this was a purely accidental association?

Now we must turn to the question of animal foods. Some of the general comments I have made about plant use and domestication apply equally to animals. Experimentation and versatility might be regarded as the rule. Sampling biasses and the differential survival of animal food debris must still be kept in mind. These late prehistoric communities were cautious in their employment of stockbreeding and the analysis of food bone from Swiss sites of the third millennium B.C. shows that from a half to a third of the animals used as food were wild. In the regions of rivers and the sea, the amount of animal protein derived from sources other than stockbreeding could have been far higher, as for example in the Baltic and northern Scandinavia. The spread of domestic stocks through Europe was probably very uneven. In the first place the distribution of the wild indigenous mammal populations was not the same, and whereas wild cattle and pigs were widely spread in Europe, sheep and goats were probably mainly restricted to Asia.

Also related to the ecology of these genera is the fact that cattle and pigs are relatively well adapted to life in forested or scrub land, whereas sheep need more open pasture land. Thus, as a general rule, it seems likely that until extensive forest clearance had taken place by Late Bronze Age times, sheep breeding was probably at a considerable disadvantage.[10] In Greece and Crete, cattle may have been domesticated as early as the seventh millennium B.C. Osteometric changes occur later in northern Europe, and one must remember that some of these changes may be simply the result of animal enclosure and founder-effect and not of intentional breeding. In the case of domestic pigs, sheep and goats, the situation is rather uncertain at present, and although we have information as to their antiquity in the Near East, the spread of these domestic stocks into northern Europe is unresolved. Higgs and Jarman[11] have put forward the hypothesis that all forms of sheep may in fact be domesticates, derived from a general capra-ovine stock, perhaps with a centre of origin somewhat north of the Fertile Crescent. Perhaps I should mention, if rather as an afterthought, that both the dog and horse could also have been used as food as well as having other uses for man. The domestic forms replaced wild canid and equid stocks which must have been widely spread in Europe. However, although the dog was domesticated early, the horse may not have been selectively bred until *c.* 2000 B.C.

In terms of the amount of animal protein food eaten by these late prehistoric Europeans it is certainly not yet possible to present a case in support of a marked increase over the pre-Neolithic situation. In this respect there could be a contrast with the intake of carbohydrate-rich foods, which must have been generally very much more used than in previous hunter-gatherer cultures. But an important by-product of this early stockbreeding must eventually have been dairy products which certainly introduced a new dimension into the range of foods.

With regard to the methodology of studying animal food debris, there has in the Old World been rather a bias towards studies of domestic varieties, although there is much information to be gained from studies of fish and molluscan remains. Shell-fish were important dietary items in parts of Europe during Neolithic and later times, although collecting may not have been as intensively practised as by some preceding groups. Evans[12] has suggested that perhaps the "most charac-teristic" shellfish economy is exemplified by "impressed-ware sites where poverty-stricken peasants subsisted on a diet of shell-fish but eked out also by domestic cattle, as for example with the Sipontiano culture of Coppa Nevigata in Italy". He also demonstrates, by reference to a Scottish prehistoric midden site, that by careful analysis of molluscan remains we can even hope to obtain data on the relative abundance of edible molluscan species in these prehistoric times (fig. 12).

In considering all these comings and goings amongst ancient Europeans, and which animals and plants were or were not domesticated or eaten, we all too often completely lose sight of one major question. That is, considering this complex mosaic of early farming, coupled with a partly retained hunting-gathering economy, what does this evidence mean in terms of a total nutritional status? The data we have to use is patchy and unsatisfactory, but we can make a few guesses from it.

First of all, the so-called Neolithic and later economies *in general* probably enjoyed a more guaranteed and stable diet than that known previously. Also, the time and effort put into the collection of food may *in general* have been less. On the other hand, prehistoric hunters, like modern ones, were remarkably well adapted to squeezing every possible ounce of edible material out of their environment, and could withstand severe 'lean' periods surprisingly well. By the second millennium B.C. the early Europeans may have lost some of the food-collecting ingenuity of their ancestors, and certainly, with population increase encouraged by their economic change, famine would have been a far greater social threat. The beginnings of agriculture probably heralded the beginnings of serious food misuse, and just as in our own society some individuals severely mishandle their nutrition, so the early agriculturalists had the opportunity to over-feed on carbohydrates. In terms of total calorie intake, and taking into account what we know of subsistance economies today, there is no reason why the adult average should not have been between 2,000 and 3,000 calories per day (i.e. the range for ourselves today). However, the ratios of protein, fat and carbohydrate to the total food intake must have been quite variable, depending upon the ecology of the community. This variation was spacial, as seen for instance in the difference between the early Swiss farmers and a northern coastal people; but also temporal, where the contrast between some Neolithic and Bronze Age communities may have been as great as between the modern Kikuyu cereal cultivators and the Masai cattle-raisers.

The question of relating the general economic structure of an early community to the actual nutritional level of the group is really a very difficult one. Perhaps the recent history of Orkney farming is a reasonable example here. Today, the Orcadians utilize their land to the fullest and especially for beef, dairy and poultry farming. Some 200 years ago, the situation was similar with the important exception that farming organization was much inferior. The latter situation resulted in considerable poverty and even starvation. Viewed by an archaeologist a thousand years hence, it is unlikely that this difference would show up in non-literary evidence.

I have now dwelt at some length on dietary change and variation, but not yet on the biosocial significance of some of these findings. It would perhaps be convenient to discuss parts of this field under three main headings: population, health and social behaviour.

The history of world population increase has been discussed in some detail in various recent publications, but nevertheless, this aspect of palaeodemography is largely guesswork. This is not surprising since population is not a static phenomenon and depends upon many factors including environment, economy, health, fertility and social stability. However, few would disagree that there must have been massive population growth during the past few centuries, the result of cheap carbohydrates, the Industrial Revolution and increased medical efficiency. Though on a more modest scale, was there also a population explosion following the development of farming economies? Did the better dietary guarantees of this period result in greater survival to reproductive age and an increased fertility? As usual, the question becomes more complex the more one considers it. Why should not a particularly favourable ecosystem have resulted in population increase even in pre-Neolithic times, and if so could the expansion have been sufficient to produce not only a population problem but at the same time sufficient labour force to have encouraged group endeavours in animal capture and plant harvesting? Which came first, the village or the farm? While the majority favour agriculture before population growth, Clark and Haswell, in their study *The Economics of Subsistence Agriculture*,[13] would seem to favour the reverse. We can at least feel certain that as farming knowledge spread north-westwards through Europe, the resulting dietary change would have assisted survival and must have encouraged some further population growth. Ways of confirming such hypotheses by recourse to archaeological finds are not easy. Atkinson[14] has attempted to consider mortality and population in the English Neolithic by reference to the skeletons and barrows, but notes that serious problems arise in this sort of cross-checking. Such burials may not represent the population as a whole, exponential growth may have continued through the Neolithic, and there may have been continued immigration into the country. I think we should add to these the fact that infant mortality is very low in the series (even allowing for the variation which might have occurred between groups[15]) and it is also important to question whether counteracting forces might even have cancelled out the factors encouraging population growth. Dietary change may well have encouraged survival, but the increasing contacts between communities and their build-up into villages and towns may well have produced new health threats. In nomadic hunter bands, disease transfer is limited by comparative isolation, but economic change heralded epidemiological change. Contagious disease could spread more easily, and even intestinal parasite egg concentrations may have reached new heights in the soils surrounding habitations. Closer contact with livestock must surely have encouraged the transfer to man of such diseases as tuberculosis, brucellosis and even anthrax. Unglazed pottery introduced another health threat, and although the increased cooking of foods added to their digestibility, unclean vessels must have encouraged food contamination and gastro-enteritis. So we see that when all these biosocial factors are taken into account, our attempts to create a Neolithic population explosion are rather left in ruins. What is just as likely is that there were mini-cycles of population expansion and decrease, with only a gradual trend to long-term increase.

We should explore this question of health in relation to the early agriculturalists a little further. The occurrence of marked abnormality, such as club-foot, hydrocephaly and dysplastic and dislocated hip,[16] certainly helps in presenting a case for the possible relaxation of infanticide following the greater availability of food. This practice is not uncommon in recent hunter groups, and was no doubt a feature of similar economies in the past, noticeable deformity being one category for elimination.

Regarding the evidence for dietary insufficiency, I have reviewed this question elsewhere[17] and do not want to expand on it too much here. Rickets, which could have resulted from over-feeding with cereals, is noticeably absent, except for one possible case in a Neolithic Dane. Early literary evidence does suggest, however, that various vitamin deficiencies occurred at times, and even influenced whole communities. But we still need to know a lot more about minor skeletal differences and changes, before we can really contribute further to the question of nutritional inadequacy. In particular, we need to know more about cortical tissue changes, bone density variation, and the frequently occurring hypoplastic defects in teeth. Changes to alveolar bone resulting from poor periodontal health need further study from the point of view of their relation to diet. Oral changes of this kind in early Norse skulls have already been tentatively related to scurvy, and one might well ask whether some of the cases of marked periodontal disease and tooth loss in some prehistoric skulls are not also the result of vitamin C deficiency. Incidentally, there are various examples of prehistoric human hair from Europe, and as elsewhere, this tends to be rather auburn. It so happens that the protein-deficiency disease kwashiorkor produces this hair colour, but before someone rushes into print with claims of an association, I have the sad news that this colour is also produced by the post-mortem oxidation of normal melanin pigment!

One final comment on health; in this case an aspect which directly affects the genetic composition of the population.[18] Richard Post[19] has pointed to another possible trend which has resulted from socio-economic changes since the Neolithic, and this is the relaxing of selective pressures. His argument is that in Palaeolithic hunters, inherited deleterious abnormalities were rigorously selected out, but with the evolution of more and more 'protective' economies, the individuals carrying such genes survived more often to reproductive age. Colour blindness and severe myopia are two defects which would perhaps not be so serious in a farming community. Post also says: "The fact that high rates of breast cancer, high frequencies of hypolactators, and very ancient histories of domestic animal milk are found in Caucasian populations and in no other suggests that problems of etiology and epidemiology may well be investigated under the hypothesis of relaxed selection."[20] Little did the early farmers know what they were letting us all in for.

Let me conclude with brief comments on possible bio-behavioural changes resulting from this move from hunting to agriculture. At the Easter Conference of the Prehistoric Society in 1964, I pointed out that there is a continuous cycle of association between inherited mental potentiality and the cultural environment, each affecting the other. Laughlin develops this point when he says: "Man's life as a hunter supplied all the other ingredients for achieving civilization: the genetic variability, the inventiveness, the systems of vocal communication, the co-ordination of social life. It could not provide the large and dense population size nor the internal genetic restructuring attendant upon the establishment of assortative mating tracks whereby the frequency of matings between persons sharing culturally defined interests and talents could be maximized."[21] In other words, as the urban revolution gathered speed, mating patterns changed, and there were perhaps greater movements of people over shorter periods of time and larger groups socially interacting. Moreover, there could well have been changes in the selection pressures acting on intelligence and aptitudes. Similarly of course, socially detrimental traits, such as warfare, sexual deviations, group hysteria and paranoid delusions, may all have taken on different importance in these prehistoric 'new societies'.

We have come a long way from the first attempts at domestication to these biosocial repercussions which have gathered momentum and have finished up as international Coca-Cola, high sugar consumption and associated heart disease, and the most serious cancer of all – population run riot. Why could these early farmers not have left well alone?

Acknowledgments

I am most grateful to Gerald Duckworth and Co. Ltd and the editors and relevant contributors to *The Domestication and Exploitation of Plants and Animals*, for permission to reproduce table 1.

Notes

1. see, for instance, J. G. D. Clark, *Prehistoric Europe. The Economic Basis* (1952); D. and P. Brothwell, *Food in Antiquity* (1969).
2. R. B. Lee and I. De Vore (eds), *Man the Hunter* (1968).
3. *Antiquity*, XXXVIII (1964), 45–8.
4. *ibid.*, XLIII (1969), 40.
5. P. J. Ucko and G. W. Dimbleby (eds), *The Domestication and Exploitation of Plants and Animals* (1969). See especially pp. 207–17 and 149–72.
6. *ibid.*, p. 214.
7. H. Godwin, *The History of the British Flora* (1956).
8. C. Gabel, *Analysis of Prehistoric Economic Patterns* (1967).
9. R. M. Adams, *The Evolution of Urban Society* (1966).
10. *Antiquity*, XX (1947), 122–36.
11. *ibid.*, XLIII (1969), 31–41.
12. Ucko and Dimbleby, *op. cit.*, p. 481.
13. C. Clark and M. R. Haswell, *The Economics of Subsistence Agriculture* (1964).
14. J. M. Coles and D. D. A. Simpson (eds), *Studies in Ancient Europe* (1968), pp. 83–93.
15. Of the total British Neolithic sample, only 5.4% are new-born infants, and 5.0% are 1–4 years of age. These percentages are suspiciously low (Brothwell, unpublished).
16. D. R. Brothwell and A. T. Sandison (eds), *Diseases in Antiquity* (1967), pp. 423–43.
17. Ucko and Dimbleby, *op. cit.*, pp. 531–45.
18. Changing patterns of infective disease are now also thought to influence successive gene pool composition.
19. *Anthropologischer Anzeiger*, XXIX (1969), 186–95; *Eugenics Quarterly*, XIII (1966), 1–29.
20. *ibid.*, p. 27.
21. Lee and De Vore, *op. cit.*, p. 320.

Causewayed enclosures

I. F. SMITH

Introduction

Forty years ago, when E. C. Curwen[1] published the first general account of Neolithic 'camps', he was able to list five partially excavated examples – Abingdon (Berkshire),* The Trundle and Whitehawk (Sussex), Knap Hill and Windmill Hill (Wiltshire) – and to class with these Maiden Bower (Bedfordshire), where W. G. Smith had recorded the destruction of typical ditch segments in 1897–9. Curwen also described a series of unexcavated sites which seemed likely to belong in the same category. Four of these have subsequently been verified, but the low earthworks within the hill-forts at Yarnbury and Scratchbury (Wiltshire) have now been shown to be partially obliterated Iron Age constructions.[2]

By the early 1950s Professor Piggott could list five more excavated sites: Hembury Fort (Devon), Hambledon Hill and Maiden Castle (Dorset), Combe Hill (Sussex) and Whitesheet Hill (Wiltshire).[3] In the following two decades there have been partial excavations at Barkhale (Sussex) and Robin Hood's Ball and Rybury (Wiltshire) and two additional sites – High Peak (Devon) and Staines (Middlesex) – have been discovered and examined. The exiguous evidence at High Peak – a flat-bottomed ditch of appropriate proportions, exposed in a single section – is supported by Neolithic occupation in the immediate vicinity. Supplementary excavations have also been undertaken at Abingdon, Combe Hill, Hambledon Hill and Knap Hill. At the time of writing definitive reports are not available for Barkhale, Hambledon Hill and Staines, nor for the most recent work at Abingdon and Combe Hill.

* See Appendix (p. 106) for list of excavated enclosures with bibliography and other information. Note added in press: the Appendix also includes a brief entry for the site on Crickley Hill, Gloucestershire, discovered in July 1971 and therefore not referred to in the main part of this paper.

Chronology

The radiocarbon date brackets, at one standard deviation, for four enclosures – High Peak (3010–2710 bc[4]), Hambledon Hill (2880–2700), Knap Hill (2875–2645) and Windmill Hill (2730–2430) – are consistent enough to suggest that the greater number of sites may have been in use during the first quarter of the third millennium bc. The fourth millennium dates obtained for the Neolithic ditch at Hembury Fort (3480–3180 and 3300–3000) imply that the period during which monuments of this type were being used must be reckoned in terms of several centuries.

Distribution

As will appear from fig. 13, the addition of three sites does not materially alter the distribution pattern known in 1954.[5] The discovery of previously unknown enclosures at High Peak and Staines points to the probability that the known distribution is misleadingly incomplete. The circumstances at High Peak, where the Neolithic ditch was buried beneath a hill-fort, reinforce the implications of Hembury Fort and Maiden Castle, where the Neolithic enclosures were also completely masked by later defences, and it seems unlikely that these three stand alone.

A Neolithic date has been suggested for low banks and an apparently causewayed ditch within the hill-fort on Beacon Hill, Burghclere, Hampshire,[6] as also for a short length of ditch with apparent interruptions in the vicinity of flint-mine shafts on Pitstone Hill, Buckinghamshire.[7] Jessup[8] suggests that a causewayed enclosure, now destroyed, may have existed at Chalk near Gravesend on the south bank of the River Thames. The unreliability of surface indications has been adequately demonstrated at Scratchbury and Yarnbury. On grounds of circumstantial evidence it may, on the other hand, be conjectured that there was a Neolithic enclosure somewhere on Ham Hill, Stoke-sub-Hamdon, Somerset. The remarkable concentration of ten stone axes, half of them belonging to the Cornish groups IV and XVI, together with examples of groups I and III, ground flint axes, leaf-arrowheads and pottery said to include a trumpet-lug,[9] recorded from the hill and its immediate vicinity is reminiscent of the similar concentrations of axe-factory products at Hembury, Maiden Castle, or Windmill Hill.

Dr St Joseph's discovery of some dozen sites with interrupted ditches which show as crop-marks on the gravels of river valleys in eastern counties[10] suggests that Abingdon and Staines may form part of a distribution pattern complementary to that known at present. Crop-marks of ditches comparable to those excavated at Staines and Abingdon have been noted elsewhere in the Thames valley,[11] in the Welland valley in south Lincolnshire[12] and in the valley of the River Lark in Suffolk.[13] Trial excavation of one such site at Cardington, Bedfordshire, in the valley of the River Ouse, is indeed said to have produced evidence for construction in the Roman period.[14] But Mr James Dyer points out[15] that the evidence adduced is not necessarily conclusive in view of the limited extent of the excavation and the possibility of disturbance during intensive Romano-British activity in the area.

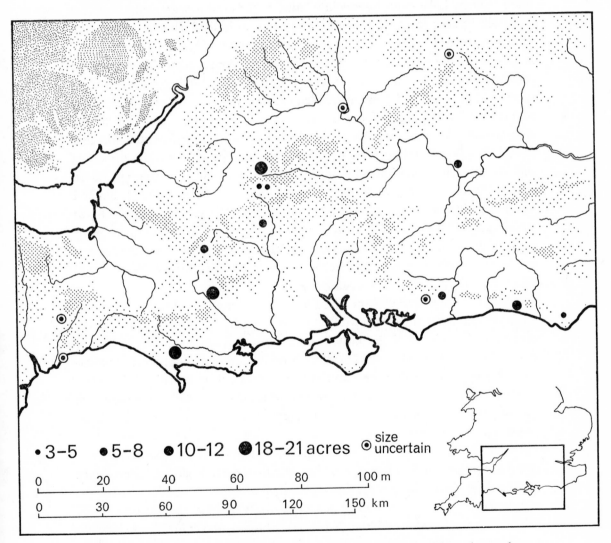

Figure 13. Distribution map of excavated causewayed enclosures. *Note:* the newly discovered example on Crickley Hill, Gloucestershire, is not included.

Siting

The two Thames valley enclosures, Abingdon and Staines, appear to be differentiated from the more numerous examples on hills or downland chiefly in respect of their low-lying situations. When this is considered together with the indications that similar enclosures may be widely scattered in valleys elsewhere the possibility emerges that choice of location may have been governed by factors other than the potential advantages of an elevated situation. The inference finds support in the siting of many hill-top enclosures in relation to the local topography.

As will be seen from the topographical notes on individual enclosures in the Appendix, those at Knap Hill and Maiden Castle stand apart from the majority in hill-top situations in that they have been set out along, rather than across, the contours. The ditches and banks at Knap Hill follow a natural contour below the summit of the knoll and those at Maiden Castle occupy a position subsequently adopted by the builders of a hill-fort. Curwen[16] first drew attention to the characteristically unconformable siting of most enclosures, particularly noticeable at The Trundle and Rybury, where the Neolithic ditch systems lie across the slopes and the partially superimposed hill-fort defences follow the contours more closely. These and other enclosures, whether also on hill-tops (Hambledon and Windmill Hill), on ridges (Barkhale and Combe Hill), a saddle (Whitehawk) or plateau edge (Whitesheet Hill), present the appearance of predetermined plans carried out regardless of topography. The vertical interval between the highest and lowest points may be considerable: about 50ft at Hambledon (plate 7) and Windmill Hill (plate 6), approaching 75ft at The Trundle.

It has been suggested that the Neolithic site at Hembury falls into a different category from other enclosures with causewayed ditches.[17] The lop-sided placing of the arc of the inner ditch (fig. 14) and its continuation at the west below the scarp edge, here marked by the line of the Iron Age rampart, support the alternative suggestion of Fox that the plan in the incomplete form in which it is known seems to represent the adaptation of the normal roughly circular arrangement to a narrow, flat-topped promontory.[18] The outer ditch at the north-east lies wholly below the scarp edge.

The tendency of the ditches to plunge down slopes may suggest that the enclosures were designed to face a particular direction; most situations offer a choice of directions. About half of the enclosures thus face east or south-east, but the remainder face west, north-west or north (see under 'Aspect' in table 1 on p. 94).

The sites at Abingdon and Staines lay beside brooks, and at Hembury there is a spring-line at the foot of the hill. The remaining 13 are situated at distances varying from a quarter of a mile to over two miles from sources of water.

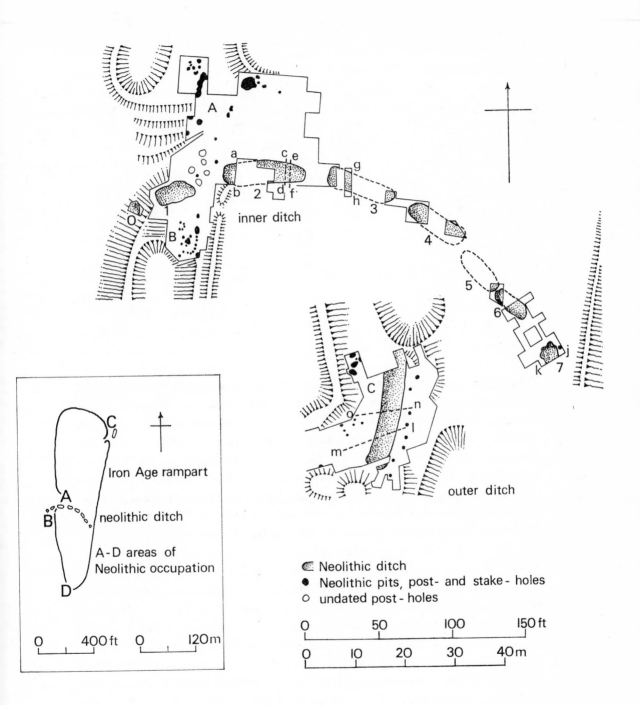

Figure 14. Plan of the causewayed enclosure at Hembury Fort, Devon (after Liddell).

Causewayed enclosure	Approx. area (acres)	Greatest diams. (feet)	No. of rings	Outworks	Aspect
Combe Hill, Sussex	3–4	550×320	Two	–	N.
Rybury, Wilts	3–4	520×470	One	One	E.
Knap Hill, Wilts	4–5	650×430	One	–	–
Whitesheet Hill, Wilts	5–6	640×450	One	–	W.
Staines, Middlesex	6–7?	540×?	Two	–	–
Barkhale, Sussex	6–7	750×550	One	–	S.E.
Robin Hood's Ball, Wilts	7–8	750×650	Two	–	S.E.
Whitehawk, Sussex	11–12	900×650	Four	Four?	E.
Maiden Castle, Dorset	17–18	1200×900?	Two	–	–
Hambledon Hill, Dorset	19–20	1050×900	One	Three	S.E.
Windmill Hill, Wilts	20–21	1270×1000	Three	–	N.W.

Table 1

Plans and sizes

Table 1 presents in summary form the data pertaining to relative dimensions and plans (defined on the ground by one or more complete or broken rings of irregularly segmented ditches, sometimes with the remnants of banks along the inner side) of the 11 enclosures for which reasonably complete plans are available. It includes Maiden Castle and Rybury, where the plans are not known in entirety, because in these instances enough evidence exists to permit classification and calculation of area. Hembury and The Trundle are omitted since it is uncertain whether their fragmentary outer ditches represent outworks or additional circuits. At Abingdon, where there were at least two ditches, much of the site had been destroyed before its recognition, and even less is known of Maiden Bower or High Peak.

As will be seen, the seven smaller enclosures show a continuous gradation in size from just over 3 acres to rather more than 7 acres. Whitehawk, with around 11 acres, stands alone between these last and the three large sites in Wessex which range from around 18 to 21 acres. (If the outer ditch at The Trundle does continue round the hill beneath the hill-fort rampart, this too must enclose about 18 acres.) Neither regional grouping nor clear correlation between size and complexity of plan is evident. The medium-sized Whitehawk, with four rings, the fourth having radial and tangential extensions, and perhaps with outworks in the form of cross-ridge dykes as well, presents by far the most elaborate arrangement.

The outworks at Whitehawk and Rybury have not been excavated; that at the latter site consists of an arc of ditch segments set round the outer side of a small knoll 240 yards south of the main enclosure. The detached ditches at Hambledon Hill, comprising two sets of double cross-dykes on the bases of spurs close to the enclosure and a third set at a distance of a quarter of a mile, have all been shown to be contemporary with the enclosure.

Timber-work

The relative paucity of evidence for post-settings associated with banks, ditches or causeways may reflect the limitations of investigation, usually confined to fairly narrow trenches, rather than the absolute rarity of such constructions. At White-hawk, hollow casts left by posts set upright in the chalk make-up are said to have existed in the banks; other post holes along the sites of the banks had penetrated the solid chalk. The charred remains of twigs, sticks and branches in the curious 'burnt layer' which was a recurrent feature of the ditches at Hembury (fig. 15) may represent the destruction of some form of light structure originally set along the banks. (At Robin Hood's Ball and Windmill Hill, holes cut in the solid chalk seem to have supported posts which antedated the outer banks. At Combe Hill post holes were sought, but not found, in the bank.)

Post holes were associated with two ditch segments at Hembury (fig. 14). A line of seven or eight holes was traced along the outer edge of the outer ditch, and further examples, sealed by a pre-Iron Age 'turf-line', surrounded segment 7 of the inner ditch. The latter arrangement recalls the undated post holes around segments of the second ditch at The Trundle. These, at first believed to indicate the former existence of roofing over 'pit-dwellings',[19] were subsequently attributed to the period of Iron Age activity within the hill-fort.[20] The narrow strips excavated round the ditch edges leave room for doubt, but the positions of the post holes suggest that they were related to the ditch segments. Possibly these ditches were surrounded by screens or fences.

Post holes on the lines of causeways in the third and fourth ditches at White-hawk appear to have supported gate-posts and fenced or revetted passages through the banks. At Hembury a group of undated post holes outside the causeway between segments 1 and 2 of the inner ditch was tentatively interpreted as the setting for a gate.

Internal features

Extensive traces of structures and activity within an enclosure have been disclosed only at Staines; interim accounts refer to numerous pits, post holes and probable palisade trenches. At Hembury Neolithic occupation was discovered in four fairly small areas (fig. 14); owing to the presence of overlying Iron Age ramparts none was fully explored. In addition to many finds on the buried surfaces, there were clusters of pits, hearths, post and stake holes. The latter formed a coherent plan only in area B, immediately within segment 1 of the inner ditch, where part of a timber structure of oval plan is said to have overlain the tail of the bank. Some 30 yards north of this, in area A, a shallow, irregular ditch was traced for a distance of 20ft in the vicinity of another series of pits. In area D, at the tip of the promontory, a layer of charcoal and 'ash' up to 6ins thick overlay the pits. Fragments of clay daub, two bearing impressions of slender withies, came from this deposit and from underlying pits. In area C Neolithic pits had been dug through the tail of the bank within the outer ditch and an occupation layer was spread upon it; one section shows this layer extending over the flattened bank to within 7ft of the ditch's edge.[21] A sherd from one of the pits in area C was found to join another from the lower fill in segment 7 of the inner ditch, some 200 yards distant.

At Windmill Hill joining parts of a vessel were also found in a ditch and pit, but the majority of pits at this site, revealed by stripping half the area within the inner ring, appear to have belonged to the pre-enclosure occupation. Investigation of a strip across the width of the enclosure at Whitehawk resulted in the discovery of a few pits and post holes, none in clear relationship to the enclosure itself. Activity at Maiden Castle, both within and without the enclosure ditches, may have been as intensive as at Hembury. Pit A23[22] was a narrow irregular ditch, apparently comparable to that found in area A at Hembury. Weathering of the exposed chalk surfaces at Windmill Hill and Whitehawk may have destroyed shallow features.

Unaccompanied crouched or contracted inhumations are recorded from the interiors of three enclosures. One is reported from Staines, two are known from Whitehawk and another two from Abingdon. At Whitehawk an adult inhumation, covered only by topsoil when found, lay close to the inner side of the second ditch. The skeleton of a child half-way down in the fill of a deep narrow hole on the edge of a causeway at this site recalls the circumstances of an inhumation 'in a small square hole' at Abingdon.

Cult centres?

Evidence that the enclosure ditches, often cut deeply into the subsoil, together with the substantial banks derived therefrom, were partially or wholly levelled during the period of use has been discussed elsewhere, with comments on the processes involved.[23] In brief, it seems that the denuded condition of the banks or, in some instances, their complete disappearance is to be explained in terms of deliberate back-filling of the ditches. Correlations exist between the scarcity or abundance of archaeological material in a ditch and the presence or absence of an adjoining bank. Levelling at an early date is stratigraphically attested at Maiden Castle, where the Long Mound had been constructed over the flattened inner bank and ditch.[24] It is worth while to consider the circumstances at Hembury in this connection because the nature of this site has sometimes been misunderstood, as previously mentioned, and because the ditch sections reveal the processes in question with exceptional clarity. This is largely due to the nature of the subsoil, where the Clay-with-flints and Greensand with chert blocks afforded both fine-grained and stony substances, unaffected by the weathering and solution which has resulted in the shrinkage and compaction of deposits in ditches dug into chalk. (The schematic presentation of the original evidence may also suggest a degree of over-simplification.) The more informative of the published sections, scattered through several excavation reports, have been brought together (fig. 15) and redrawn to a uniform scale, with uniform conventions employed. In order to eliminate irrelevant details, all the post-Neolithic layers have been conflated (see conventions, fig. 15). The position of each section can be identified on fig. 14.

Sections a–b, c–d and e–f in fig. 15 are all from segment 2 of the inner ditch; sections g–h and j–k relate to segments 3 and 7 of the same ditch. It will be seen that, apart from minor variations, the three sections across ditch segment 2 and that across segment 7 show a consistent sequence of deposits: (1) 'washed silt' (the excavator's term) on the bottom; (2) a layer of charcoal, 6ins to 2ft thick, resting against the inner side of the ditch; (3) bank material, sand or sand and clay, thrown down from the inner side; (4) a stony deposit confined to the outer part of the ditch; (5) a levelling layer of stony earth which extends over the outer lip of the ditch; (6) post-Neolithic deposits. In section a–b the sequence appears to be duplicated; a second layer of charcoal lies across the nearly-levelled ditch. In section g–h, across segment 3, the levelling layer of stony earth (5) was absent, so that a soil, formed in the hollow over the stony deposit (4), was subsequently buried beneath the post-Neolithic deposits (6). In each instance the charcoal represents wood burnt *in situ*, with consequent intense discoloration of the inner side of the ditch; in at least one segment reddening of the overlying sand and clay indicated that bank material had been thrown down while the fire was still burning.

A similar deposit of charcoal, again with evidence of burning *in situ*, was found in the south end of the outer ditch (section l–m, fig. 15); further north (section n–o) this was absent and the ditch profile was V-shaped, with sharply cut steps in the sides. This, together with the cleaner fill, suggested to the excavator that back-filling had taken place almost immediately.

Only the primary silt in the ditch bottoms can be attributed to natural agencies; all the other deposits must have been introduced intentionally. The circumstances in the outer ditch and the variations in the fill of the inner ditch suggest the repetition of a series of acts within each segment. Professor R. J. C. Atkinson has pointed out that section g–h shows recutting subsequent to infilling with bank material, presumably after an interval during which the latter had become consolidated. The segregation of the stony deposit (4) in the outer parts of all sections across the inner ditch suggests that recutting may have been a consistent feature of this ditch and that the secondary hollows were filled with material not derived from the original bank.

It may be conjectured that the 'unfinished' part of the outer ditch represents an initial stage in a sequence which in this case remained uncompleted. It invites comparison with segments of a shallow ditch which antedated three segments of the larger ditch in the third ring at Whitehawk.[25]

Recutting of ditches has been observed during the excavations at Staines[26] and can now be inferred from a number of published section drawings, e.g., at Whitesheet Hill,[27] The Trundle[28] and from some sections at Whitehawk,[29] where the 'black triangles' were especially productive of finds. Signs of secondary cutting, though common, are not always apparent. The molluscan fauna in the ditch at Knap Hill indicates that filling at this site was the result of natural weathering processes.[30] In view of the extensive investigations by Cunnington and later by Connah, the finds from Knap Hill are remarkably scanty and it seems that this enclosure was abandoned at an early stage.

Recognition of partial recutting in some ditches carries the implication that intrusive artifacts may have been deposited during these secondary disturbances. In this connection it is instructive to consider the circumstances in which Ebbsfleet ware has been recovered from seemingly primary contexts at three sites. All the finds made by Musson at Combe Hill came from a 'black triangle' in one of the two segments investigated in the inner ditch. It is evident that this deposit had been placed in a trough dug through sterile primary fill and that the pottery is therefore technically secondary. Sherds of an Ebbsfleet bowl, five to six feet deep in the outer ditch at Windmill Hill,[31] can also now be seen to have been introduced during (previously unrecognized) disturbance of the outer part of the ditch; it seems probable that the deeply buried Ebbsfleet fragments from White- hawk should similarly be considered as intrusive. Apart from these particular

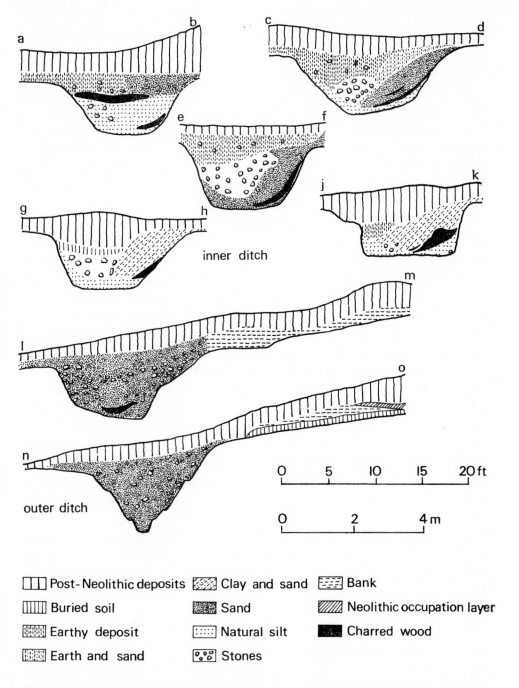

inner ditch

outer ditch

☐☐☐ Post-Neolithic deposits	▨ Clay and sand	▦ Bank
▥ Buried soil	▨ Sand	▨ Neolithic occupation layer
▦ Earthy deposit	▨ Natural silt	■ Charred wood
▦ Earth and sand	◦ Stones	

Figure 15. Diagrammatic sections of the causewayed enclosure ditches at Hembury Fort, Devon (after Liddell). See fig. 14 for positions.

instances, an explanation becomes available for the absence of stratification in the supposedly primary fill of ditches, noted at Whitehawk and especially at Windmill Hill.[32]

The rich deposits of occupation refuse at Windmill Hill were initially interpreted by the writer as the remains of communal feasts, ceremonially buried during periodical gatherings of scattered communities. A more attractive idea has been put forward by Case, who suggests that the refuse represents scraped-up settlement debris, buried because of the supposed magic powers of its fertilizing properties.[33] This hypothesis has the merit of accounting for the obviously utilitarian nature of much of the material and of opening new perspectives on the function of the enclosures in Neolithic society.

The comparison originally made by Piggott[34] between the causewayed enclosures and the curious ditch systems at Kothingeichendorf in Bavaria is given added point by Maier's reassessment of the latter and a series of allied earthworks,[35] differing in plan and cultural context, but all linked through their use as centres of a cult which involved the burial in ditches of settlement refuse together with complete or fragmentary human corpses. The occurrence of deposits of similar character in caves and fissures and the circumstance that pottery of several types may occur in intimate association in these natural cavities, as well as at Kothingeichendorf, led Maier to infer the existence of a widespread cult, shared by a number of Neolithic communities and apparently maintained over a long period of time. He also drew attention to similarities in plan between several of these ditched enclosures and Wor Barrow, causewayed enclosures or Avebury, ritual monuments in which the requirements of cult found differing forms of expression. The implied relationship between the causewayed enclosures and the henge monuments of the British Isles offers an economical explanation for the origins of the latter which finds support in a rapidly accumulating body of evidence, already too extensive to consider here.[36]

The general paucity of archaeological material in henge monuments (with the significant exceptions of three of the largest, Durrington Walls, Marden and Mount Pleasant, and perhaps the smaller Gorsey Bigbury) suggests that changes in rite accompanied the adoption of more formal plans during the period of transition. Yet, initially parallel with this sequence and sporadically evidenced over a much longer period of time, there persisted the practice of burying settlement refuse, pottery, animal and human remains, and other objects in specially prepared pits or shafts. Neolithic sites of Goodland type in Ulster;[37] the Bronze Age shafts at Wilsford, Wiltshire,[38] and at Swanwick, Hampshire, the latter with upright post and traces of blood;[39] their first century B.C. counterparts, sometimes within enclosures of archaic aspect;[40] the shafts, pits and wells of the Belgic Britons[41] – all seem in their diverse forms to be manifestations of the kind of cult practice that has been inferred in connection with the causewayed enclosures.

Economy and patterns of contact

Whatever construction may eventually be put upon the enclosures, the deposits in their ditches remain the most prolific source of information about Neolithic subsistence economy, material culture and intercommunal relationships.

The finds consistently attest a mixed economy based on stock-breeding and agriculture. Wherever animal bones have survived, those of a large breed of domestic cattle are absolutely predominant. Remains of sheep and/or goats and of pigs are recorded in association with those of cattle except at Whitesheet Hill, where the scanty finds included a single ox skull, and at Combe Hill, where sheep/goat bones were absent from the secondary deposit (see p. 98 above). At Knap Hill and Robin Hood's Ball, sheep/goat outnumbered pigs by a small margin; at Hambledon Hill the remains of pigs were slightly more numerous and this was also the case in the assemblage from the pre-enclosure occupation at Windmill Hill. But bones recovered from the ditches at Windmill Hill comprised some 60 per cent cattle, 25 per cent sheep or goat, and 15 per cent pig. These fluctuations may simply result from the small sizes of the samples available. Bones of wild animals account for a very small proportion of the total amount of bone discarded.

The impression of a single grain of Emmer in a sherd from Robin Hood's Ball appears to be the sole addition to the list of cereal identifications from cause-wayed enclosures published by Helbaek.[42] His list is further supplemented by impressions of Emmer and Bread wheat in pottery from the Neolithic barrow on Whiteleaf Hill, Buckinghamshire,[43] and of Emmer, barley and an apple-pip at Hurst Fen, Mildenhall, Suffolk.[44] The relative frequencies originally established by Helbaek are not significantly altered by these additions. Barley, chiefly of the Naked variety, accounts for 11 per cent of all impressions of cereal grains or spikes accidentally incorporated in pottery during manufacture; the remainder represent varieties of wheat. Amongst the wheats the majority of certainly identifiable impressions are those of Emmer (41 per cent); Emmer or Eincorn amount to 56 per cent; and Eincorn together with Bread wheat constitute the remaining 3 per cent. Spelt, a form of wheat which has not been identified amongst impressions on pottery, occurred as carbonized grain at Hembury, where it constituted the major component of small deposits which included

Emmer, Naked and Hulled barley, and possibly Eincorn.[45] The grains were scattered in at least six pits in the occupation area D at the south end of the promontory, where they were associated with Neolithic pottery, including part of a bowl of gabbroic ware with a trumpet-lug, and in one pit within area A grains were found still adhering to a large sherd.[46] Unfortunately, all the specimens have been stored together in one jar so that it is no longer possible to ascertain whether the Spelt came from a single deposit, but the Neolithic context seems to be certain.[47]

Impressions of flax seeds on Neolithic pottery are known only at Windmill Hill. Together with the ubiquitous hazel-nut shells, impressions of apple-pips at Windmill Hill and Hurst Fen, charred remains of crab apples at Hembury and at the settlement on Hazard Hill, Devon,[48] constitute the existing evidence for collection of wild plant foods. Marine shells were found in some quantity at Maiden Castle (limpets) and at Whitehawk (mostly mussels). Some of the latter had been collected as 'dead' shells.

Patterns of cultural contact within the earlier Neolithic have been brought into sharper focus by the work of Peacock,[49] who has demonstrated that a class of fine pottery with distinctive characteristics, long recognized to be an import at a number of sites, was most probably a trade product, dispersed from specialist workshops. In the light of this it is worth while to survey briefly some other more or less well-known evidence which may reflect other systems of contact or trade (table 2 on p. 103). It must be understood that a series of separate and complicated issues is raised by the distribution of each item included in this table and that these have hardly been touched upon here, apart from some explanatory comments. The table has been arranged so as to bring out most clearly the dispersal patterns of finished products and a raw material (Beer flint) and to emphasize the links between causewayed enclosures, contemporary settlements, and selected surface assemblages from restricted areas.

It will be seen that three classes of finished artifacts – the gabbroic pottery and stone axes from Cornwall and implements made of Portland chert – are widely distributed, each class occurring at nine sites and all three recorded from six sites. The table does not show quantitative variations and this aspect of the distributions requires brief comment. Peacock[50] has identified the outcrops of gabbro on the Lizard Head in south-west Cornwall as the source of the gabbroic pottery and has shown how the quantity of this ware which reached a given site diminished in somewhat inconstant ratio with distance from the source. Thus the small assemblage of sherds known from the early investigations at Carn Brea (15 miles from the Lizard) is composed entirely of gabbroic ware; at Corfe

	Imported pottery		Stone axes		Portland chert	Beer flint
	Oolitic ware	Gabbroic ware	Cornwall	Lake District		
Causewayed enclosures						
Abingdon, Berks				VI		
Staines, Middlesex				VI		
Knap Hill, Wilts	+					
Whitesheet Hill, Wilts	+					
Robin Hood's Ball, Wilts	+	+				
Windmill Hill, Wilts	+	+	IIa	VI	+	
				XI		
Maiden Castle, Dorset		+	IV		+	
			IVa			
			XVI			
			XVII			
			G			
Hembury, Devon		+	IIa		+	+
			IVa			
			XVII			
			G			
High Peak, Devon		+	IV		+	+
			G			
Settlements						
Carn Brea, Cornwall		+	XVI		+	
			XVII			
Hazard Hill, Devon		+	IV		+	+
			XVI			
			XVII			
			G			
Haldon, Devon		+			+	+
Corfe Mullen, Dorset		+				
Surface assemblages						
East Week, Devon			IV		+	+
			G			
Ham Hill, Somerset			IV		+	
			XVI			
			G			
East Farm, Bradford Abbas, Dorset			XVII	VI		
			G			

Table 2. Incidence of artifacts and raw materials of distant origin in causewayed enclosures, settlements and surface assemblages. (Roman numerals indicate axes of recognized petrological groups; G indicates miscellaneous greenstones.)

Mullen (145 miles distant) this ware still accounts for 13 per cent of the total. But at the two Wiltshire sites, Robin Hood's Ball and Windmill Hill (respectively 160 and 170 miles distant) it constitutes merely 1.3 per cent and 0.2 per cent of the two largest assemblages considered by Peacock.

Robin Hood's Ball and Windmill Hill have yielded proportionately much higher quantities of the oolitic pottery, a convenient term for the ware containing inclusions derived from outcrops of Jurassic limestone, which also occurs at Knap Hill and Whitesheet Hill. The inclusions in a sample of sherds from Windmill Hill, where oolitic ware comprises about 30 per cent of all the pottery, have been attributed to the Great Oolite and Forest Marble deposits of the Bath/Frome region of east Somerset. All four find-spots lie within a radius of 20–30 miles from this presumed area of origin. It now seems reasonable to consider this ware as a specialist product distributed along channels of trade. To judge from the variety of styles represented at Windmill Hill, more than one centre of production may have been in operation. A few good imitations of gabbroic ware, including a trumpet-lug,[51] suggest the exploitation of a demand created by the fine pottery from the Lizard but inadequately satisfied from that source; perhaps this is an early example of processes inferred by Peacock[52] in connection with the production of Glastonbury ware. In addition there are the highly differentiated bowls which closely resemble 'Abingdon ware'[53] and still other stylistic variants.

The stone axe distributions shown in the table, confined to the series of petrological groups with early associations, show a similar complementary pattern. Axes of the five Cornish groups and those made of greenstones, presumed to be of Cornish origin, may have been dispersed, as Peacock has suggested, together with the gabbroic pottery.[54] Again, quantity falls off in Wiltshire, where a single axe of Group IIa from Windmill Hill is accompanied by a few chance finds of axes of Groups IV and XVI elsewhere in the county. In Wiltshire there are more than twice as many axes of Lake District origin, chiefly Group VI, and Windmill Hill, with several axes of this group, is linked with Abingdon, Staines, and the much wider region to the east and north served from this source. Westwards the distribution of Group VI axes thins out rapidly; few examples reached Somerset and Dorset and there are single finds from Devon and Cornwall respectively. One of the Group VI axes from Dorset comes from a site at East Farm, Bradford Abbas, which has also produced axes of Cornish origin.[55]

The distribution of artifacts of Portland chert parallels those of the gabbroic pottery and Cornish axes, but is otherwise distinct in that quantity remains constant irrespective of distance from Portland Bill, Dorset, assumed to be the source in the absence of evidence that chert from other outcrops of Portland

Plate 1. Buried soil beneath a deposit of hillwash at Chinnor, Oxon. Scale 1.0 m.
(*Published by permission of Rugby Cement.*)

Plate 2a. Ascott-under-Wychwood. Buried soil profile overlain by limestone rubble of mound. Scale in cm (left) and inches.

Plate 2b. South Street. Buried soil profile. The upper dark layer is the modern plough soil; beneath is the chalk rubble of the barrow. Note the surface undulations of the buried soil and the relatively uniform base. Beneath are three involutions.

Plate 3a. Beckhampton Road. Section through the barrow showing the modern plough soil, mound and buried soil. Note the level surface of the buried soil and very irregular base; compare with plate 2b. Scale in inches.

Plate 3b. Kilham, Yorkshire Wolds. Buried soil beneath Neolithic barrow; note division into an upper loamy material and a lower, more clayey material, with an iron/humus 'pan' at the junction of the two layers. Chalk rubble of barrow mound above (top soil removed); natural shattered chalk below. Thickness of soil *c.* 20cm.

Plate 4. Northton. Section showing principal occupation levels. Scale in feet.

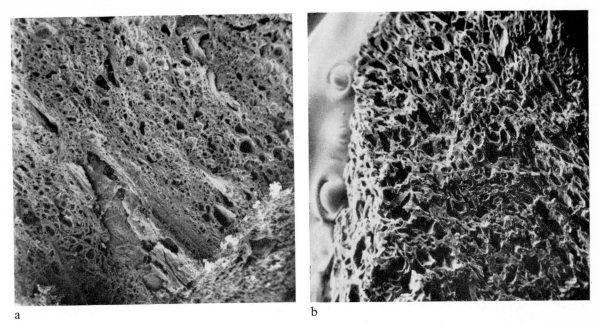

a   b

Plate 5. Low- and high-power views of cinder (? burnt bread) from a Bedfordshire Iron Age site, compared with a control sample of burnt unleavened bread, using the scanning electron microscope. a. Iron Age sample×28. b. Control × 33. c. Iron Age sample × 28. d. Control × 1600. The structural detail is seen to be remarkably similar.

c   d

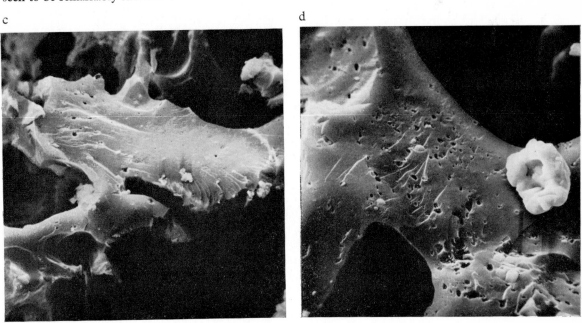

Plate 6. Causewayed enclosure, Windmill Hill, Wiltshire. (*Photo by J. K. St Joseph, Cambridge University Collection: copyright reserved.*)

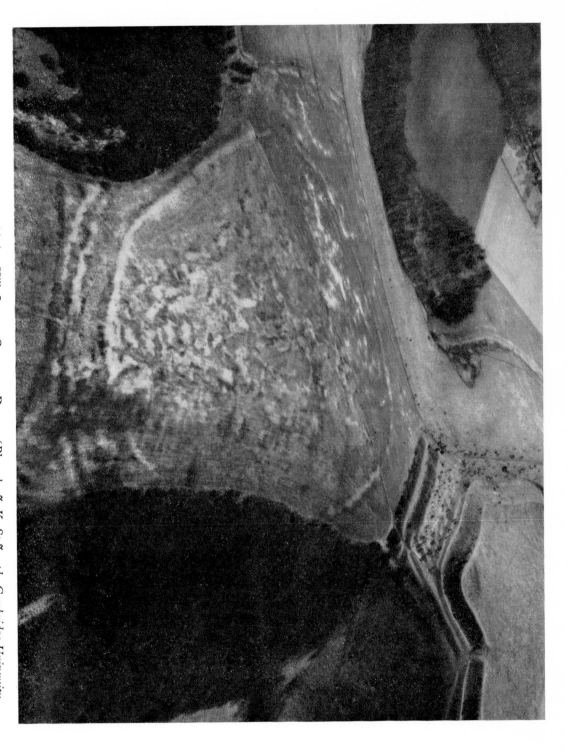

Plate 7. Causewayed enclosure, Hambledon Hill, Iwerne Courtney, Dorset. (*Photo by J. K. St Joseph, Cambridge University Collection: copyright reserved.*)

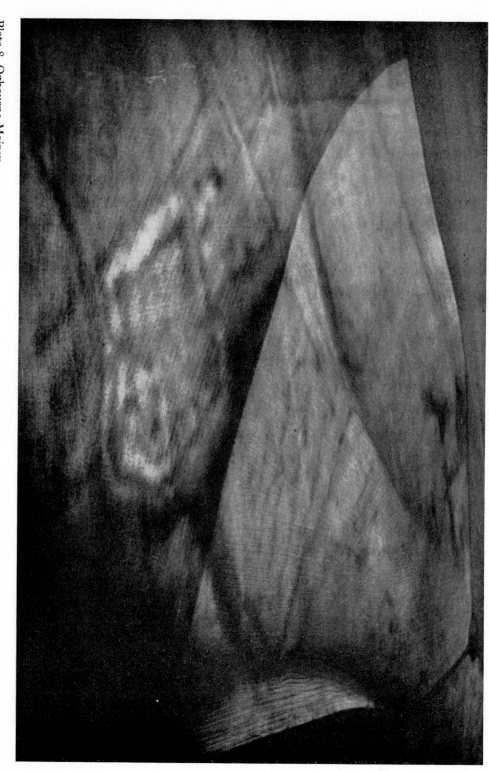

Plate 8. Ogbourne Maizey.

Beds was exploited. Neolithic artifacts of Portland chert, usually leaf-arrowheads, are represented by no more than two or three specimens at any of the sites considered. Most of the information has been tabulated by Palmer.[56]

Flint from Beer Head on the Devon coast, found at five sites in that county, was distributed in the form of raw material over distances of up to 40 miles. Beer Head seems to be the most likely source for the fresh dark flint reported from Hazard Hill[57] and from East Week, on the north-east slopes of Dartmoor.[58] Collection and transport of raw material implies an operation different in kind from those involved in the dispersal of finished products.

This tentative and intentionally uncritical sketch of patterns of contact and trade will be improved and augmented by more intensive research, notably by the important current investigation of the sources of flint axes.[59] The causewayed enclosures of Sussex should eventually be found to produce evidence for contacts with similar systems of exchange; in the meantime it may be suggested that the pottery from these sites would repay fresh examination. The high quality of the carinated bowls from Whitehawk, matched by a single (unpublished) sherd from Barkhale, may indicate that these are the products of specialist potters, even though petrological analysis may not afford independent confirmation in this instance.

Appendix
List of excavated causewayed enclosures

Bedfordshire

MAIDEN BOWER: SP 996225

W. G. Smith, *Dunstable: Its History and Surroundings* (1904), pp. 40–1; *Victoria County History, Bedfordshire*, vol. I (1904), pp. 163–70; *Proceedings of the Society of Antiquaries of London*, XXVII (1915), 143–61; *Arch. J.*, LXXXVIII (1931), 90–2, fig. 6 (finds).

On Lower Chalk at 500 ft O.D., at the edge of a plateau.

Complete plan unknown; partly masked by superimposed hill-fort and partly destroyed. Ditch segments west of hill-fort rampart were recorded in 1897–9; the accounts given by W. G. Smith (in *Dunstable: Its History and Surroundings* and *Proceedings of the Society of Antiquaries of London*, XXVII) vary in detail. Further sections have been exposed in modern quarry face (*Bedfordshire Archaeological Journal*, II, 8).

Berkshire

ABINGDON: SU 511983

Ant. J., VII (1927), 438–64; VIII (1928), 461–77; XXXVI (1956), 11–30; Ministry of Works, *Excavations: Annual Report, 1963* (1964), 9–10.

On Summertown-Radley terrace gravel, $\frac{3}{4}$ mile north of River Thames, at 200ft O.D., on spur bounded by stream-beds.

Complete plan unknown: site partly destroyed by gravel-digging before recognition. At least two ditches, 200ft apart, curved across spur which dropped gently towards south; highest point was near centre of outer arc.

Remainder of site now occupied by a housing estate.

Devonshire

HEMBURY FORT: ST 112030

Proceedings of the Devon Archaeological Exploration Society, I (2) (1930), 40–63; I (3) (1931), 90–113; I (4) (1932), 162–90; II (3) (1935), 135–75; *Antiquity*, XXXVII (1963), 228–9.

Radiocarbon dates: charcoal from segment 2 of inner ditch, 3150 bc ± 150 (BM–130) and 3330 bc ± 150 (BM–138); charcoal from 'burnt layer' overlying occupation in area D, 3240 bc ± 150 (BM–136).

On Upper Greensand capped with Clay-with-flints, at 885ft O.D. near south end of narrow, flat-topped spur.

Complete plan unknown; hill-fort superimposed. See figs. 14 and 15, and pp. 96.

HIGH PEAK: SY 103859

Proceedings of the Devon Archaeological Exploration Society, XXIII (1966), 35–59; *Radiocarbon*, XI (1969), 287

Radiocarbon date: charcoal from Neolithic pit adjacent to ditch, 2860 bc $\pm$ 150 (BM-214). Provenance of charcoal from Mrs S. H. M. Pollard, *in litt*.

On Upper Greensand capped with Clay-with-flints, at 500ft O.D. on hill rising steeply from landward to present cliff edge.

Plan unknown; hill-fort superimposed and most of site apparently destroyed by coastal erosion.

Dorset

HAMBLEDON HILL: ST 849122

Royal Commission on Historical Monuments (England), *Inventory of Historical Monuments in the County of Dorset*, vol. 3 (1970), 130–1; excavations by G. de G. Sieveking and R. W. H. Erskine (briefly reported in *Proceedings of the Dorset Natural History and Archaeological Society*, LXXIII (1951), 105–6) and by D. J. Bonney in 1958–60 are not fully published; *Radiocarbon*, VII (1965), 158.

Radiocarbon date: charcoal from bottom of ditch of southern outwork, 2790 bc $\pm$ 90 (NPL–76).

On Upper Chalk capped with flint gravel, at 600ft O.D., on domed east end of hill-top, with outworks on sloping spurs radiating south and east.

The enclosure is defined by a single ditch which curves round the summit of the hill, following the 600ft contour on the west and south-west and dropping to about 550ft on the south-east and east; it appears to be deficient along a steep scarp at the north. Two outworks (or cross-dykes), each consisting of closely spaced double ditches, lie across the bases of the south and east spurs, 40 and 30 yards respectively outside the enclosure; a similar outwork crosses the east spur at a distance of $\frac{1}{4}$ mile (see plate 7).

The interior is disturbed by gravel-digging and the enclosure itself was levelled and brought under cultivation about 1960.

MAIDEN CASTLE: SY 669885

R. E. M. Wheeler, *Maiden Castle* (1943).

On Upper Chalk, at 430ft O.D., on a saddle-backed hill.

Complete plan unknown; hill-fort superimposed. Two ditches, about 50 ft apart, embrace at west and east a pair of low knolls on a gentle east-facing slope. The north and south sides presumably run beneath the hill-fort ramparts along the scarp edges.

Gloucestershire

CRICKLEY HILL: SO 927161

Discovered in July 1971 during excavation of the Iron Age hill-fort by Mr Philip Dixon on behalf of the committee for Research into the Iron Age in the North-West Cotswolds of the Gloucestershire College of Art and Design, to whom thanks are extended for permission to include this note.

On Jurassic limestone at 800ft O.D., on a spur of the Cotswold escarpment.

Initial investigation has revealed causewayed ditches accompanied by low banks within the area of the hill-fort. There is evidence of occupation immediately behind the inner bank. Pottery and a flint industry of appropriate types are associated.

Middlesex

STAINES: TQ 025725

Archaeological News Letter, VII (1962), 131–4; Ministry of Works, *Excavations: Annual Reports, 1961* (1962), p. 6; *1962* (1963), p. 6; *1963* (1964), p. 9; *Atti del VI Congresso Internazionale delle Scienze Preistoriche e Protostoriche*, vol. II (1965), pp. 319–23.

On alluvium and gravel about one mile north of the River Thames, under 200ft O.D., on flattish land bounded by two brooks.

Two rings, about 70ft apart, were centred on a slight knoll; part of the outer ditch has been eroded by a brook.

Site now destroyed.

Sussex

BARKHALE: SU 976126

Description and plan: E. C. Curwen, *The Archaeology of Sussex* (1954), p. 89, fig. 18. Excavations: J. A. Ryle, *c.* 1930, no material result; V. Seton-Williams, *c.* 1960, unpublished.

On Chalk capped with Clay-with-flints, at 625ft O.D. on a ridge.

The single oval ring lies along a slope dropping gently towards the south-east.

COMBE HILL: TQ 574021

Sussex Archaeological Collections, LXXXIX (1950), 105–16; subsequent excavation by V. Seton-Williams unpublished.

On Chalk at 600ft O.D., on a ridge.

Two irregularly spaced rings, set across the ridge, drop downslope slightly at south and more steeply at north, where each is deficient along an abrupt scarp. The outer ring is also apparently broken by a gap of some 300ft along the south-west arc and its course is defined at the east and south-east by a few widely spaced segments.

THE TRUNDLE: SU 877111

Sussex Archaeological Collections, LXX (1929), 33–85; LXXII (1931), 100–49; E. C. Curwen, *The Archaeology of Sussex* (1954), 84–7

On Chalk at 675ft O.D., on a domed hill-top.

Complete plan unknown; hill-fort partially superimposed. Two irregularly spaced rings are set partly on the summit of the hill, partly on the north and west slopes; the second ring spirals at the west to form an extra arc. Seven ditch segments emerging from beneath the hill-fort rampart on the steep slope at the north may represent an outwork or a third ring which is masked elsewhere by the rampart.

WHITEHAWK: TQ 331048

Sussex Archaeological Collections, LXXI (1930), 57–96; *Ant. J.*, XIV (1934), 99–133; *Sussex Archaeological Collections*, LXXVII (1936), 60–92; E. C. Curwen, *The Archaeology of Sussex* (1954), 71–84, with contoured plan.

On Chalk at 390ft O.D., on a saddle between two eminences.

Four irregularly spaced rings are set along the saddle, rising over higher ground at north and south, dropping slightly at the west and steeply at the east, where the third ring lies 40ft below the top of the saddle. The fourth ring, apparently deficient on this steep scarp, has tangential and radial projections at the south-east, south-west and north-east. An outlying ditch, 40ft north of and aligned with the fourth ring, may be part of an outwork comparable with the two lines shown crossing the south end of the hill in a plan of 1821 (cf. Curwen, *The Archaeology of Sussex*, p. 73). Two further ditches, one probably tangential, lay downslope at the south-east. The enclosure has been much disturbed by a race-course, roads, allotment gardens etc.

Wiltshire

KNAP HILL: SU 122636

W.A.M., XXXVII (1912), 42–65; LX (1965), 1–23; *Antiquity*, XLIII (1969), 304–5 (radio-carbon dates).

Radiocarbon dates: from antler in primary rubble fill of ditch, 2760 bc ± 115 (BM–205); from charcoal in upper fill of ditch, 1840 ± 130 (BM–208).

On Chalk capped with Clay-with-flints, at 825ft O.D., on a steep-sided knoll at the end of a spur.

A single oval ring, set on the slope 25ft below the summit of the knoll, follows the 825ft contour from the south-west round to the north, where it has been disturbed by a later enclosure; two further ditch segments lie at the same level on a projection at the south-east.

The interior has been disturbed by flint-digging.

ROBIN HOOD'S BALL: SU 102460

W.A.M., LIX (1964), 1–27.

On Chalk at 450ft O.D., on a rounded eminence.

Two rings, 100ft apart, are set across a slope facing east.

RYBURY: SU 083640

Description, with plan and air photograph (printed wrong way up): *Antiquity*, IV (1930),

38–40. Trial excavations: *W.A.M.*, LIX (1964), 185. Subsequent discovery of Neolithic pottery: *W.A.M.*, LX (1965), 127.

Complete plan uncertain; hill-fort superimposed and interior extensively disturbed by chalk-pits. The segmented Neolithic ditch which emerges as an arc from beneath the hill-fort rampart at the east appears to continue upwards to curve round the summit of the knoll inside the west rampart. An unpublished plan by the Royal Commission on Historical Monuments (England) differs from that of Curwen (*Antiquity*, IV) in the interpretation of features within the disturbed area. The outwork, 240 yards south, is a segmented ditch, roughly semicircular in plan, set round the outer side of a smaller knoll.

WHITESHEET HILL: ST 802352

W.A.M., LIV (1952), 404–10.
On Chalk at 750ft O.D., at the edge of a plateau.
The single oval ring lies across the contours, the eastern half on nearly level ground, the western half downslope.

WINDMILL HILL: SU 087714

I. F. Smith, *Windmill Hill and Avebury: Excavations by Alexander Keiller, 1925–1939* (1965), 1–174.

Radiocarbon dates: charcoal from occupation layer beneath outer bank, 2950 bc ± 150 (BM–73); charcoal from lower fill of ditches, 2570 bc ± 150 (BM–74); charcoal from upper fill of outer ditch, 1540 bc ± 150 (BM–75).

On Middle Chalk at 640ft O.D., on a rounded hill-top.

The outermost of the three irregularly spaced rings embraces the summit the hill at the south and east, dropping at the north-west nearly to the bottom of the steepest slope. The inner and middle rings lie across the north-west slope (see plate 6).

Notes

1. *Antiquity*, IV (1930), 22–54.
2. *W.A.M.*, XLVI (1933), 198–213; LVII (1958), 17.
3. S. Piggott, *Neolithic Cultures of the British Isles* (1954), p. 20.
4. The useful convention 'bc' is adopted here, following a suggestion by Dr D. Schove in order to make it clear that dates are expressed in conventional radiocarbon years: *Antiquity*, XLIV (1970), 93. Laboratory numbers and other details will be found in the Appendix.
5. Piggott, *op. cit.*, fig. 1, map I.
6. G. J. Copley, *An Archaeology of South-East England* (1958), p. 255.
7. *Records of Buckinghamshire*, XVII (1961), 53.
8. R. Jessup, *South East England* (1970), p. 73.
9. W. J. Wedlake, *Excavations at Camerton, Somerset* (1958), p. 19.
10. J. K. St Joseph, *The Uses of Air Photography: Nature and Man in a New Perspective* (1966), p. 115.
11. *Antiquity*, XL (1966), 145.
12. *ibid.*, XLIV (1970), 144–5.
13. *ibid.*, XXXVIII (1964), 290–1.
14. Royal Commission on Historical Monuments (England), *A Matter of Time* (1960), p. 13.
15. private communication to the author.
16. E. C. Curwen, *The Archaeology of Sussex* (1954), p. 71.
17. *P.P.S.*, XXI (1955), 100; T. G. E. Powell *et al.*, *Megalithic Enquiries in the West of Britain* (1969), p. 263.
18. A. Fox, *South West England* (1964), p. 31.
19. *Sussex Archaeological Collections*, LXXII (1931), 109.
20. Piggott, *op. cit.*, p. 27; Curwen, *op. cit.*, p. 86.
21. *Proceedings of the Devon Archaeological Exploration Society*, II (1935), 135–75, fig. 9.
22. R. E. M. Wheeler, *Maiden Castle* (1943), pl. VI.
23. I. F. Smith, *Windmill Hill and Avebury: Excavations by Alexander Keiller, 1925–1939* (1965), pp. 15–17; *Palaeohistoria*, XII (1966), 471–4.
24. Wheeler, *op. cit.*, pl. V.
25. *Ant. J.*, XIV (1934), 107 and pl. XIV.
26. Ministry of Works, *Excavations: Annual Report, 1961* (1962), p. 6.
27. *W.A.M.*, LIV (1952), 407, fig. 2, cutting 1.
28. *Sussex Archaeological Collections*, LXXII (1931), pl. II.
29. *ibid.*, LXXI (1930), pl. III.
30. *W.A.M.*, LX (1965), 19.
31. Smith, *op. cit.*, fig. 4.
32. *Ant. J.*, XIV (1934), 112; Smith, *op. cit.*, p. 14.
33. *Ulster Journal of Archaeology*, XXXII (1969), 13.
34. Piggott, *op. cit.*, p. 31.
35. *Jahresbericht de Bayerischen Bodendenkmalpflege* (1962), pp. 5–21.
36. *Palaeohistoria*, XII (1966), 474; *P.P.S.*, XXXV (1969), 112–33.
37. *Ulster Journal of Archaeology*, XXXII (1969), 13.
38. *Antiquity*, XXXVII (1963), 116–20; XL (1966), 227–8.
39. *Ant. J.*, X (1930), 30–3.
40. S. Piggott, *Ancient Europe* (1965), p. 232.

41. J. M. Coles and D. D. A. Simpson (eds), *Studies in Ancient Europe* (1968), 255–86.
42. *P.P.S.*, XVIII (1952), 224–5.
43. *ibid.*, XX (1954), 219.
44. *ibid.*, XXVI (1960), 213.
45. *ibid.*, XVIII (1952), 208.
46. *Proceedings of the Devon Archaeological Exploration Society*, I(3) (1931), 109, 111; I(4) (1932), 171, 173.
47. see also *P.P.S.*, XXX (1964), 373.
48. *Transactions of the Devon Archaeological Exploration Society*, XXI (1963), 27.
49. *Antiquity*, XLIII (1969), 145–59.
50. *ibid.*
51. Smith, *op. cit.*, fig. 22, P104, P110.
52. *Ant. J.*, XLIX (1969), 53.
53. Smith, *op. cit.*, fig. 27, P194, P195.
54. *Antiquity*, XLIII (1969), 147.
55. *Proceedings of the Dorset Natural History and Archaeological Society*, LXXX (1958), 99.
56. *P.P.S.*, XXXVI (1970), 112–15.
57. *Transactions of the Devon Archaeological Exploration Society*, XXI (1963), 21.
58. *Proceedings of the Devon Archaeological Exploration Society*, V (1953), 8–26.
59. *Nature*, CCXXVIII (1970), 251–4.

Settlements in later Neolithic Britain

I. J. McINNES

This paper deals with the question of the settlements of the later indigenous Neolithic or stone-using agricultural communities of the United Kingdom. Although reference is made to certain Irish sites by way of comparison, no attempt is made to deal with Irish settlements in detail.

The evidence for house structures in the later Neolithic is confined almost entirely to what Fox would have called the Highland zone (fig. 16). At Mount Pleasant, Glamorgan, a stone and post structure beneath a cairn with a primary cremation burial in a cinerary urn has been interpreted as a rectangular house.[1] The walls of this structure were easily identifiable as they were of sandstone slabs, while the cairn was built of limestone and other rocks. Although one side of the building was almost completely destroyed by the primary cairn deposit, the wall stood to eight courses on its eastern side and from four to six courses on its southern side. A central row of posts may be presumed to have supported the roof structure and on the north the stonewalling appears to have acted as footings for a line of posts. The line of posts outside the southern stone wall was interpreted as part of a buttress formed by the red clay bank. The doorway faced east, with two post holes representing doorjambs (fig. 17A). Although a fair quantity of Neolithic pottery, including Peterborough types, came from this level, most of it was from outside the building and the excavator remarked on the absence of a hearth or any ash within the house. There were also no animal remains, but this could be due to the nature of the soil.

In this aspect the house at Ronaldsway, Isle of Man, is a complete contrast, pottery and other domestic debris being abundant.[2] This house was also partly destroyed but appears to have been about 24ft by 12 to 14ft in size (fig. 17B). The walls were formed of posts with stone footings, and the roof was supported by a double line of posts. There was a large central hearth and the entrance is

Figure 16. Principal sites referred to in the text.
1. Rinyo
2. Skara Brae
3. Northton
4. Eilean an Tighe
5. Lyles Hill
6. Lough Gur
7. Ronaldsway
8. Glencrutchery
9. Barford
10. Fengate
11. Honington
12. Streatley
13. Mount Pleasant
14. Sonning
15. Playden

presumed to have been on the south-west corner. The house was dug $1\frac{1}{2}$ to $2\frac{1}{2}$ft into the old land surface and, as the sides cut into the gravel rather steeply, the excavator suggested that this level must have been lined with some type of wooden or wattle revetment. There was no sign of stratification or sterile layers in the filling and the large amount of pottery, tools, bones etc. suggested a fairly long, steady occupation. It is likely that the site at Glencrutchery, also on the Isle of Man, was of a similar nature.

It is unlikely that the nature of the site at Eilean an Tighe, North Uist, will be fully understood. The excavator interpreted the site as a pottery kiln,[3] but the complete absence of obvious wasters amongst the large amount of pottery from the site throws some doubt upon this. As the site is submerged beneath a loch, and has doubtless suffered from wave action for some time, it is unlikely that much of the stonework is in its original position. The structure, which includes three hearth areas, appears to have been built of stone and turf, and the large quantity of pottery suggests an extensive occupation. The later Neolithic site at Northton, Harris, may be presumed to have consisted of a structure which at least had stone footings, but no perceptible pattern is visible amongst the stone tumble to indicate the form of the suggested structure. It is possible that the later Beaker settlers on the site may have indulged in some stone robbing. Again, the amount of pottery, which is of the same type as that at Eilean an Tighe, and large deposits of marine shells, indicate a fairly prolonged occupation.[4]

If Mount Pleasant and Ronaldsway represent single homesteads, Skara Brae and Rinyo are certainly more in the nature of villages or settlements of more than one household.[5]

The standard type of house at Skara Brae is internally square with rounded corners measuring some 15 to 20ft across, entered by a single doorway and having a stone-edged square hearth. The walls stand to a maximum of 10ft but begin to oversail from floor level (fig. 18A). The method of roofing is not at all clear, and complete corbelling has been ruled out as the amount of collapsed stone within the huts is unlikely to have been sufficient. The presence of whale bones in House I has suggested that these may well have been used as supports for a sod roof. Although wood is scarce on Orkney it is certainly not absent, and carbonized fragments of alder, birch, pine and oak at Rinyo may indicate a wooden roofing structure. The internal fittings of the houses – beds, boxes, hearths and cupboards – indicate a considerable degree of sophistication. Such fittings are of course only known at Skara Brae and Rinyo. This may be put down to the nature of the Caithness flagstone; the facility with which it may be fractured makes it ideal for building such structures. But it should be borne in mind that dressers and built

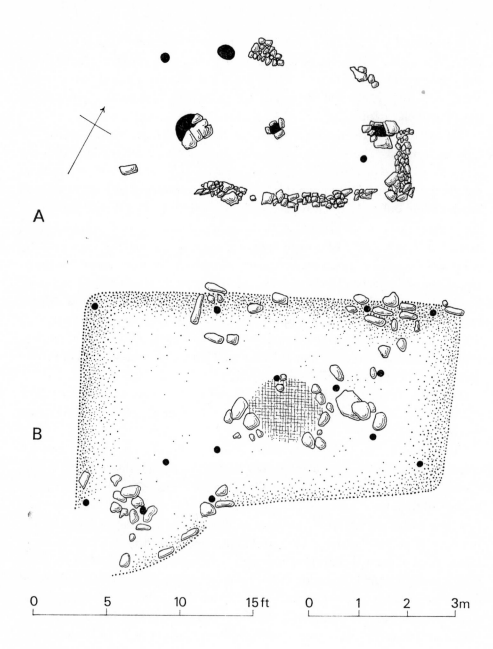

A

B

Figure 17. Plans of houses at (A) Mount Pleasant and (B) Ronaldsway.

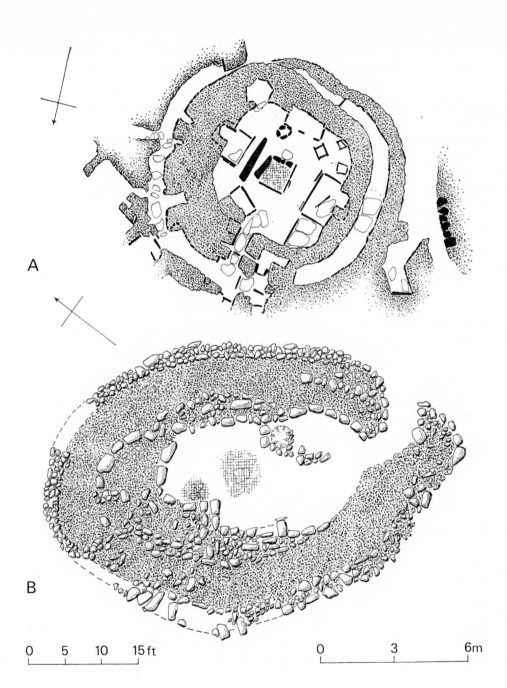

Figure 18. Plans of houses at (A) Skara Brae and (B) Ness of Gruting.

beds are only of use to a settled community. Such objects, even in wood, would be an encumbrance to a people involved in any type of seasonal movement.

Although many of the 60 houses listed by Calder in his paper on Stone Age House sites in Shetland must be of a date well beyond that which this paper might reasonably include, there is some indication that the earliest may come within the scope of the later Neolithic.[6] Henshall has shown that the Stanydale Temple is of the same constructional technique and design as the tombs of her Zetland group.[7] The house at Ness of Gruting[8] comes within the same complex of buildings and appears to be contemporary with Stanydale. The pottery from Ness of Gruting seems to be related to the Hebridean sequence with what appears to be influence from Beaker wares.

The large house at Gruting is oval in plan, 19ft by 14ft 6ins, with an apsidal extension 7ft 6ins by 6ft 9ins (fig. 18B). The walls are massive and built in a technique similar to that employed at Stanydale and in tomb construction. There is a central hearth and, like the Ronaldsway house, the Gruting house is dug into the old land surface to a depth of some 3ft. The presence of beds or benches along the side walls suggests comparison with the much more sophisticated constructions at Skara Brae and Rinyo. This Shetland house type must have lasted about a thousand years, for at Jarlshof, in the last phase of the oval houses, bronzes were being cast.[9] No doubt these houses were built to such a pattern, and continued to be so built for a millennium to satisfy local conditions, and it is unlikely that the settlements of Shetland will reveal much about the situation prevailing in the southern half of the country.

The majority of sites in the Lowland zone giving evidence of occupation in the later Neolithic are either pits containing sherds and domestic debris or occupation deposits, concentrations of pottery and flints sometimes associated with hearths or areas of blackened soil. The size of these pits is very variable. At Enborne Gate, Newbury, Berks.,[10] a pit containing Peterborough pottery, fragments of sarsen and flint flakes, was 5ft in diameter and 4ft deep. In contrast, the pits at Iver, Bucks.,[11] were only 1ft in diameter and 15ins deep, but also contained Peterborough sherds and flints. The complexity of the sites, too, varies. At Grantham the pit was 7ft long and 2ft deep with apparent signs of stake holes round the edge.[12] Stake holes also surrounded one of the pits at Winterbourne Dauntsey, Wilts. At Selsey, Sussex, and Downton, Wilts.,[13] what were described as shallow depressions may be regarded as the bases of pits, the upper parts of which have eroded. An examination of pits covered by later barrows might be expected to give some evidence as to the original size of pits. At Overton Down 6a, the pit beneath the barrow was 2ft wide and 1ft 6ins deep;[14] at Aldro barrow 30 the pit was only 14ins wide and 1ft deep.[15] At Acklam Wold barrow 211, although the pit was 2½ft wide it was only 10ins deep.[16] As this pit was covered with a barrow with Food Vessel primaries it is unlikely that any great degree of natural erosion would have occurred before the erection of the barrow.

Frequently these pits have been described as cooking holes, for example at Clacton,[17] on account of the presence of pot boilers and calcined flints within them. The pottery at Astrop, Northants., was found in pits full of black earth, calcined stones and ashes.[18] The post barrow pit at Fussells Lodge also contained burnt flakes and pieces of charcoal,[19] and similar fillings occurred in the pits at Winterbourne Dauntsey, Wilts., Cassington, Oxon., and Wykeham, Yorks.[20] At Puddlehill, Dunstable, Beds.,[21] calcined stones and flints were confined to the smaller of the two pits and the excavators regarded the largest pit as having been used for storage and the two smaller pits for cooking. Smith, however, in her commentary on the pottery from this site, pointed out that there was no sign of burning on the sides of the smaller pits, and there is no suggestion in any of the other reports that such signs of burning have been found in pits elsewhere. It is most likely, surely, that the burned stones were, as Smith has suggested, merely part of the domestic rubbish.

Smith has further suggested that these pits should be regarded as grain storage pits, pointing out that their distribution is confined to a limited area of the known distribution of Neolithic settlement, particularly being concentrated south of the Jurassic ridge. With the exception of two shallow pits at Scotstarvit, Fife,[22] all these pit sites are found on chalk, limestone, gravel or sand, in other words on light, easily tillable soils. This applies even to the most northerly of these pits at Grandtully, Perths.[23] This site is situated on a side morain of gravel, and the pit, which measures 3½ft in diameter and 4ft deep, is a respectable size even by southern standards.

The evidence for these pits being grain storage pits is scanty. None of the pottery from the pits has been found to have grain impressions, nor have actual examples of grain been found in any of the pits. (The wheat found at Townhead, Rothesay,[24] is excluded as this cannot be directly related to the later Neolithic pottery from the site, earlier undecorated wares also being present, and neither type of pottery being clearly associated with the grain.) However, daub has been found in both the pits at Cam, Glos., bearing what may be the impressions of withies and which may represent the internal lining of a storage pit.[25] Daub was also found in the pits at Risby Warren, Lincs.,[26] Sutton Courtenay, Berks.,[27] and Fussells Lodge, Wilts.[28] The burnt clay found in the pits at Stanton Harcourt,

Oxon.,[29] was interpreted originally as the remains of an oven and it is worth noting that a clay oven was found in more than one hut at Rinyo.[30]

If some at least of these pits are accepted as storage pits for grain it would be reasonable to expect to find some other evidence of settlement in the immediate vicinity. This is not to say that the actual fields in which the crops were grown need to be near the main settlement. Certainly some sort of shelter would be likely near the fields as the growing crop would require protection from birds, wild cattle and deer, but this could be undertaken by one or two individuals with only the minimum of shelter. Once the grain had been harvested and winnowed one would expect it to be stored within the settlement area itself, storage being undertaken for consumption in the winter and spring months.

Although it is usual for there to be a scatter of domestic debris about the pits this is not always the case. At Heath Row[31] the excavator stripped a substantial area about the pits in the hope of finding some evidence of house-structure or a hearth, but found that the pottery and flints were confined to the pits.

At Puddlehill, Beds., the excavator was more fortunate in that some 200ft from the pits, beside a spring, was a layer of charcoal containing flint scrapers, broken animal bones and pot sherds.[32] The dimensions of this layer of charcoal are not recorded but it seems likely that this area represents the actual settlement with the storage pits some little way distant.

Areas of charcoal or discoloured earth are frequently found on occupation sites without pits. The site at Eaton Socon, Beds., for example, consisted only of fire-blackened stones, black soil and wood ash with which were associated flint flakes and a single Mortlake rim.[33] At Creeting St Mary, Suffolk, the pottery and flints were found in an area of blackened sand[34] and at Downton, Wilts., the excavator remarked on the absence of a living site, that is, no definite post holes, but remarked on patches of discolouration in the vicinity of a shallow pit.[35]

Hearths are not infrequently associated with these areas of discolouration, for example at Craike Hill[36] and Driffield West Reservoir, Yorks.[37] At Scotstarvit, Fife, a hearth and two shallow pits containing fragments of Peterborough Northern pottery, burnt animal bones and pitchstone flakes, must represent some form of occupation. A hearth alone associated with domestic debris may not represent any more than the most temporary of occupations; such seems to be the case at Shippea Hill, Cambs.[38] and Selmeston, Sussex.[39]

At Honington, Suffolk, although no hearths were found, a number of pits were associated with a series of oval dark-coloured patches (fig. 19A). These patches were thought by the excavator to represent the floors of tents or huts.[40] The highest concentrations of implements and sherds occurred in these discoloured

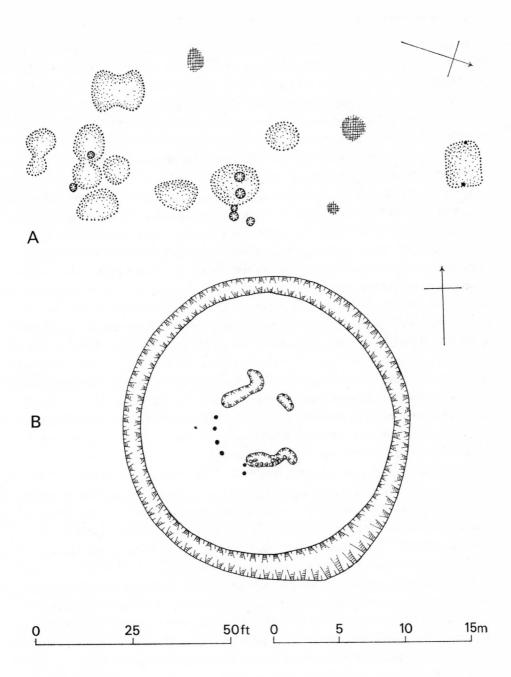

Figure 19. Plans of settlements at (A) Honington and (B) Playden.

areas, although there was also a scatter of worked flints outside them. There were no post holes or other structural evidence. In addition to the huts, a number of small holes and dark patches were noted, and in some of the former, animal bones were found, often showing traces of burning. Certain of the pits were identified as cooking holes, mainly on account of the presence of burnt stones in those pits nearest to the huts. The proposed huts at Honington are approximately 10ft by 8ft in extent and it is possible that the saucer-shaped depressions at Selsey Bill, Sussex, may represent a similar, if less extensive, site.[41]

Apart from the stake holes surrounding pits at Grantham and Winterbourne Dauntsey there is very little structural evidence on other late Neolithic settlement sites. Various scoops and hollows occurred at Grandtully but these did not form any recognizable pattern. Single post holes have been found at Edingthorpe, Norfolk[42] and Puddlehill, Beds. Many of the occupation sites already mentioned have been discovered in adverse circumstances, during the course of gravel working or the excavation of a later superimposed and destructive site, and a single post hole could easily be overlooked under such circumstances. Although no-one would wish to create a house out of a single post hole it is unfortunately possible to do so. One of the houses at Lough Gur, Site D House I, consisted of a single central post hole with surrounding bank of stones, for the support, no doubt, of the walls, the completed structure resembling a charcoal burner's hut.[43] In a paper on stone tepi rings of the Blackfeet Indians,[44] Kehoe showed how a ring of boulders was used to weigh down the skin of the tepi when it was occupied for a period of time. When the site was abandoned only a circle of stones remained, with a small heap of ashes the sole evidence of human occupation. The writer went on to say that tepis were weighted down by logs and brush in wooded areas and by cut sods in unglaciated, boulderless regions. It is possible therefore to construct something on the lines of the Lough Gur house with a central upright pole and with the walls supported by logs or sods, which would result in only a single post hole remaining in the archaeological record.

Although stone foundations were widely used in the Highland zone, the upper part of the houses already described must have been of perishable material. Since the weight of the roof was taken on the central posts in the houses at Mount Pleasant and Ronaldsway the walls need have been nothing more substantial than wattle, and even where timber was abundant the piling up of sods against a wattle wall would have given much-needed warmth and protection. It has already been suggested that stone footings may be replaced by turf or sleepers, and Evans in his study of Irish sod and turf houses[45] has indicated that where the purlin form of roofing was used it was not necessary for the purlin props to be sunk into the ground. Indeed he has suggested that it would not be easy to adjust the props to the required height if they were sunk into the ground. Similarly, it is not necessary to sink cruck blades into the ground where this type of construction is used.

Evans postulated the existence of a sod house at Lyles Hill where there were no post holes.[46] The site consists of a hearth measuring about 4ft in diameter. Flints and sherds were very numerous both inside the hearth and in the dark earth on all sides. They became infrequent 2 to 3ft from the edge of the hearth, but the charcoal spread continued over an area 15ft by 8ft. The amount of pottery recovered from this single hearth site argues for more than temporary occupation, and there remains the possibility of a sod hut, roofed with sod-covered branches resting on the wall tops, or a primitive type of cruck construction imbedded in the sod walls. This would leave no traceable remains other than discolouration and a thickened surface. In an area of subsequent cultivation such remains would rapidly be destroyed by ploughing or even grazing animals. A later Neolithic site at Streatley, Beds., appears to have been of a similar nature;[47] a circular area of discolouration, apparently of turves, with an entrance on the east (fig. 20).

The use of turf as a building material suggests the existence of open areas of grassland. Although pollen evidence indicates the continued existence of forests, it is evident that grassland or heath, however limited in extent, must have been available, and that Neolithic builders had the tools and technology to cut large quantities of sods. In Ireland, at Knowth and New Grange, large quantities of turves were used in construction, layers of these alternating with layers of stones.[48] In the United Kingdom too there is evidence of sod or turf being used in the construction, not only of round barrows, but also of long barrows such as Thickthorn and Holdenhurst.[49] At Thickthorn there was a small turf enclosure beneath the barrow, and turves were used to revet the mound at Holdenhurst. In Yorkshire the Neolithic round barrow at Seamer Moor was partly constructed of turves.[50] There can be no doubt that turf was available for building at the beginning of the third millennium. How much more is this likely to have been the case after a millennium of agriculture, which is likely to have included ploughing, as the find beneath the South Street long barrow has shown.[51]

The structure at Playden, Sussex was enclosed by a circular ditch,[52] the enclosed area being 65ft in diameter (fig. 19B). In the centre were three narrow hollows 2ft wide and 1ft 6ins deep, one lined with stone walling two courses high. A large quantity of charcoal and burnt timbers came from the base of the ditch, along with sherds of Neolithic and later pottery. The timbers in the ditch were up to 1ft in diameter and 5 to 6ft long. Patches of wood ash and charcoal indicate possible hearths and one patch had four pot-boilers lying beside it. It is suggested that this central area represents a hut site, the hollows forming bedding trenches for wooden uprights (fig. 19B). The site was destroyed by fire and the burnt timbers dumped in the ditch. The timbers on the west side were either left standing or were re-erected at this stage. The whole central area was then covered with a layer of white sand, not a natural deposit in the neighbourhood. A pavement of sandstone blocks was laid over the central area and the site seems to have become a flintknapping area, with a considerable layer of occupation material building up upon the white sand layer.

One of the sites at Barford, Warwicks., Site C, has been interpreted as a settlement.[53] This was a multiperiod site consisting of a sub-rectangular ditch and a mass of post holes. The post holes did not however form any distinct pattern. There was a noticeable paucity of domestic debris on the site.

The site at Sonning, Berks., was also outlined by a sub-rectangular ditch, with possible traces of an internal bank on the southern side (fig. 21B).[54] The internal area contained five shallow depressions, a pit and numerous 'holes'. These holes varied from 6ins to 2ft 6ins in depth and 6ins to 2ft in diameter, but formed no distinct pattern. In view of the presence of fragments of bone in these pits it is unlikely that they are post or stake holes. Like Barford, there was a noticeable absence of domestic debris on the site. The excavator therefore regarded the site as a sacred or funerary one and drew parallels with the rectangular enclosure at Dorchester, Oxon.[55] Domestic debris was also noticeably sparse at Mount Pleasant and in the first phase at Playden. The recent excavations at Fengate (fig. 21A)[56] have revealed a square ditched enclosure some 153ft by 48ft which undoubtedly ante-dates the Beaker settlement in the area and, if the Fengate site is regarded as a settlement, it is possible that the sites at Barford C and Sonning may represent something similar.

The lack of positive evidence for house structure in Lowland Britain, in areas of known settlement, is a problem which is likely to remain with us. Whatever type of house structure belongs to the later Neolithic it does not seem to have been anything akin to the massive constructions of the Neolithic long houses across the Channel. Not that the material was unobtainable or that the ability to fell and erect massive timbers was lacking, witness the timber circles at Woodhenge[57] and Arminghall.[58] Childe postulated the existence of a timber long house at Easton Down[59] disturbed by later Beaker pits, but there seems little evidence to suggest that this linear postsetting is any earlier than the Beaker structures. A possible rectangular post structure has also been suggested by the single line of

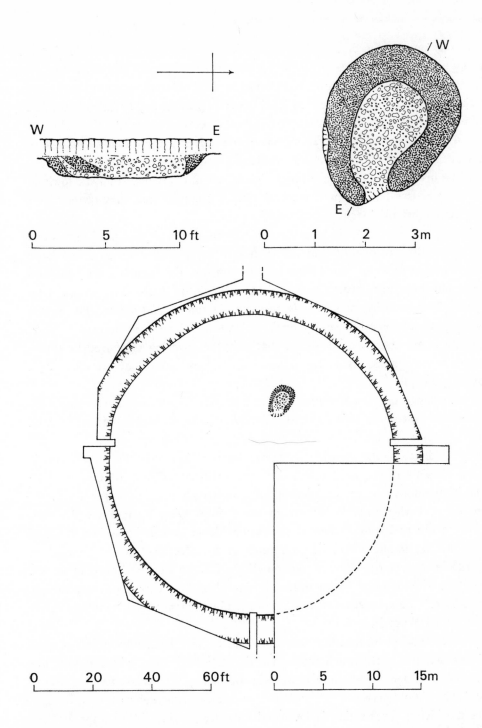

Figure 20. Plans and section of Streatley.

post holes outside the bank at Durrington Walls, the greater part of this house having weathered away, leaving only that part protected by the slip of the bank.[60] Lack of evidence for wooden structures may be ascribed to the natural weathering of chalk shown by the variation in level between present-day surfaces and those protected by barrows, upwards of 18ins having been recorded.[61] Nevertheless, such a degree of weathering cannot have been uniform, there being evidence of both posts and stake holes on chalk – massive posts, such as those already referred to in the henges, and also stake holes 6ins or less in diameter. If all the lowland Neolithic houses have been weathered away it suggests that they cannot have been very substantial structures in the first place.

One type of structure which leaves a minimum of trace is that used to this day by tinkers. Built of pliable branches such as alder or willow which do no more than penetrate three or four inches into the topsoil, the branches are bent into hoops and the whole covered with canvas, although no doubt skins would serve as well. The resulting structure is surprisingly roomy and warm. The fire is always outside the cabin so no form of protected hearth is necessary. Such structures have the great advantage that only the covering skin need be transported, a new framework being obtained at the new site. They are ideal for a travelling people.

Such a suggestion for Neolithic houses indicates the existence of a temporary or seasonal pattern of settlement. Unfortunately the economic evidence which might support the idea of a seasonal pattern of shifting settlement is lacking. Direct evidence of the growing of cereals by the later Neolithic population is scanty. Grain rubbers were found at Combe Hill and Enbourne Gate.[62] Two grain impressions, one unidentified on a Peterborough vessel from the Thames[63] and one of barley on a Peterborough sherd from West Kennet are the only examples of actual grain.[64] The osteological evidence indicates the dominance of cattle and pig among domesticated animals in the later Neolithic.[65] There does seem to be a greater interest in pigs on Rinyo Clacton sites with, of course, the exception of Rinyo and Skara Brae. Pig was absent at Rinyo and very rare at Skara Brae.[66] This, however, may be explained by the scarcity of woodland in the windswept Orkney islands.

The part played by hunting does not seem to have been very great, as wild animals are noticeably much rarer than domesticated ones, where figures are available. Red deer bones were present in the pits at Winterbourne Dauntsey[67] and Acklam Wold barrow 211[68] and amongst the domestic debris at Gop Cave.[69] Direct evidence for hunting is indicated however by the pit-fall traps at Mye Plantation, Wigtown, with which were associated sherds of Rinyo Clacton

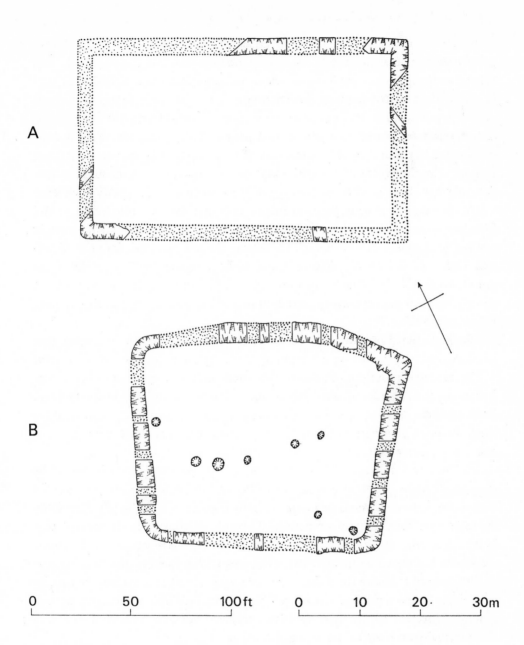

Figure 21. Plans of enclosure at (A) Fengate and (B) Sonning.

pottery.[70] The use of bones of small mammals and birds to decorate Peterborough pottery suggests that these were taken in some numbers, and the possibility that fishing and trapping or shooting of waterfowl were important activities is suggested by the fact that so much Peterborough pottery has been found in rivers or in pits beside them.[71] The development of petit tranchet derivative arrowheads may possibly be related to a similar occupation. Their presence on sand-dune sites in the north and in the main areas of occupation, and therefore of forest clearance, on the Wolds of Yorkshire and the Downs in the south, suggests that they may have been used in the hunting of geese feeding on the grassy open land.

The presence of marine shells at inland sites may indicate movement to and from the seashore, as such objects are unlikely to have been traded, certainly not as a food source. A limpet shell came from the late Neolithic levels at Windmill Hill,[72] mussel at Woodhenge[73] and scallop, mussel and oyster from the pits at Woodlands.[74] Oyster shells were used to grit pottery at Hills Road, Cambs., and cockle-shell impressions occurred on one of the Rinyo Clacton sherds from Pakenham, Suffolk.[75]

The importance of cattle in the economy would favour the argument that late Neolithic settlements were temporary due to seasonal patterns of movement.

The repeated rebuilding at Skara Brae does indicate prolonged occupation. Eventually the site became semi-subterranean due to the build up of the midden. Even after the site was suddenly abandoned it was revisited. The site at Skara Brae, although geographically in the Highland zone, must have been an ideal one for primitive settlement based on herding. The absence of large forests meant there was no need to clear tracts of land preparatory to settlement. The machair provides excellent grazing for cattle, and its high lime content coupled with a heavy rainfall would facilitate the growing of crops (although there is no evidence that such activity occurred). The sea, of course, is an ever-present larder. A similar situation prevails at Northton in Harris where the Neolithic settlement is situated on the machair, in an area known today as the Bull Pasture.

The detailed evidence from these northern sites merely emphasizes the paucity of evidence in the south and it may well be that late Neolithic settlements were of a more permanent nature than has been suggested but built in such a way as to leave virtually no trace in the archaeological record.

During the excavation of the deserted medieval village at Borup in Denmark there was no evidence of house structure in the initial season of excavation; the field systems were plotted and the areas in which houses should be expected examined – concentrations of pottery, hearths and wells suggested the presence of farmsteads. The reasons for the unfruitful result appeared in the following year when a third possible farm site was excavated.[76] The wall posts along the length of this building had stood on stones and apparently supported the roof, for no trace could be found of internal post settings. The aligned stones of the farms excavated the previous season had clearly been removed because of a longer period of cultivation over that area of the site. This type of structure is still to be seen in Scandinavia and must represent the ultimate archaeological nightmare.

Notes

1. *Transactions of the Cardiff Naturalists Society*, LXXXI (1953), 75–92.
2. *P.P.S.*, XII (1947), 136–69.
3. *P.S.A.S.*, LXXXV (1950–1), 1–37.
4. unpublished: information from Mr D. D. A. Simpson.
5. V. G. Childe, *Skara Brae*, (1931); *P.S.A.S.*, LXXIII (1939), 6–31; *P.S.A.S.*, LXXXI (1947–8), 16–42.
6. *P.S.A.S.*, XCVI (1963), 37–86.
7. A. S. Henshall, *Chambered Tombs of Scotland*, I (1963), 151.
9. *P.S.A.S.*, LXXXIX (1955–6), 340–67.
9. J. R. C. Hamilton, *Excavations at Jarlshof*, Shetland (1956), p. 22.
10. I. F. Smith, *The decorative art of Neolithic ceramic in S. E. England and its relations* (1956). Thesis for Ph.D., University of London.
11. *Records of Buckinghamshire*, XIII (1934–40), 287.
12. *Ant. J.*, XV (1935), 348.
13. *W.A.M.*, LVIII (1962), 116.
14. *P.P.S.*, XXXII (1966), 122–55.
15. J. R. Mortimer, *Forty Years Researches in British and Anglo-Saxon Burial Mounds of E. Yorks.* (1905), p. 68.
16. *ibid.*, p. 93.
17. *P.P.S.*, II (1936), 179.
18. *Oxford Archaeological Society Report* (1912), p. 114.
19. *Arch.*, C (1966),17.
20. *W.A.M.*, XLVI (1934), 445–53; *Oxoniensia*, V (1940), 1–12; *Y.A.J.*, XL (1962), 619–21.
21. *P.P.S.*, XXX (1964), 367–81.
22. *P.S.A.S.*, LXXXII (1947–8), 255.
23. *Antiquity*, XXXI (1967), 220–1.
24. *Transactions of the Bute Natural History Society*, X (1930), 50–4.
25. *Trans. Bristol & Glos. Arch. Soc.*, LXXXVII (1968), 25.
26. *P.P.S.*, XXIII (1957), 43.
27. *Ant. J.*, XIV (1934), 265.
28. *Arch.*, C (1966), 17.
29. *Oxoniensia*, XX (1955), 19.
30. *P.S.A.S.*, LXXXI (1947–8), 15.

31. W. F. Grimes, *Excavations on Defence Sites*, I (1960), p. 186.
32. *P.P.S.*, XXX (1964), 362.
33. *Procs Camb. Ant. Soc.*, LVIII (1965), 141.
34. Smith, *op. cit.*
35. *W.A.M.*, LVIII (1962), 121.
36. *Ant. J.*, XXXVIII (1958), 224.
37. unpublished information from Driffield Museum.
38. *Ant. J.*, XIII (1933), 266–96.
39. *Arch. J.*, XCI (1934), 32–58.
40. *Procs Camb. Ant. Soc.*, XLV (1951), 30–43.
41. *Ant. J.*, XIV (1934), 40–52.
42. *Norfolk Archaeology*, XXXI (1957), 395–416.
43. *P.R.I.A.*, LIV (1954), 385.
44. *American Anthropologist*, V (1958), 861–73.
45. Evans in J. G. Jenkins (ed.), *Studies in Folk Life:* Essays in honour of Iowerth Peate (1969), pp. 79–90.
46. E. E. Evans, *Lyles Hill* (1953), p. 29, fig. 9.
47. Smith, *op. cit.*
48. *Antiquity*, XLI (1967), 304; XXXVIII (1964), 288.
49. S. Piggott, *The Neolithic Cultures of the British Isles* (1954), p. 59.
50. *P.P.S.*, XXVII (1961), 345.
51. *Antiquity*, XLI (1967), 289.
52. *Ant. J.*, XV (1935), 152–64.
53. *Transactions of the Birmingham Archaeological Society*, LXXIII (1969), 19.
54. *Berkshire Archaeological Journal*, LXI (1963–4), 4–19.
55. R. J. C. Atkinson, C. M. Piggott and N. K. Sandars, *Excavations at Dorchester, Oxon.* (1951).
56. *Current Archaeology*, XVII (1969), 156.
57. M. E. Cunnington, *Woodhenge* (1929).
58. *P.P.S.*, II (1936), 1–51.
59. *P.P.S.*, XV (1949), 77–86.
60. *Ant. J.*, XXXIV (1954), 155–70.
61. Mortimer, *op. cit.*
62. Smith, *op. cit.*
63. *ibid.*
64. J. Murray, *The First European Agriculture* (1971).
65. *ibid.*
66. V. G. Childe, *Skara Brae* (1931), p. 203.
67. *W.A.M.*, XLVI (1934), 446.
68. Mortimer, *op. cit.*, p. 68.
69. *Arch. J.*, LVIII (1901), 335.
70. Piggott, *op. cit.*, p. 306.
71. Smith, *op. cit.*
72. *Idem, Windmill Hill & Avebury* (1965), p. 135.
73. Cunnington, *op. cit.*, p. 77.
74. *W.A.M.*, LII (1948), 289.
75. Smith, *op. cit.*, in n. 71 above, p. 212.
76. A. Steensberg, *Atlas Over Borups Agre* (1968), p. 50.

Beaker houses and settlements in Britain

D. D. A. SIMPSON

A perennial problem associated with the makers of Beaker pottery is the scarcity of domestic sites. We know a great deal about their graves, and the main distribution pattern of Beakers in Britain and Europe is provided by funerary finds, but the actual settlements of their makers have remained strangely elusive, in particular in terms of structural remains. The majority of Beaker finds from non-sepulchral contexts in Britain come from coastal sites, notably from areas of sand dunes: sites such as Risby Warren in Lincolnshire, Hedderwick and Gullane in East Lothian and in the west Walney Island in Cheshire, Glenluce in Wigtownshire and Ardnamurchan in Argyll. Also, in the west in Ireland, are inland sites such as Sheepland, Co. Down, and Ballynagilly, Co. Tyrone. Few of these sites have been subject to extensive excavation and this is particularly true of the coastal settlements, where occupation layers have been exposed largely through the process of natural erosion. Even where excavations have taken place on an extensive scale as, for example, at Ballynagilly, no definite house sites are generally recovered. The Beaker settlement at Ballynagilly lay on a low hill of glacial gravel and sand rising some 50ft above the peat bogs which surround it.[1] The features so far recovered consist of a series of hearths and pits and a number of unrelated post holes. These and the extensive scatter of artifacts showed three main concentrations, which the excavator suggested might mark the presence of houses. This is the rather cloudy picture presented by the majority of such settlement sites; hearths, pits and occasional post holes. Caves produce further potential domestic sites, but in no case is there unambiguous evidence of domestic use. In chamber I of the Tooth Cave, Gower,[2] for instance, a discoidal knife, spatula, and flint knife of sub-leaf-shaped form, similar to examples associated with Beakers in graves, might indicate a domestic assembly; but the second chamber contained sherds of a collared urn associated with human remains. Cave

sites in the Kilmartin Valley[3] are more obviously sepulchral in function while
the Yorkshire Windypits[4] are best interpreted as religious sites related to the
later ritual shafts. Dr Isobel Smith has listed 14 further sites which have produced
what are probably storage pits containing Beaker pottery, but unassociated with
any other structure.[5] All but two of these storage pit sites occur in the lowland
zone of Britain, as with the Early and Middle Neolithic examples, and suggest a
dichotomy in economy, at this early stage, between cereal production in the south
and east and stock raising in the north and west.

A variety of reasons have been put forward to account for the apparent
absence of such houses. On the one hand it has been suggested that the Beaker folk
were nomadic, not staying in one place long enough to warrant the construction
of substantial dwellings, but content to live in light tents. This is belied, however,
by the presence of wheat and barley impressions on Beakers and by the occurrence
of this pottery in what Dr Smith has argued very convincingly to be grain storage
pits, indicating a sedentary existence for at least part of the year. Again, in chalk
and limestone areas where erosion has removed about 18ins of natural from the
tops of the downs and wolds, only substantial post holes would survive. This
argument is supported to some extent by the discovery of settlements beneath
barrows as at Swarkeston in Derbyshire and Arreton Down in the Isle of Wight,[6]
both with post structures, and Reffley Wood in Norfolk[7] and Chippenham in
Cambridgeshire.[8] Furthermore, one may be looking in the wrong place; on the
tops of the downs where the barrows lie and not in the valley bottoms where,
perhaps significantly, the henges frequently do. In such a low-lying situation it
would hardly be surprising, particularly in chalk and limestone areas, that few
traces of settlements have been found, covered as they must be by many feet of
hillwash and water-deposited material, to be discovered only by chance. Support
for this theory is provided in an earlier context from the pit beneath the Skendleby long barrow in Lincolnshire.[9] The pit contained occupation debris and molluscan species indicating a damp, wooded environment and this contrasted with the
snail assemblage from elsewhere on the site, which indicated a dry heathland.
The excavator inferred, therefore, that the occupation material had been brought
from a settlement in the valley bottom to the site of the barrow on the chalk ridge.

Whatever the reasons for the scarcity of such sites, and to these one might add
the failure to recognize them for what they are, there are still a number of Beaker
settlements which have produced either stone or timber settings capable of interpretation as buildings. There are nine in all (fig. 22). Six are what could be
considered as western sites: Northton, Harris, Woodhead, Cumberland, Gwithian
in Cornwall, Easton Down in Wiltshire and Lough Gur and Downpatrick in

Figure 22. Principal sites referred to in the text.

1. Rinyo
2. Skara Brae
3. Northton
4. Woodhead
5. Downpatrick
6. Antoft's Windypit
7. Beacon Hill
8. Willington
9. Swarkeston
10. Lough Gur
11. Tooth Cave, Gower
12. Easton Down
13. Belle Tout
14. Gwithian

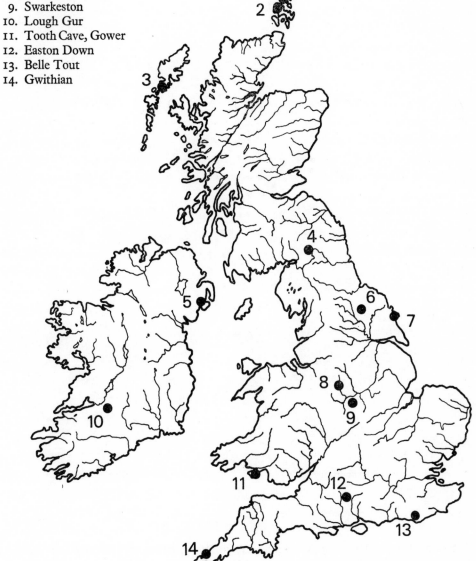

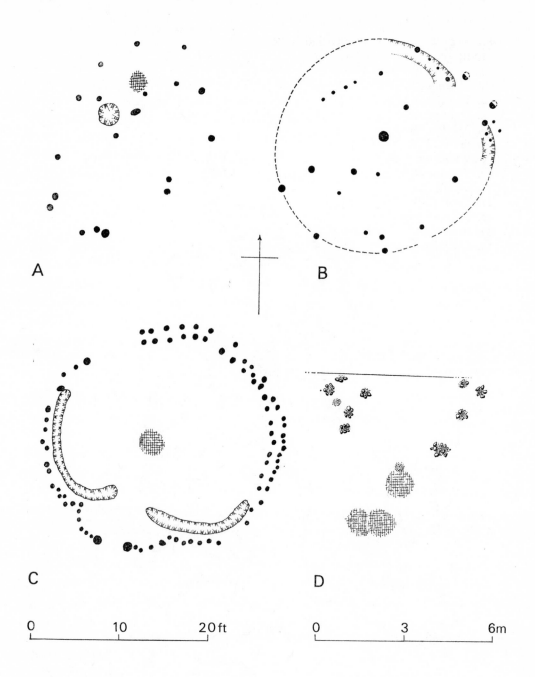

Figure 23. Plans of houses at (A) Lough Gur, (B) Downpatrick, (C) Gwithian and (D) Beacon Hill.

Ireland. The remaining three sites are Swarkeston in Derbyshire, Beacon Hill, Flamborough in Yorkshire, and Belle Tout, Birling Gap, in East Sussex.

Certainly the best known and most often quoted Beaker site producing recognizable house plans is Lough Gur in Co. Limerick.[10] The Beaker contribution to this settlement should not, however, be over-emphasized. Of the published section of the site, sites A and B, both rectangular, have produced only Western Neolithic material. Site C, three circular houses, 21ft in diameter, had Western Neolithic wares in their earliest levels and a small quantity of Bell Beakers in the upper levels. Site E, a rectangular house, was undateable and Site F, rectangular, has one sherd only of Beaker; the rest of the pottery was Lough Gur Class I and II wares. Site G, also rectangular, contained Class II wares exclusively. Only site D can be claimed as a site of Beaker houses, and here one had two oval timber-built houses with maximum diameters of 22ft. W/MR and N/MR sherds predominated on this site (fig. 23A).[11]

The other possible Irish site, at Downpatrick, Co. Down, was not in fact published as a Beaker settlement.[12] It consisted of a small house 13ft in diameter, defined by post holes and having an internal clay hearth. A fragment of a Tievebulliagh axe was found in one of the post holes. The second and larger house (fig. 23B), 32ft in diameter, was defined by a gully on the north-east, in which small posts or stakes had been set, and by individual post holes in the south-west. On the north-east, the gulley was broken by a gap, 4ft wide, outside which were two posts almost certainly defining a porched entrance. A considerable quantity of pottery was associated with both houses, although no vessels were restorable. The majority of the vessels were decorated with twisted cord impressions, in addition there were a number of comb-impressed fragments. All these sherds the excavator classed as cordoned urns, but stated in the report that some resembled Beaker pottery. A re-examination of these sherds suggests that some indeed do represent Beakers and the presence of cordons is a feature of a number of Beaker assemblages; the cordoned urn itself may owe much to such antecedents.

Neither of the Irish sites produced evidence for the economy of the occupants of the houses. No grain impressions occurred on any sherds, although two pits adjacent to the larger house at Downpatrick, surrounded by stake holes, might be grain storage pits like those listed by Dr Smith, and ox teeth at the same site indicate cattle raising.

The majority of the structures at Easton Down, Wiltshire,[13] consist of a series of roughly oval pits up to 10ft in length 6ft in width, sunk into the chalk to a depth of 18ins (fig. 25B). All are surrounded by stake holes although no stake holes or hearths are found within the depressions. It appears unlikely that these do in fact represent house sites and one must bear in mind that the excavation report was written at a time when Bronze and Iron Age populations in Europe were generally considered to have lived in 'pit dwellings'. More convincing as the remains of a building is a V-shaped trench 6ins deep and 17ft in length with stake holes set in its base and offset from it on either side. The dating of this feature is uncertain however, and although Beaker sherds were found in adjacent pits its relationship with these cannot be determined from the published account.

Beacon Hill, Bulford, Flamborough, was a stratified occupation site, part of which had been destroyed before excavation took place (fig. 23D).[14] Three main horizons were distinguished: a Mesolithic level succeeded by Western Neolithic and finally a Beaker one. Associated with the Beaker material (E, FN and AOC forms) were groups of stones set upright in the subsoil, which the excavator interpreted as the packing for posts. They formed one end of a roughly oval house about 15ft wide and of unknown length. No structures were found inside the area delimited by the post holes, although a hearth in the same horizon lay outside the house. The acid soil conditions had destroyed all organic remains.

At Swarkeston, Derbyshire, again only a part of the settlement area, that beneath the actual barrow, was excavated (fig. 25A).[15] Here, there were two groups of structures. Firstly, two rows of slightly converging stake holes were traced for some 40ft; the setting was 2ft 6in at the narrowest point. The excavator suggested it may have served as a bird trap. The second feature is a group of post holes forming a rough square of 12ft, with a smaller rectangular setting to the south-east. All the pottery was found outside this structure, suggesting that it was kept tidy. A hearth and three pits also belonged to this complex. No organic material survived. The pottery appears to belong to Clarke's southern Beaker series.

More doubtful, perhaps, as a house structure is the site at Woodhead in Cumberland.[16] This consisted of a stone bank, 2ft 6in wide and 26ft in diameter, with an entrance on the south-east (fig. 24D). Inside the ring were two post holes and between these and the bank was a shallow pit, 6ft 4in long and 4ft wide, containing occupation debris and charcoal fragments. On the floor of the ring was a jet button and a pulley ring, types normally associated with Beakers. The two posts, it was suggested, were intended for stepping a pole, supporting a roof of skins. The site bears a certain resemblance to the enclosed cremation cemeteries of the Highland Zone of Britain and, in this case, the pit could have held an inhumed burial. A rather similar ring cairn with a Beaker burial has recently been published from Burnt Common in Devon.[17] The distinction, however, between the houses of the living and those of the dead may be a narrow one, and the site is worthy of consideration in any survey of Beaker settlements.

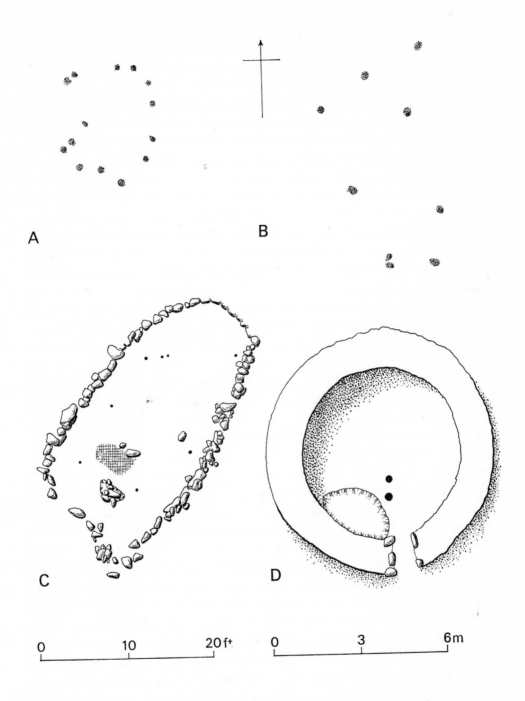

Figure 24. Plans of houses at (A) and (B) Belle Tout, (C) Northton and (D) Woodhead.

At Gwithian, the layer VIII Beaker horizon produced two successive timber structures.[18] The earlier structure consisted of a setting of posts giving a diameter of 15ft and a large central post. A pair of outlying post holes marked the porched entrance. A hearth is set off-centre. This house was replaced by a larger building of oval plan with a maximum diameter of 25ft (fig. 23C). The post holes of the Phase I house were filled in with small stones and sealed by the floor of the later building, some of the posts of which cut the Phase I posts. This later house was defined by a double ring of stake holes and by gully slots. A large pit and hearth lay within the setting. The building lay within a rectangular palisaded enclosure. In the gullies of House II and employed as packing material were fragments of a number of saddle querns. Remanent magnetic readings for the two hearths suggested a period not exceeding 50 years between the two houses. In addition to the evidence for cereal production attested by the querns, a pair of large posts outside the house may well be the supports for a corn-drying rack. In addition, there were bones of sheep, cattle and pigs (although the relative proportions of each species have not yet been worked out) and large quantities of shell-fish, particularly limpets. The pottery from the houses and from Layer VIII generally included European Bell Beaker and coarser wares, decorated with crudely executed chevron designs in plaited cord, made, Professor Thomas has suggested, by indigenous Neolithic groups in imitation of Beakers. A number of these vessels have cordons.

Far to the north, in the coastal sand dunes at Northton, on the south-western tip of the Island of Harris is a complex stratified site showing intermittent occupation from Neolithic to Medieval times.[19] In the lower of the two Beaker occupation levels were found the remains of two oval stone structures and a number of burials. The better preserved building was 28ft long and 14ft wide (fig. 24C). Both structures were orientated north-east/south-west. The walls were of dry stone construction and survived *in situ* to a maximum height of 3ft. Tumbled material within the enclosure would have added no more than 3ft at the most to the height of the structure. The rather insubstantial nature of this dry-stone walling suggests it was never intended as a totally free-standing structure but served largely as a revetment to a large hollow, excavated in the sand, and this was confirmed by the relationship of the midden to the house. On the floor of the house were two occupation layers separated by a thin deposit of sterile sand. On the axis of the building was a hearth and, adjacent to it, a pit containing a red deer antler. The only other internal feature was a series of stake holes, somewhat irregularly placed, 2 to 3ft from the inner stone face. These appear to be too flimsy to have supported a roof structure more substantial than mere animal skins.

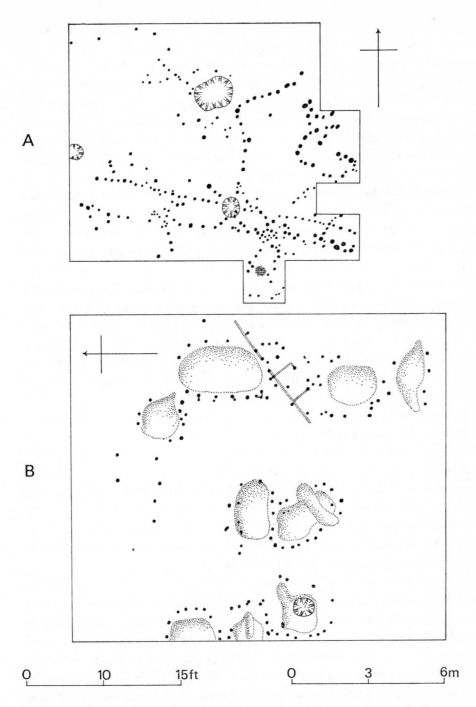

Figure 25. Plans of settlements at (A) Swarkeston and (B) Easton Down.

Large quantities of sherds of both plain and elaborately decorated Beakers of Clarke's Northern British series were found on the floor of the huts and in the associated middens. A great many of these vessels would be perfectly at home in a short cist; they were not specifically domestic 'looking'. The animal remains showed a predominance of sheep followed by cattle and red deer. Shell-fish and crab also figured prominently in the diet. There was no evidence at all for cereal production, either in the form of milling equipment or grain impressions on the thousands of surviving sherds, although bronze working was attested by a small splash of metal produced in the casting process.[20]

The final site, at Belle Tout, Birling Gap, is in many ways the most remarkable (fig. 24).[21] This consisted of two rectangular enclosures now partially destroyed by coastal erosion, which were excavated in 1909 and again in 1968 and 1969. The surviving enclosure was defined by a bank and ditch which had undergone a number of structural alterations. At least one rectangular building of indeterminate length, defined by gully slots and flint rubble, antedated the earthwork. Within the enclosure were the eroded and weathered remains of five further structures. Three were circular in plan, 12 to 15ft in diameter, defined by individual post holes in two cases and by flint packing, presumed to have come from an eroded bedding trench, in the third. The remaining buildings were a rectangular arrangement of gully slots and flint rubble of unknown length and a trapezoidal structure defined by eroded post holes some 30ft long. At least one of the buildings had an internal storage pit and the excavator suggested that each of the other structures had a group of three such external pits.

Finally, at Willington, Notts., excavations currently (1970) in progress have revealed the ground plans of two and possibly three buildings associated with Beaker pottery.[22] The largest structure, defined by individual post holes, was apparently 50ft long by 30ft wide.

Deliberately excluded from this survey are the oval stone-built house at Carrigillihy, Co. Cork,[23] and the two rectangular structures on Coney Island, Lough Neagh, with sherds of Bowl Food Vessel.[24]

This completes the list of known Beaker houses. Two other groups of sites need also to be considered; firstly the Late Neolithic houses of Orkney and Shetland and secondly mortuary houses. The stone houses of Rinyo and Skara Brae were almost certainly contemporary with Beaker houses and share a number of characteristics with them, including a sub-circular plan, similar internal area, and the provision of a pit or pits adjacent to the hearth (fig. 26).[25] One must bear in mind, too, Dr D. L. Clarke's contention that Rinyo-Clacton or Grooved Ware is a development from his insular Beaker forms.[26] Northwards again in Shetland there is a large series of stone-built oval houses morphologically similar to the contemporary heel-shaped cairns.[27] The multiple carinated vessels, decorated with incised chevrons, from sites such as Ness of Gruting appear again to be copies and developments from Beaker wares, which they also resemble in fabric. Both in general plan, size, and the internal provision of a pit and hearth, they resemble some of the sites already discussed. Of particular interest is the site known as the Benie Hoose,[28] where a typical small oval house was apparently remodelled with the addition of a crescentic façade and almost closed forecourt, presumably converting it into either a tomb or a temple (fig. 26B). Here, again, one sees the close links between dwelling houses and religious and funerary structures.

Timber structures, apparently funerary in intent, have been found beneath a number of round barrows in southern Britain and Yorkshire.[29] The majority of these are simple circles of stakes or posts of comparatively small size, forming settings of too great a diameter ever to have been roofed – they appear generally to have served as a revetment for mound material or to have delimited the central burial area. A good example was found beneath one of the barrows on Earl's Farm Down, near Amesbury, excavated by Mrs Christie.[30] Beneath Amesbury barrow 61,[31] and as yet unpublished, was a stake hole circle, within which was evidence of extensive burning which had consumed structures, perhaps of the mortuary house class. The only dating evidence from the site was a number of Beaker sherds from the ditch.

What do appear to be mortuary houses are two small post or stake settings of square plan beneath barrow II and barrow IX at Beaulieu in Hampshire.[32] There was no direct evidence for dating either of these structures, but they were inferred to belong to the Beaker period. It has generally been assumed that such mortuary houses beneath barrows reflect in plan the houses of the living, but if these are in fact Beaker structures their form is at considerable variance with known Beaker houses in Britain and certainly very much smaller; about one-eighth of the area of the average Beaker house (fig. 27). An equally doubtful association is that of a long, rectangular setting of oak posts, 45ft long and 20 ft wide, beneath a large round barrow at Dalry in Ayrshire.[33] The only dating evidence here was a Beaker in a pit grave outside the enclosure, but beneath the barrow.

That the makers of Beaker pottery were capable of erecting large timber structures is, however, clearly demonstrated by the timber circles found within a number of henge monuments and by the Sanctuary on Overton Hill.[34] It is generally accepted that some of the post settings within henges represent roofed structures and there seems no reason to doubt that some of these may, in fact, have been dwelling houses. The term 'henge' has come to embrace a very

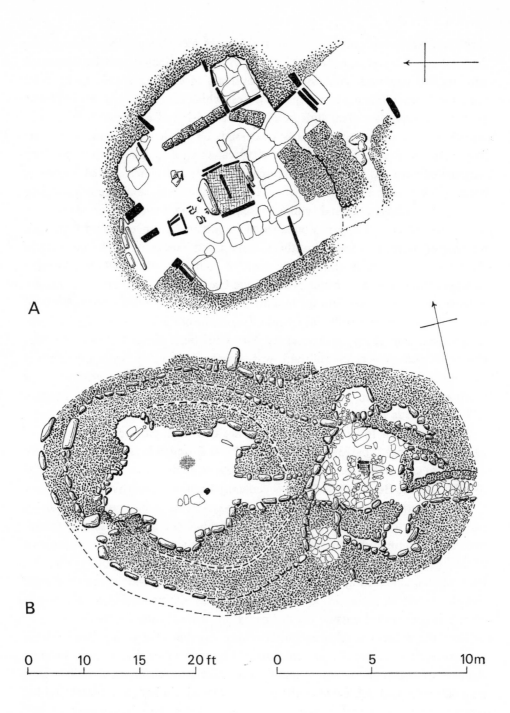

Figure 26. Plans of house at (A) Rinyo and (B) the 'Benie Hoose'.

considerable range of site, both in dimensions and in internal features, linked only by the shared characteristics of a circular bank and internal ditch broken by one or more entrances. The very considerable quantities of pottery and other occupation material at such sites as Woodhenge,[35] Durrington Walls,[36] Gorsey Bigbury,[37] and Dorchester Big Rings,[38] look much like domestic refuse. At the Sanctuary on Overton Hill, the earliest structure was a small round hut about 11ft in diameter. It is really only in its final phase, with the double stone circle linked to Avebury by the West Kennet Avenue, that the site takes on a wholly religious character. The occurrence of burials here or at Woodhenge, for example, need not detract from the possibly utilitarian function of such sites. The occurrence of the burial of an aged female beneath one of the hearths at Skara Brae in no way detracts from the secular character of the building. In sites such as the Sanctuary one may be witnessing the transition in function between a secular and a religious structure, as represented at the Benie Hoose in Shetland. One must always bear in mind that, in a primitive society, the division between the sacred and the profane, between the real world and the spirit one, is ill-defined; there seems no objection to considering some henges as domestic sites and others, with broadly similar morphological characteristics, as religious monuments, as the dwellings of spirits; one could apply the same argument to the megalithic tombs of the north and west.

Returning to the actual house sites, what conclusions and generalizations if any can be drawn from them? Although few in number, they seem to present a considerable variety of plan and construction. In general, however, if one excludes the doubtful mortuary house sites, they are all circular or oval in plan and show a close similarity in ground area; this is particularly noticeable at Gwithian, Downpatrick and Lough Gur, each with an area of 450 sq ft. The variations in building material as between stone and wood, or a combination of both, can be explained in terms of varying environmental conditions. With the exception of the Phase I house at Gwithian, none appears to have central post holes. For the Gwithian Phase II house, Professor Thomas suggests a reconstruction similar to Phase II houses on the Goldberg,[39] for example, with stakes or withies looped over to form a domical roof (fig. 29). The same might apply at Swarkeston, Belle Tout, and Lough Gur. At Woodside and Northton a tent-like roof seems most probable. The other consistently recurring feature is a pit adjacent to the hearth. This is found at Northton, Gwithian, Lough Gur, Downpatrick, Woodside, Belle Tout and, in a stone form, at Rinyo and Skara Brae, and is duplicated in contemporary houses on the Continent. The function of such pits is uncertain; they presumably served as some form of storage pit. Most contained fragments of charcoal and

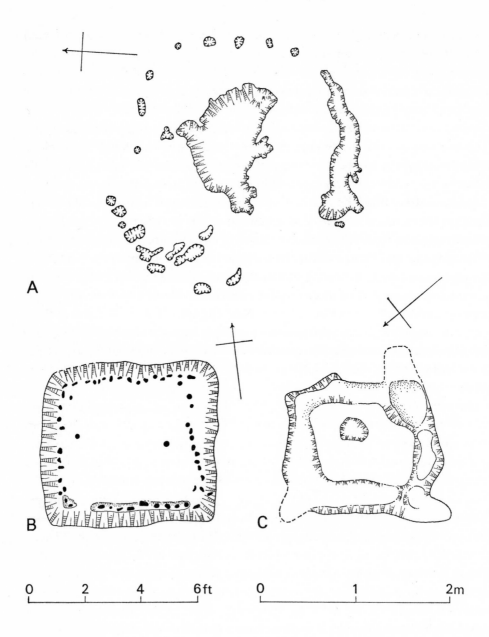

Figure 27. Plans of (A) Neolithic hut at Waulud's Bank and (B) and (C) mortuary houses, Beaulieu.

occupation debris and, at Northton, a red deer antler. At Skara Brae and Rinyo, on the other hand, a number of the stone boxes sunk in the floor had been caulked with clay and probably served to keep fish and shell-fish alive until they were required. The only other constant feature is that these houses occur in isolation or, at most, in pairs. There were two houses at Northton, two at Downpatrick and a second possible house at Gwithian. The notable exceptions are the agglomerations at Rinyo and Skara Brae. In some cases this may be the result of small-scale excavations, although not, for example, at Northton where the limits of the Beaker middens were broadly defined, with no trace of any further structures.

It appears, therefore, that one is dealing with quite small social and economic units in these settlements (apart, of course, from the henges); how large or small in terms of numbers of individuals it is extremely difficult to say. Childe and others have estimated that the average Danubian long house would have accommodated an enlarged family group of some 20 individuals. Now, the average Danubian long house has an area of some 2,000 sq ft, or 100 sq ft per person. This estimation appears, in part, to be based on the size and known population of Iroquois Indian lodges, perhaps not a very fair comparison in view of the differing economies of the two groups and the specialized social significance of the Iroquois long houses. If one used the Danubian figures, then the average Beaker house would accommodate four persons. In the Danubian houses, too, it is uncertain how much accommodation was required for livestock; the variation in a single house plan between one section of the house defined by separate timbers and the other by close-set timbers in a continuous bedding trench implying some dichotomy of function within the building. In the case of the British Beaker houses, the narrowness of the entrances and the flimsy nature of the structures suggest that they were designed exclusively for human habitation, and not for a mixed population of men and animals. At Gwithian, for example, the palisade around the house was presumably to prevent animals from leaning against the house, or even eating it.

To use a further ethnographic parallel to estimate the numbers living in a Beaker house, one could cite the house structures of the extreme west of Scotland.[40] Until two centuries ago the population of this area enjoyed a basically mixed-farming, Iron Age economy, inferior in some respects to that of southern Britain in the last centuries B.C., and under environmental conditions not dissimilar to that of Prehistoric Britain in the second millennium B.C. The basis of the economy was the raising of cattle, supplemented by the cultivation of small strip fields in which oats and a few root crops were grown. The nature of the economy required a partially transhumant existence in which cattle were moved from largely coastal and sheltered settlements in the winter, where they were fed in part on hay, to upland pastures in the summer. Out of this way of life there developed two major house types; a permanent dwelling, a rectangular black house (fig. 28B) in the sheltered coastal area or valley bottom in which men and animals passed the autumn, winter and spring; and small stone-built circular huts, serving as temporary residences for the men herding the cattle, hunting and so forth in the summer months (fig. 28A). Such variations of size and plan of houses within a single, quite primitive culture is, incidentally, a salutary warning that one should not perhaps place too much cultural emphasis on the formal variation of houses within a single chronological period.

The average black house has an area of some 600 sq ft, one-third of which is devoted to animals, leaving some 400 sq ft for human occupation, which almost invariably consisted of a single family, man, woman and children. It was rare to find a larger unit in a black house; when the children grew up, they simply built another house some little distance away from the parents' home. The living area in the black house is very similar to that of our Beaker houses, particularly Downpatrick, Northton, Gwithian, Lough Gur, the Shetland and Orkney houses. At Rinyo and Skara Brae, the pair of beds in each house confirm the size of the unit. All these structures, therefore, could be permanent or semi-permanent dwellings for a single family. The two occupation layers at Northton (reminiscent of the two floors in the Early Neolithic house at Haldon in Devon) might indicate seasonal movement. The small round houses of the Hebridean sheilings, occupied for only a short period in the summer months, have areas of 70 to 100 sq ft. This

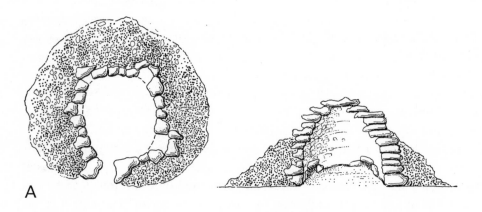

A

Figure 28. (A) Plan and elevation of beehive hut, Harris, and (B) plan of black house, Skye.

compares with the structures at Swarkeston and Farway Cairn, Devon,[41] undated but possibly Beaker, and these might be interpreted as light summer huts intended only for temporary occupation.

If one looks for antecedents in Britain and Europe for the house type I have been describing, then these are difficult to find. In Britain, there are even fewer surviving house plans of Early and Middle Neolithic date than there are for the Beaker period, but the evidence from such sites as Haldon, Clegyr Boia and the pre-camp phase at Windmill Hill, as well as a number of other unpublished sites, suggests a rectangular house plan, although there appears to have also been a round house at Clegyr Boia, and Site C at Lough Gur consisted of two round houses associated with Middle Neolithic pottery. One of the closest parallels, both in plan and in the provision of a pit within the house, comes in the form of a small circular hut from Waulud's Bank in Bedfordshire,[42] but the Peterborough pottery associated with it need not be earlier than the first Beaker settlements in Britain (fig. 27).

The Continental evidence is equally thin on the ground. In the south-west, three small circular structures, defined by stone footings 8ft in diameter, at Penha Verde, Sintra, Portugal, have been claimed as house sites (fig. 30),[43] but other similar structures in the same area have been interpreted as tombs.[44] In an unpublished area of the Beaker levels at Vila Nova de San Pedro were found circular, paved areas which Dr Savory interprets as the make-up of hut floors.[45] At Le Lizio in Brittany[46] both round and rectangular house plans have been

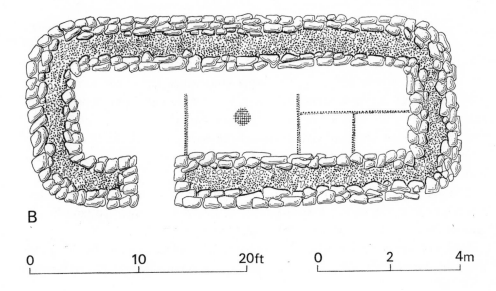

B

0   10   20ft   0   2   4m

recovered from a site that has produced Chassey, Beaker and Iron Age material, but the relationship between structures and small finds is difficult to determine from the published account, and similar ambiguity exists in connection with the settlement at Fontbouisse, Gard.[47]

In central Europe, the evidence is again either sparse or ambiguous. Hajek mentions huts represented by post settings in Moravia without adding detailed information or plans.[48] At Jensteju,[49] Lovosice,[50] Brno-Obrany,[51] Letonice,[52] Strelice,[53] Tesetice,[54] and Vanonci[55] in Czechoslovakia, sub-rectangular or oval hollows from 12 to 20 ft in length have been interpreted as the ground plans of semi-subterranean houses. At Tesetice and Jensteju, hearths were associated with these structures, giving some weight to their identification as dwellings, but at Letonice, two skeletons lay on the floor of the structure, some 6ft below ground level, and the total absence of post holes associated with these sites makes their interpretation difficult. At Oltingen, near Basle, a series of circular scoops and hollows, about 30ft in diameter, have produced Beaker material but, again, no post holes were recorded with any of these features (fig. 30).[56] At Mulheim, near Coblenz, were found a number of small square houses with rounded corners and slightly sunken floors, defined by settings of small post holes or stake holes.[57] These houses have ground areas of about 250 sq ft, considerably less than the British Beaker houses. A possible link, however, is provided by the consistently recurring feature of a pit adjacent to the hearth. Such an arrangement and similar size and ground plan is provided by a number of Late Neolithic houses in Central Europe, the best known group being those of Phase III at the Goldberg (fig. 29).[58]

Two very much larger Beaker houses have recently been excavated, although not yet published, at Molenaarsgraaf in the Netherlands (so far the only Beaker houses from Holland).[59] The smaller house, the complete ground plan of which was recovered, is over 60ft long; the larger house must have been nearer 100ft. Associated with the smaller house was a Veluwe Beaker. Both houses are of elongated oval plan with a row of posts down the centre, supporting a ridged roof. An irregular series of pits bordered the north wall of the house and is reminiscent of the irregularly placed pits, flanking the long houses of the linear pottery cultures.

A similar long house, 40ft by 20ft, is in process of excavation (1970) a few kilometres from the classic Mesolithic site of Ertebølle in north Jutland.[60] The pottery from this site is mixed Corded Ware and Bell Beaker.

In addition to these domestic sites, we have the evidence of a number of timber mortuary houses beneath round barrows, accompanying Single Grave Corded

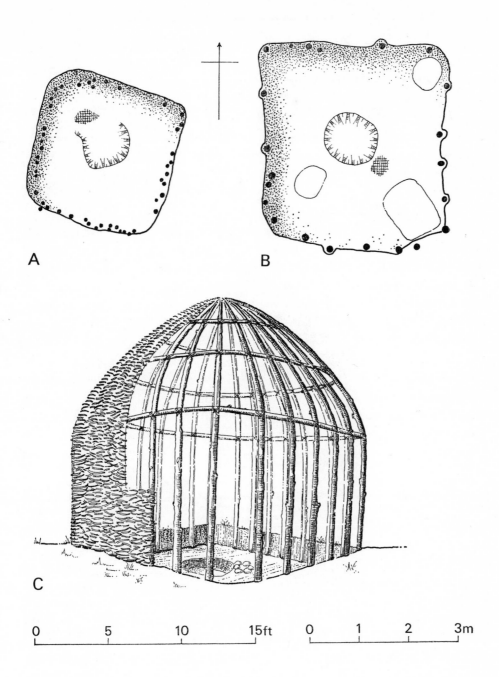

Figure 29. Plans and reconstructions of houses on the Goldberg.

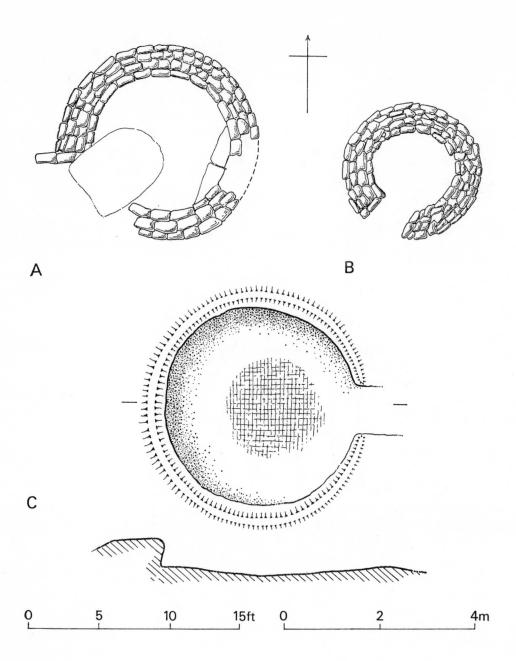

Figure 30. Plans of structures at (A) and (B) Penha Verde and (C) Oltingen.

Ware burials. These are invariably rectangular or square in plan.[61] Lastly, one could mention the palisaded cattle kraal at Anlo in the Netherlands[62] and the earthwork at Le Lizio, Brittany,[63] which invite comparison with the enclosure at Belle Tout in Sussex.

The evidence, such as it is, from the Continent suggests that Beaker groups adopted the house types – as they did with other aspects of their material culture – from the indigenous populations of Late Neolithic central Europe, whether they be long houses or the smaller square buildings. The same may be true in the British Isles. The henge certainly represents an indigenous development among a local Middle Neolithic population, adopted by the makers of Beaker pottery in Britain, and the same may apply to house types. The concept of circularity, both in religious, funerary and domestic sites, appears to have been introduced and developed in Britain from a western source before the arrival of Beaker groups and this tradition of circularity, particularly in the west, was to remain virtually unbroken for a further two, or perhaps it should now be three, millennia.

Notes

1. *Guide to the Prehistoric Society Ulster Conference, 1967.*
2. *B.B.C.S.*, XXII (1967), 277.
3. unpublished; information from Mr J. M. Davidson.
4. Dalesman, XVIII No. 2 (1956).
5. *P.P.S.*, XXX (1964), 352–81.
6. *P.P.S.*, XXVI (1960), 263–302.
7. *Later Prehistoric Antiquities of the British Isles* (1953), p. 40.
8. *Proceedings of the Cambridge Antiquarian Society*, XXXVI (1936), 134–42; XXXIX (1940), 33–68.
9. *Arch.*, LXXXV (1935), 37–106.
10. *P.R.I.A.*, LVI, C (1954), 297–459.
11. Beaker classification follows that of D. L. Clarke, *Beaker Pottery of Great Britain & Ireland* (1970).
12. *Ulster Journal of Archaeology*, XXVII (1964), 31–58.
13. *W.A.M.*, XLVI (1933), 225–42.
14. *Y.A.J.*, XLI (1963), 191–202.
15. *Journal of the Derbyshire Archaeological & Natural History Society*, LXXX (1960), 1–48.
16. *Transactions of the Cumberland & Westmorland Archaeological Society*, XL (1940), 162–6.
17. *Proceedings of the Devon Archaeological Society*, no. 25 (1967), 22, fig. 2.
18. unpublished: information from Professor A. C. Thomas.

19. *Antiquity*, XL (1966), 137–9.
20. identified by Dr R. F. Tylecote.
21. *P.P.S.*, XXXVI (1970), 312–79.
22. interim note; Trent Valley Archaeological Research Committee, July, 1970.
23. E. E. Evans, *Prehistoric & Early Christian Ireland* (1966), p. 76.
24. *Ulster Journal of Archaeology*, XXVIII (1965), 84.
25. V. G. Childe, *Skara Brae* (1931); *P.S.A.S.*, LXXXI (1946–7), 16–42.
26. Clarke, *op. cit.*
27. *P.S.A.S.*, LXXXIX (1955–6), 340–97.
28. *P.S.A.S.*, XCIV (1960–1), 28–45.
29. P. Ashbee, *The Bronze Age Round Barrow in Britain* (1960), pp. 60–5.
30. *P.P.S.*, XXXIII (1967), 336–66.
31. *W.A.M.*, LVI (1956), 238.
32. *P.P.S.*, IX (1943), 1–27.
33. *P.S.A.S.*, X (1870–2), 281.
34. *W.A.M.*, XLV (1931), 300.
35. M. E. Cunnington, *Woodhenge* (1929).
36. *Ant. J.*, XLVII (1967), 166–84.
37. *Proceedings of the University of Bristol Spelaeological Society*, VI (1949), 186–99.
38. R. J. C. Atkinson, C. M. Piggott and N. K. Sandars, *Excavations at Dorchester, Oxon.*, I (1951), p. 103.
39. V. G. Childe, *Prehistoric Migrations in Europe* (1950), p. 125, fig. 99.
40. *Antiquity*, XII (1938), 261–89.
41. *Proceedings of the Devon Archaeological Society*, no. 25 (1967), 33, fig. 5.
42. *Bedfordshire Archaeological Journal*, II (1964), 1–15.
43. *Communicoes dos Servicos Geologicos de Portugal*, XXXIX (1958), 37–60.
44. *ibid.*, pp. 87–128.
45. H. N. Savory, *Spain & Portugal* (1968), p. 182, and private communication from Dr Savory.
46. *Révue Arch.*, II (1933) 199–219.
47. *Gallia*, V (1947), 235–57.
48. *Archeologicke rozhledy*, III (1951), 29.
49. *Pamatky Archeologicke*, XXXI (1936–8), 121–2.
50. unpublished: information from Dr E. Neustupny.
51. unpublished: information from Dr J. Ondracek.
52. *Časopis Moravského zemského Musea*, XLI (1956), 74.
53. *Obzor praehistoricky*, IX (1930–5), 149.
54. *Sbornik praci Filosof. fakulty brnenske university*, V (1956), 5.
55. *Časopis Moravského zemského Musea*, VIII (1908), 7.
56. *Praehistorische Zeitschrift*, V (1913), 162, fig. 4.
57. *P.P.S.*, XV (1949), 82.
58. V. G. Childe, *Prehistoric migrations in Europe*, p. 125, fig. 99.
59. unpublished: information from Dr L. P. Louwe Kooijmans.
60. unpublished: information from Dr J. A. Jensen.
61. S. Piggott, *Ancient Europe* (1965), p. 87, fig. 43; p. 88, figs. 44–5.
62. *Palaeohistoria*, VIII (1961), 59–90.
63. *Révue Arch.*, II (1933), 199–219.

Early prehistoric agriculture in Western Europe: some archaeological evidence

P. J. FOWLER

Fertility, an abstract concept involving ideas and urges not only to regenerate but also to increase the bounty of the natural world in which Man finds himself and of which he is, in his own view, one of the most important parts, was the major preoccupation of those early and small populations inhabiting western Europe from *c.* 5000 B.C. onwards. In the sense that agricultural Man consciously and deliberately tried to induce fertility for his own benefit, he became deeply involved with both the practical and mysterious aspects of the fertility cycle, developed the perceptions of husbandman, herdsman and seer to cover all conceivable eventualities, and adapted to a mode of living based on the assumption that Nature would provide in a reasonably predictable ratio directly related to the joint effort of gods and men. Although, in cultural terms, archaeology has traditionally sought to distinguish between what went before – during what might be called the 'passive fertility' phase of human economic development – and what happened when Man became a food-breeder ('active fertility') by such terms as Mesolithic and Neolithic, the usefulness of such concepts based largely on the discovered fraction of the surviving, largely mineral, artifactual material, is limited and even negative.[1] Man did not live by fish and flint chips alone; and since all farmers, whether gathering the harvest from forest or field or water, were seasonally-orientated, the thought required for the preparation and cropping of planned food supplies probably stimulated human awareness at least as much as changes in what any given man actually did each day.[2]

The psychology of agrarian adaptation, however, is one of the facets of European development which we cannot explore here. The much more limited and mundane aim is briefly to review some of the tangible archaeological evidence bearing directly on the processes of agriculture in western Europe before the Celts. The technical aspects have of course already been comprehensively discussed, both in general surveys[3] and in detailed studies of particular types of evidence;[4] and modern synoptic views of the development of European agriculture in a cultural context are readily available.[5] Nevertheless, with debate and uncertainty currently in full spate concerning not only the chronology, processes and techniques of prehistoric agriculture but also the very nature of what 'going Neolithic' involved,[6] a summary restatement of the nature of some of the strictly archaeological evidence on which our generalizations are based might be useful. Consciously omitted therefore are environmental factors as evidenced by soils, pollens and fauna (see Evans above, pp. 11–26), crops[7] and certain implements like spades,[8] sickles,[9] and grinding stones[10] on which little useful can be added in a brief survey, stock-raising and domestic animal types,[11] diet (see Brothwell above, pp. 75–87), folklore and modern survivals,[12] and the various specialist studies authoritatively discussed in a recent symposium.[13] More positively, we shall discuss the 'documentary evidence', ploughs and fields, and suggest two lines for further research, beginning with a word on how we portray early agrarian development and related factors.

The conventional method of indicating past succession is illustrated by the columnar time chart.[14] The rigidity of this presentation can be mitigated somewhat with arrows indicating lateral movement[15] or by more ambitious, almost alimentary, exercises.[16] In contrast, we have the type of map whereby cultures/communities are represented on the 'amoeba' principle.[17] One advantage of this type of map is that it can show time/space relationships because, like real amoebae, elements can split and spread further in any given direction.[18] Then there is the 'prevailing wind' type of map in which, although the evidence plotted is as objective as possible, the method of presentation carries certain implications.[19] In the particular case quoted, although the general trend indicated by the radiocarbon dates is not in dispute, the map clearly implies that everything started in the Near East and proceeded north-west in a fairly steady progression; whereas in fact there is considerable dispute about the primacy of the Near East in certain aspects of the development of an agricultural economy[20] and there must also have been many local variations and even reversals of Neolithic trends throughout Europe. Waterbolk,[21] for example, has already suggested that the early development of agriculture in Wessex was inspired by what had previously happened in northern Ireland, and any such movement even of ideas would of course be directly against the trend indicated in this map.

So far, our examples have been of prehistory occurring, like so much English medieval history, in a vacuum or in just a geographical context. Archaeological attempts to indicate the various climatic factors affecting if not determining agricultural developments have hitherto tended to be rather crude; in one case, for example,[22] we see a clear zoning of Western Europe into horizontal west–east bands. Obviously this is a cartographic generalization and, by implication, very much an over-simplification of the processes involved as agrarian economy took root. We obtain an entirely different impression of agrarian Europe if we look at it, on the other hand, from the point of view of agricultural productivity (fig. 31). The available data obviously in part expresses national differences in efficiency and investment but the models, and therefore the visual picture, expressing that data can be very different[23] from our usual archaeological presentation. Not only do we have in these cases two very different-looking types of map, but we also see

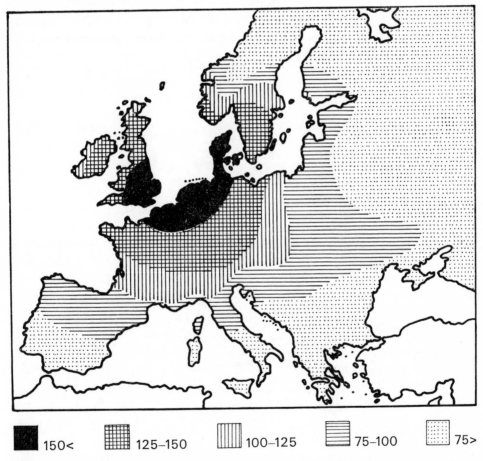

150<   125–150   100–125   75–100   75>

Figure 31. Intensity of modern agriculture in Europe. The index of 100 is the average European yield per acre of eight main crops.

that the productive regions are south-east Britain, the Low Countries and
Denmark (incidentally, precisely the area covered by surviving 'Celtic' fields).
The presentation therefore emphasizes a different area from that traditionally
associated with the essentially linear development of Neolithic economy up the
Danube and over the loess soils.

This introductory excursion may well be platitudinous but it is not irrelevant
since it is essential to bear in mind the variety and limitations of the visual and
theoretical frameworks by which we express our academic interpretations and, all
too easily, from which we accept our ideas of what was involved, what it was like.

From Italy to Scandinavia there are many examples of rock-carvings illustrating
agriculture, fields, settlements, implements and techniques. Amongst the best
known are those at Val Camonica[24] where the pictures span a fairly long prehistoric period (fig. 32). It is of course difficult to date any one picture precisely

A

B

Figure 32. Rock engravings from (A) South Sweden and (B) Val Camonica. Not to scale.

but there seems no doubt that some of them go back well into the second millennium B.C. A typical scene shows two oxen being led by a man holding what appears to be a hooked stick, possibly even a (spare?) crook-ard, but there is no indication of the method of harness between plough-beam and the oxen. The plough itself is probably a sole-ard with a stilt which is being held by the ploughman; behind comes a woman, carrying a child on her back, bending down and using a mattock. This scene[25] represents in all essentials the type of evidence from all the local carvings and it is remarkable how consistent this type of evidence is from all parts of Europe. The plough types, for example, are very limited, the two-ox team is almost universal, and there can be very little doubt that these were the basic features of early agriculture in the whole of western Europe, producing, in respect of ard-marks and perhaps fields, similar archaeological phenomena (see below, pp. 161–70).

The evidence from Val Camonica allows a plough typology to be presented, apparently showing a development from a crook-ard to a sole-ard. The associations here, however, do not always run so obviously with fertility and ritual as they do in the Scandinavian rock-art. The value of this evidence for understanding the agricultural scene is best exemplified by the Bedolina rock map, rather later in date than our period here, which shows a whole layout of houses, fields, trackways and varieties of crops.[26]

Most of the relevant petroglyphs in Scandinavia are concentrated in the Bohuslan area of western Sweden (fig. 32);[27] agricultural scenes hardly exist in the rock-art of Norway[28] or Denmark.[29] In Sweden they usually occur with a multitude of animal and human figures, boats, and symbolic features like discs and groups of dots. At Aspeberget, for example, the plough team occurs in a procession of animals following a boat. Here again the evidence of plough type is convincing in that only two main types, the crook- and the sole-ard, are shown, with the exception of two examples of a stave-ard; but in all essentials the evidence is the same as that in Italy and the Alps. It is just possible that some of the vaguely rectangular and sub-divided features actually represent fields, though on the other hand the rock-carvings imply, if correctly interpreted, that hunting and herding clearly played a large part in the contemporary economy. Again, individual scenes here are difficult to date but there seems little doubt that the art begins in the second millennium B.C. In any case, in default of earlier remains of actual ploughs, the best we can do is to use this pictorial evidence and extrapolate backwards. There seem good positive grounds for doing this anyway because it is at least arguable that there were no essential changes in agricultural techniques, like inventing the plough or developing permanent field systems (but possibly the invention of manuring?) within the second millennium B.C. Although of course neither ploughs or fields were everywhere in use throughout western Europe by, say, 2000 B.C., they had surely been invented long before, so that, when such artifacts impinge on the archaeological record in the centuries after that, the pictorial evidence, and as we shall see, the artifactual evidence of the ploughs and fields themselves, indicates a *terminus ante quem* rather than providing a contemporary evidence of a technological and indeed social break-through.

Two of the rock-carvings provide interesting sidelights on early agriculture, its motivation, and its symbolism within the 'fertility' syndrome. A Swedish petroglyph at Tegneby[30] shows one of the two known examples of a stave-ard.[31] The ard is attached to the tail of a horse, a unique example in the rock-carvings of this animal providing the traction; and while it is tempting to take the combination of rarities – plough-type, tail attachment, and draught animal – as indicating something special, perhaps ritual, it may be that the practice depicted is not even purposefully cruel, as the English Parliament thought in 1635 when confronted with this particular manifestation of the 'Irish problem', but is simply a very effective way of ensuring that the horse did not go on pulling when the rather vulnerable share hit an obstruction.[32] However, since the ploughman is dressed up in some form of bird garment and is also bearing a prominent, albeit reversed, phallus, the fertility overtones are unmistakeable, even though the details of the ploughing practice may not be quite so aberrant as they seem at first sight. Nevertheless, the importance of the ritual connections of cultivation, i.e. the emphasis on fertility, is supported by another scene in which the ploughman, carrying a branch and possibly a sack with seed in it, is beginning to plough what is clearly meant to be the highly significant third furrow.[33] The ard in this scene appears, incidentally, to be of a developed beam type.

With one exception all these examples are in Norway or Sweden, only one being known from Denmark. The other main type of evidence for the plough itself is of course well-known: the complete ploughs or parts of ploughs found in bogs principally in Denmark, though there are several in Holland.[34] Until very recently, these have all been regarded as Late Bronze Age or later with the emphasis on the last few centuries B.C.[35] This situation has now been radically altered by a C-14 date of 1490 B.C. for the Hvorslev ard, one of the best known examples of a crook-ard, previously dated on palaeo-botanical evidence to the Late Bronze Age.[36] Interestingly Glob[37] had already suggested on typological grounds that this particular ard type in general is probably amongst the earliest European ploughs. This new dating evidence could well mean that other examples of this and other simple types, such as those in the rock-carvings, could go back into the early or mid-second millennium B.C. One result of this is that we can now see that these wooden ards really were the type of implements producing the ard-marks which are such a common phenomena under European barrows. From the evidence of both the rock-carvings and the actual ard finds, therefore, we seem to have in prehistoric use four main types of plough – the crook-, the sole-, the bow- and the stave-ard – of which the crook-ard is almost certainly the earliest and in use by the mid-second millennium at latest.

As a cultivating implement, this ard-type is so simple, merely needing a person using a mattock to turn round so that he is going frontwards instead of backwards, that there seems no need to derive the basic idea (which is common sense) or the actual ard-type from the Near East or anywhere else. Surely it is possible to conceive of such an implement as having been invented several times and in different places during the early development of agriculture, provided of course that the *need* to aerate and pulverize the soil existed through the introduction of the idea of 'positive fertility'. One could even go further and suggest that the first use of a dragged implement, as distinct from a pushed or spade-like imple-ment, may possibly have been in central or north-western Europe where early farmers, perhaps for the first time, encountered denser vegetation and wetter, heavier, soils than further south-east. This is in no way to deny the primacy of the Near East in developing the practice of food production, but simply to query the usual assumption that, whatever the mechanics of the move of a 'Neolithic' economy into western Europe, the complete Neolithic equipment that we see manifested archaeologically moved in with the idea from the outside, i.e. from the Near East. Waterbolk[38] has argued for the importance of the Hungarian Plain as the area where Near Eastern elements adapted to a European environment, a process represented archaeologically by, for example, stone axes implying the challenge, and the acceptance of the challenge, of tree-felling. North-western Europe, for its part, was surely ripe to receive, to adapt to, 'positive fertility' as its response to a changing environment in which mixed deciduous forest replaced pine and hazel, rain increased and raised bogs appeared with the resultant dimi-nuition of the traditional food supplies of fish, waterfowl and wild grazing animals like the auroch and the red deer.

Of course we do not know that the plough was used at all in the initial stages of cereal food production (in itself an argument for the independent development of an ard within a north-western European context?) and indeed the accepted idea is that slash-and-burn techniques were employed, vitiating the need for a plough. Unfortunately, this method of cultivation does not leave obvious archaeological evidence – none of the early ard-marks are associated with 'slash-and-burn' evidence – and it is assumed largely on the basis of modern primitive survivals and, by implication, from pollen analyses. Even if, as seems likely, this technique was used for initial clearance and perhaps crop-growing, it was a phase which need not have lasted very long. Indeed, it is difficult to see already settled hunting/fishing communities by their lake- and river-sides changing to a nomadic existence just because they caught on to the idea of growing instead of chasing food. Surely their instinct would be to exploit their locale and such a response could well have produced the circumstances in which it was simply necessary to think of an ard. In theory, given the need, this would not have been too difficult. Three progenitors were immediately available: branches broken off a tree-trunk (which is really all a crook-ard is); the mattock or some such grubbing implement, either 'natural', e.g. of wood or antler, or of two hafted pieces; and the hafted, stone-headed axe which is, after all, different only in function and not design compared to an ard. It only needed someone to hit on the idea of dragging one of these through the ground for the principle of the plough to have been invented and Man has more than adequately shown his capability of conceptual leaps rather more demanding than that.

To return to the evidence, however, we would be in a much better position to understand the early development of the ard if the argument over the function of the 'shoe-last axes' could be resolved, as surely it can by microscopic examination such as Semenov[39] has demonstrated for other stone implements. Glob[40] accepts their function as shares and makes the important point that the associations of these axe/shares are in a Bandkeramik context, taking them, and presumably the crook-ard too, back to the earliest phase of the western European Neolithic. A date in the fifth millennium B.C. can therefore presumably be considered for the beginnings of plough agriculture if these 'axes' are accepted as shares (fig. 33) (though much later in date, the blade-end of an axe-hammer actually in one of the ard-marks at Gwithian, Cornwall, strongly suggests that at least a stone tip had been fitted to a wooden share in one case[41]). Such an acceptance does not leave very long for a slash-and-burn phase, as already argued above on other grounds, but it does leave a very long gap – about three thousand years! – before we are presented with our earliest surviving plough, preserved by the peat at Hvorslev. Indeed, we must confess that we really know very little about the most important tool of the early farmers, a fact starkly emphasized by a recent attempt[42] at primitive plough classification which illustrates all manner of variation in the relationships between the plough components. It is somewhat depressing to think that the plough has an undocumented history in Europe at least as long as the period from which the classified examples come.

Nevertheless, now that the crook-ard is at least tangibly attested in a mid-second millennium context instead of merely in the last prehistoric centuries, we at least have one implement to set beside the other well-known early agrarian phenomena of western Europe, the ard-marks; and conversely, recent work which has produced many new examples and, in at least one case, refreshingly early dating evidence, provides some positive archaeological evidence to take the story back well before the Hvorslev C14 date. Ard-marks have usually been called plough-marks or furrows in British archaeology, largely one suspects because most examples found until recently have been medieval or later and therefore there has been no need to distinguish between marks made by a mould-board plough and a prehistoric ard. Here, by definition, unless something is very wrong in our understanding of prehistoric agriculture, they will be called ard-marks, following Continental practice. These marks are actually grooves, usually filled with a soil different in colour from the surrounding material (which is of course why they are noticed), forming a criss-cross pattern in plan. They are interpreted as having been made by an ard-share, accidentally or otherwise, in a soil below the topsoil as the ard passed backwards and forwards, and then similarly at right angles, during the preparation of the seed-bed. Over one hundred examples of ard-marks have now been recorded in Europe, most of them from underneath barrows and therefore regarded as belonging to the first half of the second millennium B.C.

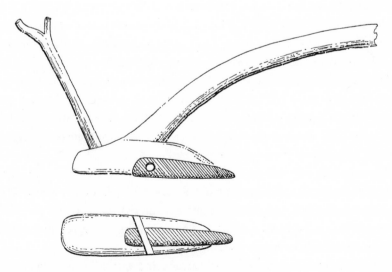

Figure 33. Reconstruction of crook-ard with stone share.

Their European distribution is generally very similar to that of the ploughs and indeed of 'Celtic' fields but one suspects this is really a coincidence produced by several factors such as chance survival and archaeological expertise. Individually, several examples give the lie to generalizations about only light soils having been cultivated by early farmers and, taken with the ancient field distribution and the evidence of disturbed soil profiles and pollen counts from them from pre-barrow land surfaces, they indicate that large areas of what has been regarded as marginal land were productive in prehistoric times and indeed are probably marginal precisely because of this previous usage.[43]

Although the barrows beneath which so many of the ard-marks have been found really provide only a *terminus ante quem* for the marks themselves, in western Europe as a whole only a few examples have been claimed to be Neolithic. Most of them were beneath grave-mounds and have tended to be regarded as dating to the first part of the second millennium B.C. or the late third millennium B.C. at earliest. Typical examples under Early Bronze Age barrows are four from Bornholm, Denmark,[44] and potentially earlier examples, in the sense that they occurred beneath 'Late Neolithic' barrows and therefore have a culturally earlier *terminus ante quem*, were recorded at Lundehøj beneath a megalithic tomb[45] and South Borup, apparently associated with 'Neolithic-type pottery'.[46] A similar association occurred under a barrow with a probably Early Bronze Age primary burial at Lerchenfeldt,[47] and similar associations in non-barrow contexts have been noted in two Dutch examples at Schokland and Zandwerven,[48] the latter tenuously associated with a radio-carbon date of *c.* 2100 B.C. In a few other cases, the ard-marks have a dating bracket from their context: at Ostenfelde, for example, they overlay graves with TRB pottery beneath an Early Bronze Age barrow.[49] All these examples are of criss-cross ard-marks, implying a cross-ploughing technique; parallel ard-marks along one axis only (the temptation to call them one-way ard-marks is resisted in view of the technical use of the term 'one-way plough') seem to be wholly exceptional, at least in a pre-Iron age context, the only early examples, neither certain, apparently being beneath barrows at Ballermosen[50] and at Amesbury G. 70, Wilts.[51]

At the moment, the earliest example of criss-cross ard-marks in Europe is beneath the South Street long barrow at Avebury, Wilts.[52] where a date of 2810 ± 130 B.C. (BM 356) was obtained from charcoal on the surface of the buried soil beneath the barrow mound. The ard-marks occurred in the surface of the subsoil beneath this buried soil.

The South Street example is in fact rare from every point of view, not least in its being under a barrow in Britain. In this respect the British evidence differs markedly from that on the Continent; whereas in Britain ard-marks have been beneath only three barrows, on the Continent nearly all the examples come from under barrows. In fact, only one of those published was actually inside a visible field system,[53] thereby emphasizing the remarkable fact that despite the undoubtedly agricultural basis of early Neolithic economy, there is in fact no direct evidence in the form of surviving fields or ploughs for perhaps the first two, even three, thousand years of its development in Europe.

Under the South Street long barrow the pattern of ard marks indicated several phases of ploughing in a criss-cross pattern along a general north-west/south-west orientation and at right-angles to this. The grooves are discontinuous but are remarkably deep; their spacing is about 30cm. A line of possible holes crossed them, perhaps representing a sub-division of the ploughed area after cross-ploughing. Clearly we are seeing here a technique in use which was already well-developed, and this pre-supposes that agriculture involving this technique could be considerably earlier. These marks were not produced by the first experimental ploughing. It is not known what the depth of soil was when the ploughing took place but as it was presumably from at least the surface of the surviving burial soil, the ard must have been cutting an extraordinarily deep furrow. The grooves alone were as much as 15 cm deep into the subsoil. Along the central axis of the barrow were two superimposed buried surfaces indicating that some lynchetting may have occurred. Indeed the barrow may be where it is because it was built on a slight rise, resulting from the earlier Neolithic cultivation, which was perhaps the only slight relief in what is a markedly flat locality.

The South Street excavation was also remarkable because it produced a second, and later, set of ard-marks outside the mound, running across the top of the partly-filled ditch and beyond. These marks were much more regular and better preserved, although occurring only c. 35cm below the present surface. Their associations were with Beaker pottery, a C-14 date of 2000 B.C. and, in terms of the molluscan assemblage, a very marked phase of land-clearance. This one site then provides us with the two earliest examples of regular ploughing in Britain and probably in Europe in that the dating evidence is positive rather than merely providing a *terminus ante quem*. It must be suspected, however, that some of the Continental European examples occurring under Late Neolithic or Early Bronze Age barrows may well belong to the third millennium B.C. or even earlier.

The other examples from Britain are well-known,[54] though definitive publication of most of them is still awaited (fig. 34). The best example is at Gwithian, Cornwall,[55] partly because the ard-marks were so well preserved in blown sand, partly because at least two phases of cultivation were represented, and partly because here, unlike nearly all the other European examples, the evidence occurred inside arable fields (see above, p. 163). The stratification at Gwithian was impeccable, with the ard-marks occurring most notably in layer 5 and, less continuously, in layer 3, respectively Early Middle and Late Middle Bronze Age.[56] The evidence from layer 5 was particularly interesting because at the base and on top of the plough soil the marks could be clearly seen in plan and in section, showing in places how the plough had been tilted to leave asymmetrical grooves. The other point here is that it was just possible to see the marks within the thickness of layer 5, thereby showing that the technique represented by the ard-marks

Figure 34. Criss-cross plough-marks in England.
1. Carrawburgh
2. Walker
3. Rudgeway
4. South Street
5. Overton
6. Amesbury
7. Fritham
8. Gwithian

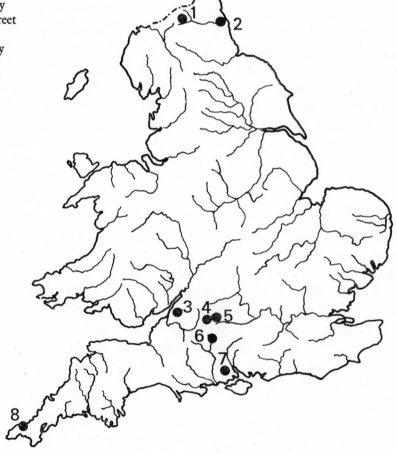

was the normal method of cultivation and not simply something that was done at the beginning and the end of cultivation. The fact that the marks showed up as a once-only pattern on the top of layer 5, and had actually been preserved as grooves in the surface of the plough soil filled with blown sand, strongly suggests the unlikely hypothesis that the field had been abandoned when it was actually being ploughed. Of considerable significance in thinking about the actual ways in which a field was prepared as a seed bed is the additional evidence associated with the layer 5 ard-marks and showing up in exactly the same way, i.e. as a hole in the plough-soil filled with blown sand, were the spade-marks, concentrated around the edges of a field. The type of spade indicated by this evidence is similar to the Cornish shovel and the all-purpose implement still widely used in Ireland today.[57] This associated evidence suggests very much that, while the bulk of the field was cross-ploughed using an ard pulled by two oxen, the headlands were dug by hand.

The several other instances of prehistoric ard-marks in Britain have been listed elsewhere.[58] With one exception in Gloucestershire on the M5 motorway in 1970, there are no significant additions so far, though new examples can be confidently expected. A possible way of using this evidence has already been suggested:[59] the pattern of ard-marks was used to estimate the length of time it took to plough a field and the distance that a plough-team would have travelled. The suggestion is very tentative and clearly requires corroboration elsewhere; but to obtain this it is necessary to expose fairly large areas of ard-marks within a field, and so far only Gwithian, Cornwall, and Overton Down, Wilts., have produced the appropriate evidence. As has been already indicated one of the significant facts about these ard-marks is that they are almost always about the same distance (c. 30 cm) apart, and experiment has now suggested why this is so (see below, p. 175). It would seem on the evidence of the ard-marks alone that there was no basic change in plough-type or cultivation technique from the establishment of cross-ploughing with a crook-ard or equivalent sometime probably in the fourth or even fifth millennium B.C. down to the introduction of a mould-board plough, possibly in the last centuries B.C. or more likely during the Roman domination of western Europe. Agriculture has always been regarded as a very conservative form of economy and it would certainly seem to be so in this respect for the last millennia of prehistoric Europe.

The other important point which is now quite clear from the whole of western Europe is that the incidence of ard-marks is very much the result of the accident of survival and the observation of excavators. Such marks can be expected on virtually any type of sub-soil. The example in clay at Aptrup, Denmark,[60] has often been quoted and that on Boulder Clay at Walker, Northumberland,[61] is a comparable British example. The new example in Gloucestershire is also on clay and emphasizes the point. Overall, the ard-mark evidence suggests that our traditional generalizations about the places, such as light soils, where early agriculture is almost exclusively supposed to have occurred may be a little too facile. Pollen analyses repeatedly make this point;[62] and so too does the distribution map (fig. 34) of criss-cross ard-marks in Britain, even though that map is patently one showing where archaeologists have recognized such evidence rather than where the prehistoric nucleii of British agriculture alone existed. The non-validity of distribution maps showing discrete archaeological evidence for making deductions about agrarian developments generally has already been demonstrated,[63] especially with regard to ancient fields.

Until very recently it would not have been possible to include fields as a topic in a summary of early agriculture down to about 1400 B.C. for the very simple reason that, throughout Europe, the surviving remains of prehistoric fields, with very few exceptions, were regarded as being of late Bronze Age date at earliest and more particularly of the last centuries B.C. and first centuries A.D. From the whole of that area, the evidence was that the 'oltidsagre' of Scandinavia, the 'eisenzeitlicke fluren' of Germany, and the 'Celtic fields' of Britain were almost entirely of the millennium from about 500 B.C. onwards, a point underlined by the inclusion of Celtic fields by the Ordnance Survey on the map of *Roman Britain*. Nevertheless, there were a number of hints, even within the Celtic field tradition, that their origins went back earlier. Their association with settlements like Itford Hill[64] put them, even at the time of excavation, back into the first half of the first millennium B.C., and with the back-dating of the Deverel-Rimbury culture during recent years, they have now been pushed even further back into the latter part of the second millennium B.C. The excavation of the settlement site at Shearplace Hill, Dorset, with its radio-carbon date of *c*. 1200 B.C. was crucial in this respect.[65]

On the Continent, however, no early date has so far been claimed for the various types of field remains, the most controversial point being that the oblong type of field familiar in Denmark especially was the product of a mould-board plough in the last centuries B.C. The field types and the dating evidence are well covered in recent surveys,[66] but field survey and excavation in Britain, Scandinavia and Holland are now probably as widespread as ever and fresh results and thinking can be confidently expected. In Holland, for example, recent work has shown that the extent of ancient fields is much greater than previously thought and by implication was probably very extensive. On the whole, however, chronological evidence including C-14 dates still strongly suggests that the layout of the visible field systems belongs in the main to the middle of the first millennium B.C. at earliest. The evidence in Britain, on the chalklands anyway, is generally similar. However, without in any way wishing to gainsay that most of the ancient fields in western Europe which we can still see on the ground or on air photographs belonged to the millennium from about 600 B.C. onwards, it is nevertheless possible to suggest that the type of agriculture represented by these fields, and with it some of the fields themselves, originated at a much earlier date.

Several factors suggest that a system of small rectangular fields goes back, not only to the Middle Bronze Age, but even earlier to a pre-Wessex culture date. The early and consistent ard-mark evidence, particularly now that it has appeared in typical fields both in Cornwall and Wiltshire, is one of the clearest pointers: the evidence from the fields is similar to that from beneath barrows. It is just possible that the whole idea of laid-out field systems should be associated with the development of Beaker peoples in western Europe, but cross-plough agriculture, as we have already seen at South Street, demonstrably goes back at least a thousand years before that and indeed into the mid-fourth millennium on current C-14 recalibration; but so far there is no tangible evidence of actual fields being laid out in a regular system at such an early date even though, by implication, they not only could have been but should have been as the most obvious reason to explain the regularity, the incidence, of criss-cross ard-marks. When the evidence from beneath a Middle Neolithic barrow in Wiltshire, beneath a late Neolithic barrow in Denmark, actually in a Bronze Age field in Cornwall and actually in a Celtic field in Wiltshire, is so similar, naturally one wonders whether the absence of permanent field boundaries in the first two cases is not simply fortuitous.

There is, of course, evidence of fields different from and apparently earlier than the conventional appearance and date of Celtic fields. In the north of Britain, for example, and specifically in Shetland, early fields have been identified around the late Neolithic structures at, for example, Brouster.[67] Here irregular areas are demarcated by low dry-stone walls, the absence of surface stones, and in part by the heaps of stones dotted around in an irregular manner, the heaps presumably being the result of clearance; and in places it is possible to see that there is one dwelling placed in each cleared area. Although this is circumstantial evidence for agriculture, these cleared areas were not necessarily cultivated with a dragged implement; and it is a little dubious whether they should in fact be called field systems since they are simply irregular areas not necessarily cultivated for very long. There is an important functional and economic distinction between permanent arable fields and land cultivated briefly or sporadically. Similar fieldwork problems are associated with first millennium A.D. settlements in, for example, the

Stavanger area of south-western Norway.[68] The other point about the north British evidence is its date. It could be argued that the associated pottery suggests a date in the early/middle second millennium B.C. rather than very much earlier, so that the evidence indicates a primitive type of agriculture which might be expected in any rocky area rather than an early stage from which the Celtic field systems developed. Nevertheless, as direct archaeological agrarian evidence from a culturally Neolithic context, this material appears to provide a remarkably full glimpse of early food-producing communities at work and, if correctly ascribed to the Neolithic, is almost certainly unique in Europe.

Recent work in Ireland has produced new evidence of early agriculture, both in the form of fields and from palaeobotanical studies. The latter is producing the earlier dated evidence represented by declines in tree pollen, notably of oak and elm, related to C-14 dates in both the third and fourth millennia B.C.[69] Early field walls have been known for some time.[70] Probably the best known example was at Millin Bay, Co. Down, where one such wall went underneath a megalithic tomb. Current work in the west of the island, e.g. Counties Mayo and Kerry,[71] is revealing whole stretches of early landscape divided up into walled fields, subsequently covered over and preserved by blanket peat from the later second millennium B.C. onwards. These field systems must be of earlier Bronze Age date at latest and could well go back into the third millennium B.C. The value of these two types of evidence is demonstrated in the detailed surveys recently completed at Goodland, Co. Antrim.[72] The widespread existence of these early field systems has also been demonstrated by the occurrence of field walls beneath some of the Bronze Age stone monuments at Beaghmore, Co. Tyrone, an example already described as "possibly the earliest in Ireland". It is just possible, however, that some of the several field types recently revealed by aerial photography of Ireland may also go back to an early date.[73] It is, after all, clear from the excavations at Lough Gur, Co. Limerick, for example, where evidence of cereal production came from both Neolithic and Bronze Age occupation, that some sort of early arable, whether or not in regular fields, must have existed in the vicinity, presumably on the lower slopes of the hills around the lake. It is perhaps worth remarking incidentally on the superficial similarity in plan between, on the one hand, the irregular but almost lobate arrangement of cultivated areas around the Neolithic sites in Shetland and, on the other, the fields laid off from some of the raths and similar sites in Ireland. Though air photography has been chiefly responsible for demonstrating the Irish evidence, particularly from ploughed-out sites, some field complexes, e.g. a particularly good example in the Deer Park near Sligo, clearly exist as visible earthworks.

It is, however, worth returning to the Celtic fields of southern Britain, to see if they too can fit into a discussion about the earlier stages of agriculture in western Europe. It is already accepted that a type of regular field system goes back at least to the Middle Bronze Age in Britain and this could now also be true on the Continent. At Nijnsel, Holland, for example, a recently excavated agricultural settlement with a round house, granaries, and other features is directly comparable with the settlements on Cock Hill[74] and Itford Hill, Sussex, and presumably by the Dutch site too a field system or systems once existed.[75] The other main type of landscape evidence taking an organized agrarian system back into the Middle Bronze Age at least seems to be a specifically southern British phenomenon and that is of course the linear ditches or 'ranch boundaries' best known on the Wessex chalk. Their nature and probable function was long ago demonstrated by Hawkes[76] and a Middle Bronze Age date for many of them is generally accepted. In many cases, Celtic fields are directly associated with them so this would seem to take some of the systems back to that date too. But an earlier date for the fields is also indicated in a number of cases where the linear ditches actually cut across pre-existing field systems. This is true on Martin Down, Hants., for example, where much of the ditch excavated by Pitt-Rivers cuts through a subsequently recognized field system.[77] Other examples occur on Salisbury Plain.[78] While in some cases this may simply represent a local change in land use from arable to pasture, and while accepting that the dating of any individual ditch is a particularly difficult matter, all the evidence together – and a comprehensive survey still needs to be made and published – clearly indicates that Celtic field systems existed in the Middle Bronze Age and perhaps earlier. The problem and the potential is well illustrated on Fyfield Down, Wilts., where one such ditch sharply divides fields from pasture and would seem to date from the Bronze Age, taking the arable fields back to that date.[79] The same point is made on Stockbridge Down in Hampshire.[80] It is worth remarking incidentally, particularly in view of the implications for a thoroughly-organized landscape provided by these ditches, that the way in which they relate to hills subsequently crowned by hill-forts, as for example Sidbury, Wilts., and Quarley and Danebury, Hants., strongly suggests that, whatever the date at which these hill-forts as we now see them were built, they were capitalizing on pre-existing focal points.

It is through the excavation of actual fields in Britain during the last few years that we have learned, following Continental examples,[81] a great deal about the structure and dating of Celtic fields: walls, fences, ditches and baulks are all now structurally demonstrated on the Wessex chalk. In the south-west, where ancient field systems have for long been known on the granite plateaux of Dartmoor,

Bodmin Moor and west Cornwall, recent work has clearly indicated that the early fields there are of second millennium date in many cases.[82] In part, this recognition stems from the work at Gwithian,[83] though its credibility has recently been re-emphasized by the discovery of a bronze palstave in the Horridge field system.[84] One of the important points about the Gwithian excavations was that they showed not only impeccable stratification and ard-marks but also the existence of two superimposed Bronze Age field systems. The settlement associated with the earlier (layer 5) has not yet been identified with complete certainty but, in plan, the field system itself, although occurring on sand by the seashore, bears marked similarities to the single farm-and-fields layout familiar from Dartmoor.[85] A similar stratified sequence, also indicating Early Bronze Age agriculture, has recently been demonstrated at Stannon Down in north Cornwall.[86] Interestingly, at Gwithian as on the chalk downs, the field boundaries were varied: ditches (the 'toft' boundary?), a stone bank (from field clearance?) and lynchets (originally baulks subdividing the arable?) were all present. Furthermore, the very important evidence of manuring using seaweed is at present the earliest known reasonably certain example of this technique.[87] In general then, at least some of the typical stone-walled settlements and their associated field systems on Dartmoor (e.g. Foales' Arrishes, Dean Moor) and further west were in being during the early second millennium B.C. and perhaps originated earlier; some, however, certainly were in use, perhaps starting anew in some cases, in the first millennium B.C. by which time superficially similar but earlier sites had been abandoned and forgotten. In this respect the Middle or Late Bronze Age hoard of gold objects from Towednack, St Ives, is relevant because it had been buried in an already existing field bank.[88] Two bronze hoards found amongst Celtic fields have also been recorded in Wessex: Lulworth, Dorset, and Ebbesbourne Wake, Wilts.[89]

One other point is clear from recent distribution maps of Neolithic and Bronze Age monuments in the south-west. On Dartmoor, for example, there is a general correlation in the distribution of settlements and of round barrows even though the former do not occur as high as the latter.[90] By implication, those much larger areas where barrows also occur but which have not yet been subject to detailed ground survey might also contain or have contained contemporary settlements and might, therefore, have also been cultivated in the second millennium or earlier. The likelihood of such settlements existing is also suggested by the detailed parish-by-parish survey currently being carried out in Cornwall where it is now abundantly clear that previous quantitative knowledge of the number and distribution of settlements and fields as well as other types of monument was badly deficient.[91]

Is there any chance that the characteristic Celtic fields of the chalk downs further east also go back to a 'barrow horizon'? In fact, there is, because just as the linear ditches often bear a chronological relationship to such fields, sometimes post-dating them, so fields and barrows are similarly related. Usually, as Bowen[92] has demonstrated, fields are later than barrows: there are numerous cases of both round and long barrows having been used as the corners of Celtic fields.[93] In a few cases, however, with varying degrees of probability, it appears that round barrows are on top of Celtic fields and, therefore, could well push the beginnings of a regular, rectangular field layout back into or even before the Early Bronze Age.

One of the most convincing of such examples is amongst the Poor Lot barrow cemetery in Winterbourne Abbas, Dorset.[94] There, on the hillside overlooking the focal area of the barrow group, is a triple bell barrow, itself a rarity but one of two such examples in the same group. A south-east/north-west contour lynchet approaches the barrow from the south-east and, though modern cultivation has obscured the actual point of contact, its continuation would join with the ledge or shelf on which the mounds rest. Another lynchet, also following the contours, appears from beneath the westernmost barrow to link with other, typically Celtic field, lynchets to the north (fig. 35). It can hardly be reasonably doubted in this case that the triple barrow is overlying the corner of a Celtic field, belonging to a system of such fields of which fragments survived until recently in the adjacent area. No visible ditch surrounds the mounds and the fact that what was apparently a quarry scoop for them was still visible at the time of the survey might further suggest that the field was abandoned before or at the construction of the barrow. If the ground observation here is correct, then presumably this impressive funerary monument was placed here precisely because the platform provided by the Celtic field corner enabled it to be prominently displayed to those looking up the slope from the valley-floor and the focal barrows below. A similar though slightly different relationship exists between a barrow and a Celtic field on Pentridge Hill in Cranborne Chase, Dorset (fig. 35): there a fine round barrow lies to one side and above the corner of a field defined by a lynchet 2 metres high. It is very difficult to explain the formation of the lynchet if the barrow was already in existence, and it seems probable that the barrow, itself 2.6 metres high on its western side above a north falling slope, was built after the field had already been in use for a considerable time.

In neither of these cases is there direct evidence of the barrows' date but they are likely to belong to the middle of the second millennium and the triple barrow especially would normally be regarded as a special 'Wessex culture' type. The

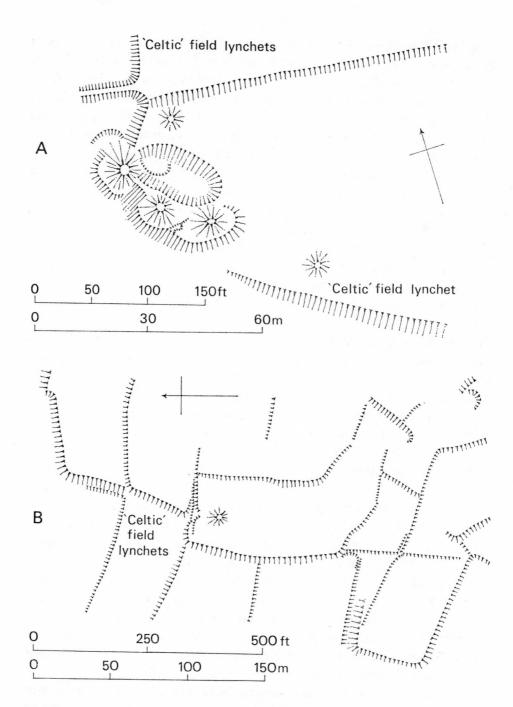

Figure 35. Plans of barrows and Celtic field lynchets, Dorset: (A) Winterbourne Abbas; (B) Pentridge (after R.C.H.M., by permission).

fields must, therefore, be contemporary or earlier. A similar date is also suggested by two examples in the Fyfield Down Nature Reserve, Wiltshire. At the south end of the Down, a bell barrow[95] appears to be inside a Celtic field as is shown by Dr St. Joseph's superb air photograph[96] and supported by ground examination; while on the adjacent Overton Down a disc barrow, or more strictly a bell-disc barrow from which Bronze Age sherds have been recorded,[97] appears fairly convincingly to be cut into pre-existing lynchets. Again a 'Wessex culture' or earlier date for the fields is suggested. In none of these cases is there evidence on the ground of the various features, e.g. a lynchet on the outer edge of the barrow ditch, which in the case of the Grafton barrows led to the demonstration that, despite superficial appearances, the fields were later than the barrows.[98] In view of these examples, caution should presumably be used before assuming that destroyed barrows represented by 'ring ditches' on air photographs in areas containing ancient fields are necessarily earlier than these fields. On Avebury Down, for example, one such 'ring ditch' is clearly inside a Celtic field, and though it is possible that the field overlies it, it is just as likely that the barrow was built on an area which had already been divided up into prehistoric fields and has since been flattened by medieval/modern cultivation.

This evidence for actual fields and therefore, by implication, field systems pre-dating round barrows of the first half of the second millennium B.C. need not really occasion surprise since it was precisely anticipated ten years ago.[99] Further-more, a few sites like the probable Middle Bronze Age settlement enclosure on Ogbourne Maizey Down[100] were constructed on top of well-developed lynchets of a Celtic field system (plate 8); and the existence of cultivated soils underneath both long and round barrows has already been demonstrated in several excava-tions. The new point here is that regular field systems of the Celtic field type them-selves actually pre-date the barrows. By implication, this might well be a wide-spread phenomenon since it would now seem reasonable to think that the known instances where a cultivated soil has occurred under a barrow possibly indicate the former existence of proper field systems and not just sporadic and unorganized cultivation. The same may be true of course where such a soil has been noted under Neolithic earthworks, e.g. at Windmill Hill, Wilts.[101]

Since the idea of regular systems of rectangular fields can now be demonstrated with some confidence to have existed, at least in southern Britain, in the first half of the second millennium B.C. at latest, it is relevant to consider briefly how such systems were laid out. For several good reasons, fieldwork and excavation have tended to concentrate on the individual field – its shape, size, lynchet height and so on – rather than on an overall view of the whole system and its structure.

Partly as a result of this, we tend to have a 'cellular' view of the field systems in which, rather like a honeycomb, field is added to field to build up the network of little rectangles in a piecemeal development. Yet, despite the paucity of good published plans of complete field systems in Britain, there is evidence here and, more cogently, in Europe that in practice the opposite happened, i.e. that large areas were cleared, perhaps in swathes, and were then subdivided into small rectangular plots to create the characteristic Celtic field landscape familiar from so many air photographs. This view of the field pattern was suggested long ago by Curwen[102] and it is timely to revive it (fig. 36). A glance through the published field system plans from western Europe easily detects in many of them evidence, in the form of long, often straight, parallel and continuous field boundaries, of large continuous land blocks forming the basic, original skeleton within which the detail of the individual fields has been infilled (fig. 37). Although such an interpretation of field system patterns involves something of a change in our attitude to them, again it need come as no surprise: the evidence has been there all the time. Hawkes,[103] Bowen[104] and others have already pointed out in relation to Wessex that "the tradition of dividing land into large blocks goes back at least to the Bronze Age"; to the middle of the second millennium one could now add without exaggeration. Similar claims have recently been advanced, less confidently but convincingly, for Dartmoor.[105] Hawkes [106] stressed the importance of the Wessex 'ranch boundaries' as the earliest evidence in Europe for land division, perhaps for practical reasons (arable/pasture as already mentioned above, p. 169), perhaps to divide properties. In the present context they are also significant in showing the contemporary farmers' ability, conceptually and technically, to think and act 'big' in landscape terms, surely by communal effort rather than by individual enterprise. And if this is a correct view of the pastoral/property background, then the creation of an arable field pattern by working from the whole area to (or in?) major blocks, subsequently split up into workable units, provides the ploughman's counterpart. The rather disturbing thought about this model is that it is very like the old-fashioned explanation of the origins of the medieval 'open' field system, particularly as viewed by the Germanic school! Nevertheless, the re-interpretation of some prehistoric field patterns suggested here clearly has far-reaching social implications, and if their development did involve large-scale, well-organized communal effort we may be glimpsing here the ordinary, seasonal perhaps rather than day-to-day, agrarian background which provided the framework within which the larger and superficially more impressive Neolithic and Bronze Age monuments were conceived and executed. It makes more sense than seeing the temples and tombs as exceptional monuments appearing in a social vacuum, and it is a view by no means vitiated by all the evidence for the existence of the single farmstead as the smallest social unit.

Finally, two approaches to agrarian prehistory which are capable of further development can be mentioned as likely to lead to a deeper and more accurate understanding of what farming 5,000 years ago involved. In the first place, a great deal more can be learnt from experiment.[107] The corpus of experimental knowledge is now building up after trials in ploughing, growing and storing crops,[108] using tools, and in reconstructing buildings.[109] On the last, extremely interesting results have been obtained in Denmark and there too a research establishment is enquiring further into the practical sides of prehistoric farming.[110] So far British work has been largely based on ideas about pre-Roman Iron Age agriculture but, as has already been shown, this has a direct bearing on what went before so it is by no means irrelevant here. On the ploughing side, the most interesting results so far have been connected with the acquisition of empirical knowledge about the harnessing of draught animals to an ard, about what an ard can and cannot do, and about the amount and type of wear which occurs on a share during cultivation. In addition, the reproduction of ard-marks and their subsequent excavation and examination has thrown valuable light on both their formation, and, in detail, on the sort of evidence to look for when such phenomena are being excavated from an ancient context. Of particular value has been the demonstration that a very efficient way of preparing a seed bed with an ard is to plough several times along the same groove drawn out at about 30 cm or slightly more from its neighbours. This seems to have a pulverizing effect beneath the surface of the field, and enables most of the area of the 'field' to be broken up relatively easily when the gaps between the deep grooves are then ploughed at a shallower depth and furrows at right angles are subsequently drawn across the field. There seems little reason to doubt that this explains the superficially odd but consistent spacing of ard marks which has been noted now from so many sites.[111] The work on the shares themselves has demonstrated the peculiarities of wear which again indicate the sort of evidence to look for from surviving ancient exemples. In particular, it is quite clear that in gravel or other stony soils the share could wear down very quickly indeed. It would be possible, therefore, for a share to be much later in date than the actual framework of a plough to which it was attached.

Another profitable line of experiment, this time in southern Britain, has been in the storage of grain in pits. Again, despite the Iron Age prototype, this is relevant to the Neolithic at least in view of the widespread occurrence of pits in Neolithic contexts.[112] Experiments both in Wiltshire and in the Cotswolds have clearly demonstrated the feasibility of storing grain underground and, perhaps just as significantly, have justified the validity of the empirical approach to ancient agriculture. It is now proposed to try and combine the smaller experiments together into a single project involving the actual running of an ancient farm, not just as a static reconstruction but as a working model.[113] Such an experiment should produce as in no other way a fund of practical knowledge gained from experience of the problems and efficacy of farming itself; and it should also produce some explanations of the phenomena such as lynchet formation which form the archaeological evidence on which our theoretical knowledge is so very largely based. Such information, rather than theoretical models, can fairly be compared with information from ethnographic sources. For example, around much of the Mediterranean even today ard agriculture is still being practised, and it is with this sort of evidence that we should compare our experimental results rather than use the surviving primitive data to explain our archaeological observations.

Another and completely different development can also increase our understanding of early agrarian societies. As archaeologists we should be learning from and using some of the techniques for landscape and settlement analysis currently being practised in geographical circles.[114] Attempts have been made in Wiltshire and Cornwall using only archaeological material to analyse settlement types and patterns[115] but one immediate difficulty is that there are relatively few areas

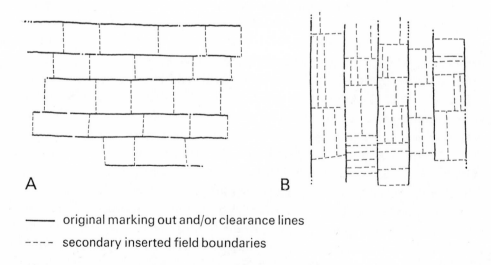

A   B

——— original marking out and/or clearance lines

- - - - secondary inserted field boundaries

Figure 36. Theoretical method of Celtic field system layout.

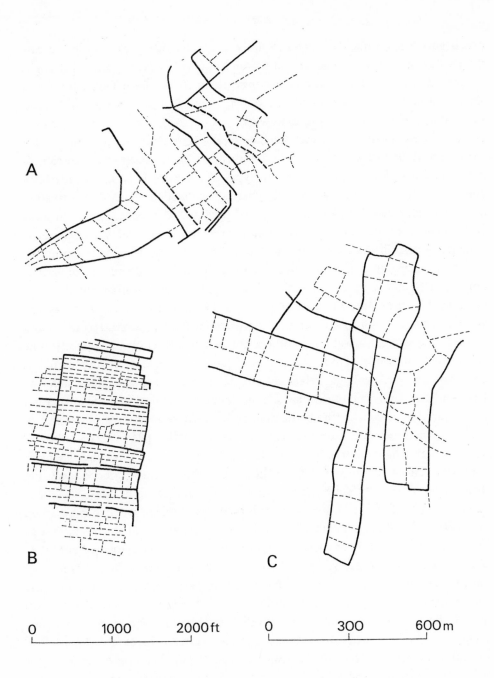

Figure 37. Elementary analysis of Celtic field systems to show block layout. (A) Valley of Stones, Dorset; (B) Byrsted Hede, Denmark; (C) Windmill Hill, Crawley, Hants.

which have been sufficiently well-explored archaeologically to supply the raw
material in an adequate, reliable and usable form. Other areas where this might
be done are, for example, in the Federsee basin in southern Germany where
about 100 prehistoric settlements are known[116] and in the two parts of Jutland
where much of Mathiassen's detailed work[117] has provided a great mass of information, the implications of which have not really been fully worked out. In this
last case a whole series of maps and tables provide data, whatever its deficiences
now, which could be subject to various types of analysis. This has already been
done in Sweden in the Stockholm area, where again detailed survey and excavation
has produced settlement patterns for several periods and already pointed to some
of the deductions that can be drawn from them.[118] But the sort of work that can be
done using established techniques, including computer analysis, is not simply a
matter of putting on to maps a series of dots representing distributions of various
types of monument in the several chronological periods. Rather should it be
possible, for example, to interpret this data in the light of productivity measured
against the relationship between settlements, their fields, natural resources and
markets: the straightforward type of analysis demonstrated by Chisholm.[119] The
classic model for this sort of approach was of course provided by von Thunen, but
even his 'analysis', though relatively simple, is more sophisticated than the
Highland/Lowland type of division familiar in archaeological literature. It is not
just a question of considering settlement/arable field relationships but rather of
taking into account all the environmental factors in relation to a living community,
e.g. water, grazing land, building material, fuels and so on. In this comprehensive
context, some of the apparent anomalies, e.g. an apparently unnecessarily big
distance between a settlement and its arable, can become explicable.

The irony of all this of course is that it is precisely at this moment in time, when
our means of analysis demand so much more precise and definable data, that so
much of that data has been or is being destroyed. Even well-preserved sites now
tend to exist in a cultural vacuum divorced from their contemporary landscape
and, for much of western Europe, it is extraordinarily difficult to produce the
information about the incidence of settlements, their relationships to one another,
and all the other factors which made up their total natural and cultural environment. Nevertheless, while of course it is a step forward to be able to produce
pictograms like that for some features of the 'Little Woodbury' economy[120]
for the essential parts of any given past economy,[121] instead of or as well as the
implement typologies and cartographic conventions of earlier work, we must
recognize even new archaeo-economic models for what they are and not blind
ourselves into thinking that they represent anything more or less than our

imposition of imperfect comprehension on to incomplete evidence. It is at least one advantage of the experimental approach that it leads to re-creation rather than destruction of this evidence and sometimes even to practical use in modern agricultural terms.[122]

Notes

1. cf. H. T. Waterbolk, *Science*, CLXII (1968), 1093–1101.
2. cf. P. J. Ucko and G. W. Dimbleby (eds), *The Domestication and Exploitation of Plants and Animals* (1969), p. 557.
3. J. G. D. Clark, *Prehistoric Europe* (1952), chaps IV and V.
4. e.g. P. V. Glob, *Ard og Plov i Nordens Oltid* (1951); A. G. Haudricourt and M. J. Delamarre, *L'Homme et La Charrue à travers le Monde* (1955); E. C. Curwen and G. Hatt, *Plough & Pasture* (1953); *Gwerin*, I no. 1 (1957), 171–81; *P.S.A.S.*, XCVI (1963), 264–317; *Transactions of the Dumfries and Galloway Natural History and Antiquarian Society*, XLV (1968), 147–83, for ploughs. H. C. Bowen, *Ancient Fields* (1961); M. Müller-Wille, *Eisenzeitliche Fluren in den festländischen Nordseegebieten* (1965), for fields. *P.P.S.*, XVIII (1952), 194–233, for crops.
5. e.g. S. Piggott, *Ancient Europe* (1965). V. H. Jankuhn, *Vor- und Frühgeschichte von Neolithicum bis zur Völkerwanderungszeit* (1969).
6. e.g. *Antiquity*, XLIII (1969), 176–86, 31–41; Ucko and Dimbleby, *op. cit.*; *Antiquity*, XLIV (1970), 105–14, 38–45.
7. *P.P.S.*, XVIII (1952), 194–233.
8. A. Gailey and A. Fenton (eds), *The Spade in Atlantic and Northern Europe* (1970).
9. S. A. Semenov, *Prehistoric Technology* (1964); A. Steensberg, *Ancient Harvesting Implements* (1943); W. F. Grimes (ed.), *Aspects of Archaeology* (1951), pp. 39–48.
10. *Antiquity*, II (1937), 133–51; XV (1941), 15–32.
11. *P.P.S.*, XXXIII (1967), 84–106; e.g. *Naturwissenschaftliche Beiträge in Veröffentlichungen des Stadtlichen Amtes für Denkmalpflege Stuttgart, Reiche A, Vor- und Frühgeschichte Heft 10/11* (1968).
12. e.g. Grimes, *op. cit.*, pp. 49–65; E. E. Evans, *Irish Folk Ways* (1957).
13. Ucko and Dimbleby, *op. cit.*
14. A good, up-to-date example is in *Prehistorie en Vroegste geschiedenis van ons land* (Leiden, Rijksmuseum, 1969), 81; more familiar is S. Piggott, *Neolithic Cultures of the British Isles* (1954), fig. 64; or with C-14 dates, P. J. Fowler, *Wessex* (1967), fig. 2.
15. e.g. Clark, *op. cit.*, table B.
16. e.g. *P.P.S.*, XXXI (1965), 123, fig. 8.
17. e.g. V. G. Childe, *The Dawn of European Civilisation* (1950), maps I–IV; S. Piggott, *Ancient Europe*, p. 57, fig. 26; p. 59, fig. 28.
18. e.g. splendidly S. Piggott, *ibid.*, p. 146, fig. 79.
19. e.g. *P.P.S.*, XXXI (1965), 65, fig. 2.
20. Ucko and Dimbleby, *op. cit.*

21. Waterbolk, *op. cit.*

22. Clark, *op. cit.*, p. 10, fig. 2.

23. e.g. M. Chisholm, *Rural Settlement & Land Use* (1969), fig. 7; *Geographical Magazine*, XLII no. 5 (1970), 360–1.

24. E. Anati, *Camonica Valley* (1964).

25. *ibid.*, p. 117.

26. *ibid.*, pp. 106–7.

27. Müller-Wille, *op. cit.;* P. Gelling and H. E. Davidson, *The Chariot of the Sun* (1969).

28. A. Hagen, *Rock Carvings in Norway* (1965).

29. P. V. Glob, *Helleristninger i Danmark* (1969).

30. P. V. Glob, *Ard og Plov i Nordens Oldtid* (1951), figs. 61–3; Gelling and Davidson, *op. cit.*, fig. 35C.

31. The other at Finntorp is now difficult to see though Glob, *ibid.*, fig. 60, shows it clearly in its context.

32. Evans, *op. cit.*, pp. 3, 131.

33. Gelling and Davidson, *op. cit.*, p. 79, fig. 35d; *Agricultural History Review*, VII (1959), 27–37.

34. Glob, *op. cit.*, pp. 68–9.

35. Müller-Wille, *op. cit.*

36. *Tools & Tillage*, I (1968), 56–8.

37. Glob, *op. cit.*, pp. 28–9.

38. Waterbolk, *op. cit.*

39. Semenov, *op. cit.*

40. Glob, *op. cit.*, pp. 82–8.

41. Gailey and Fenton, *op. cit.*, pp. 10–17.

42. *Tools & Tillage*, I (1968), 3–27.

43. cf. *P.P.S.*, XXXV (1969), 203–19; *Advancement of Science* (1965), 88–97. The plentiful literature on ard-marks is discussed with many references to the individual examples in Glob, *op. cit.*; *Bericht der Römisch-Germanischen Kommission*, XXXVII (1957), 148–214; *Procs. W. Cornwall Field Club*, II (1961), 200–15; Müller-Wille, *op. cit.* For the British evidence, see *Antiquity*, XLI (1967), 289–301.

44. Müller-Wille, *op. cit.*, nos. 50–3.

45. *ibid.*, no. 49.

46. *Kuml*, (1964), 7–14.

47. *ibid.*

48. Müller-Wille, *op. cit.*, nos. 9 and 16.

49. *ibid.*, no. 30.

50. *ibid.*, p. 114.

51. *Antiquity*, XLI (1967), 293.

52. *Antiquity*, XLI (1967), 289; XLII (1968), 138–42; XLIII (1969), 144–5

53. Müller-Wille, *op. cit.*, no. 76.

54. *Antiquity*, XLI (1967), 289–301.

55. *Procs. W. Cornwall Field Club*, II (1961), 200–15.

56. Gailey and Fenton, *op. cit.*, pp. 10–17.

57. *ibid.*

58. *Antiquity*, XLI (1967), 289–301.

59. *W.A.M.*, LXII (1967), 16–33.

60. *Kuml*, (1964), 7–14.

61. *Antiquity*, XLI (1967), 292.
62. e.g. *Advancement of Science*, LXIII (1965), 88–97.
63. e.g. Clark, *op. cit.*, fig. 46; C. Thomas (ed.), *Rural Settlement in Roman Britain* (1966), p. 62.
64. *P.P.S.*, XXIII (1957), 167–212.
65. *ibid.*, XXVIII (1962), 289–328.
66. Müller-Wille, *op. cit.*; Jankuhn, *op. cit.*
67. *P.S.A.S.*, LXXXIX (1956), 340–97.
68. *Stavanger Museums Årbok* (1966), 53–96.
69. *Report VI International Congress on the Quaternary*, II (1964), 461–71; *Journal of the Royal Society of Antiquaries of Ireland*, XCIX (1969), 165–8; *Antiquity*, XLV (1971), 97–102.
70. H. C. Bowen, *Advancement of Science*, LVI (1958), 369–71.
71. *Journal of the Kerry Archaeological and Historical Society*, III (1970), 5–14.
72. *Journal of the Royal Society of Antiquaries of Ireland*, XCIX (1969), 39–53.
73. E. R. Norman and J. K. St Joseph, *The Early Development of Irish Society – The Evidence of Aerial Photography* (1969).
74. *S.A.C.*, XCIX (1961), 78–101.
75. *Berichten van de Rijkdienst voor het Oudheidkundig Bodemonderzoet*, XVIII (1968), 117–29.
76. *Procs Hants. Field Club*, XIV (1939), 136–94.
77. H. C. Bowen, *Ancient Fields* (1961), fig. 34.
78. O. G. S. Crawford, *Air Survey & Archaeology* (1924); P. J. Fowler, *Wessex* (1967).
79. *Current Archaeology*, no. 16 (1969), 124–9, Map A.
80. O. G. S. Crawford and A. Keiller, *Wessex from the Air* (1928), pl. xxv.
81. e.g. *Geografiska Annaler*, XLIII (1961); summarized in Müller-Wille, *op. cit.*, figs 16–17.
82. *Archaeological Review*, IV (1970), 3–13, gives a good general survey.
83. *Procs W. Cornwall Field Club*, II (1961), 200–15; Gailey and Fenton, *op. cit.*, pp. 10–17.
84. *P.P.S.*, XXXV (1969), 220–8.
85. *ibid.*, XX (1954), 87–102.
86. *Cornish Archaeology*, IX (1970), 17–46.
87. *Procs W. Cornwall Field Club*, II (1961), 209–10.
88. *Man*, XXXII (1932), 177–86.
89. Bowen, *op. cit.*, p. 18.
90. *Exeter and its Region* (British Association, 1969), figs 21–2; cf. also *P.P.S.*, XXXV (1969), 203–19.
91. *Archaeological Review*, IV (1970), 3–13.
92. Bowen, *op. cit.*, p. 29.
93. Royal Commission on Historical Monuments (England), *Dorset* II (1970), pt 3.
94. *ibid.*, pp. 461–3.
95. *Victoria County History of Wiltshire*, I Pt 1 (1957), Fyfield 1.
96. Bowen, *op. cit.*, pl.v.
97. *Victoria County History of Wiltshire*, I Pt 1, West Overton 9.
98. Bowen, *op. cit.*, fig. 2e.
99. *ibid.*, p. 30.
100. *P.P.S.*, VIII (1942), fig. 3; and author's air photographs.
101. I. F. Smith, *Windmill Hill & Avebury: Excavations by Alexander Keiller, 1925–1993* (1965), pp. 35–40.
102. E. C. Curwen, *Air Photography & the Evolution of the Corn Field* (1938), p. 26.
103. *Procs Hants. Field Club*, XIV (1939), 136–94.

104. A. L. F. Rivet (ed.), *The Roman Villa in Britain* (1969), p. 26.
105. *Transactions of the Devonshire Association*, C (1968), 277–91.
106. *Procs Hants. Field Club*, XIV (1939), 136–94.
107. *American Anthropologist*, LXIII (1961), 793–816; *P.S.A.S.*, XCIX (1967), 1–20.
108. *Bulletin of the Institute of Archaeology, University of London*, VII (1968), 1–14.
109. *Trans. Bristol & Glos. Arch. Soc.*, LXXXVI (1967), 60–73; LXXXVIII (1969), 29–33.
110. H. O. Hansen, *Reports from Experiments in Lejre 1968*, I (1969); *Tools & Tillage*, I (1969), 67–92.
111. *Antiquity*, XLI (1967), 289–301.
112. *P.P.S.*, XXX (1964), 352–81.
113. *Prehistoric Farm at Butser Hill* (1970).
114. R. J. Chorley and P. Haggett, *Models in Geography* (1967); *Tydschrift voor sociale en economische geografie*, LI (1960), 317–26; P. Haggett, *Locational Analysis in Human Geography* (1965).
115. *W.A.M.*, LXIII (1968), 27–38; *Cornish Archaeology*, VII (1968), 5–14.
116. R. R. Schmidt, *Jungsteinzeitsiedlungen im Federseemoor* (1930–7); W. Zimmermann (ed.), *Der Federsee. Die Natur- und Landschaftsschutzgebiete Baden-Württembergs*, II (1961).
117. T. Mathiassen, *Studier over Vestjyllands Oltidsbebyggelse* (1948); *Nordvestjaellands Oltidsbebyggelse* (1959).
118. B. Ambrosiani, *Fornlamnagar och Bebyggelse* (1964).
119. Chisholm, *op. cit.*
120. Rivet, (ed.), *op. cit.*, fig. 1.3.
121. C. Gabel, *Analysis of Prehistoric Economic Patterns* (Studies in Anthropological Method) (1969).
122. L. Shanan *et al.*, 'Ancient Technology and Modern Science applied to Desert Agriculture', *Endeavour*, XXVIII (1969), 68–72.

Index of sites

Page numbers of illustrations are given in italics.

Abingdon, causewayed enclosure, 89–105 *passim*, 106

Aclam Wold, 211, Neolithic pit, 119, 126

Aldro 30, Neolithic pit, 119

Allt Volagir, birch forests at, 59

Amesbury G.70, ard marks, 162

Anlo, kraal, 151

Aptrup, ard marks, 165

Ardnamurchan, Beaker settlement, 131

Arminghall, timber circles, 124

Arreton Down
  Beaker settlement, 132
  round barrow, 64, 68

Ascott-under-Wychwood, 18, 43, 46, 48, 49
  chambered tomb, 62, 65
  land-snail diagram, *32–3*
  plan of subsoil hollow, *36*
  sections of subsoil hollow, *37*
  soil profile, *30*, 31ff.

Aspeberget, rock engravings, 157

Astrop, Neolithic pits, 119

Avebury, henge, 62, 65

Ballermosen, ard marks, 162

Ballynagilly, settlement site, 23, 131

Barford, Neolithic settlement, 124

Barkhale, causewayed enclosure, 89–105 *passim*, 108

Beacon Hill
  Beaker house, *134*, 136
  causewayed ditch, 90

Beaulieu, mortuary houses, 141, *144*

Beckhampton Road, long barrow, 62, 66

Belle Tout, *137*, 140

'Benie Hoose', Neolithic house, 141, *142*, 143

Blashenwell, tufa deposit, 14

Bohuslan, rock engravings, 157

Borup, medieval house, 128

Brno-Obrany, Beaker house, 148

Brook, forest clearance, 23, 27, 63

Brouster, Neolithic settlement, 167

Burnt Common, ring cairn, 136

Byrsted Hede, field system, *176*

Cam, Neolithic pits, 119

Cardington, crop marks, 91

Cassington, Neolithic pits, 119

Cherhill, tufa deposit, *14*

Chippenham, Beaker settlement, 132

Clacton, Neolithic pits, 119

Clegyr Boia, Neolithic house, 147

Cock Hill, Bronze Age settlement, 169

Combe Hill
  causewayed enclosure, 89–105 *passim*, 108
  grain rubber, 126

Cotswold-Severn tombs, siting, 19, 22

Craike Hill, Neolithic settlement, 120
Creeting St Mary, Neolithic settlement, 120
Crickley Hill, causewayed enclosure, 107

Dartmoor, Mesolithic forest clearance, 17
Deer Park, field system, 168
Dorchester Big Rings, henge, 143
Downpatrick, Beaker house, 132, *134*, 135, 143, 154, 146
Driffield West Reservoir, Neolithic settlement, 120
Durrington Walls
    henge, 62, 67, 126
    hillwash, 23
    occupation debris, 143

Earl's Farm Down
    round barrow, 64, 68
    stake circle, 141
Easton Down
    Beaker pits, 135, *139*
    Beaker settlement, 124, 132
Eaton Socon, Neolithic settlement, 120
Ebbesbourne Wake, Bronze Age hoard, 170
Ebbsfleet, occupation sites, 12
Eilean an Tighe, Neolithic settlement, 115
Enbourne Gate
    grain rubber, 126
    Neolithic pit, 118
Ertebølle, Beaker house, 148

Fengate, Neolithic settlement, *127*
Foales' Arrishes, field system, 170
Frogholt, pollen, 63
Fussells Lodge, Neolithic pit, 119
Fyfield Down, field system, 169, 173

Glencrutchery, Neolithic settlement, 115
Glenluce, Beaker settlement, 131
Goldberg, Neolithic houses, 143, 148, *149*
Goodland, field system, 168
Gop Cave, Neolithic settlement, 126

Gorsey Bigbury, occupation debris, 143
Gower, Tooth Cave, 131
Grandtully, Neolithic pits, 119, 122
Grantham, Neolithic pit, 118, 122
Gullane, Beaker settlement, 131
Gwithian
    ard marks, 160, 163, 164, 165, 170
    Beaker house, 132, *134*, 138, 143, 145, 146

Haldon, Neolithic house, 146
Hambledon Hill, causewayed enclosure, 89–105 *passim*, 107
Harris, beehive hut, *146*
Heath Row, Neolithic pits, 120
Hedderwick, Beaker settlement, 131
Hembury
    causewayed enclosure, 89–105 *passim*, *93*, 106
    ditch sections, *99*
High Peak, causewayed enclosure, 89–105 *passim*, 107
Holdenhurst, long barrow, 123
Honington, Neolithic settlement, 120, *121*
Horridge, field system, 170
Horslip, long barrow, 63, 66
Hvorslev, ard, 158, 160

Itford Hill, Bronze Age settlement, 169
Iver, Neolithic pits, 118

Jensteju, Beaker house, 148
Julliberrie's Grave, long barrow, 64, 67

Kilham, long barrow, 63, 64, 68
Kilmartin Valley, Beaker from, 132
Knap Hill, causewayed enclosure, 62, 64, 67, 89–105 *passim*, 109
Knowth, chambered tomb, 123

Le Lizio, Beaker houses, 147, 151
Leichenfeldt, round barrow, 162
Letonice, Beaker house, 148

Lough Gur, houses, 122, 132, *134*, 135, 143, 146
Lovosice, Beaker house, 148
Lulworth, Bronze Age hoard, 170
Lundehøj, ard marks, 162
Lyles Hill, sod house, 123
Lyonesse surface, 12

Maiden Bower, causewayed enclosure, 89–105 *passim*, 106
Maiden Castle, causewayed enclosure, 89–105 *passim*, 107
Marden, henge, 64, 67
Martin Down, field system, 169
Millin Bay, field walls, 168
Molenaarsgraaf, Beaker houses, 148
Mount Pleasant, Neolithic house, 113, *116*, 122
Mulheim, Beaker houses, 148
Mye Plantation, pit-fall traps, 127

Ness of Gruting, Neolithic house, *117*, 118
New Grange, chambered tomb, 123
Nijnsel, Bronze Age settlement, 169
Northton
    Beaker house, *137*, 138, 143, 145, 146
    settlement, 13, 22, 52ff., 65, 115, 132
    land-snail diagram, *54–5*
    shell-fish assemblage, *60–1*
Nutbane, long barrow, 15

Oakhanger, forest recession, 17
Ogbourne Maizey Down, field system, 173
Oltingen, Beaker houses, 148, *150*
Ostenfelde, ard marks, 162
Overton Down, ard marks, 165
Overton Down 6a, Neolithic pit, 118

Peacock's Farm, Buttery Clay, 12
Penha Verde, Beaker houses, 147, *150*
Pentridge Hill, field system, 171, *172*
Pitnacree, round barrow, 19

Pitstone Hill, flint mines, 90
Playden, Neolithic settlement, *121*, 123
Poor Lot, field system, 171
Puddlehill, Neolithic pits, 119, 120

Reffley Wood, Beaker settlement, 132
Rinyo
    Neolithic houses, 115, 140, *142*, 143, 145, 146
    ovens, 120
Risby Warren
    Beaker settlement, 131
    Neolithic pits, 119
River Lark, crop marks, 91
Robin Hood's Ball, causewayed enclosure, 89–105 *passim*, 109
Ronaldsway, Neolithic house, 113, *116*, 122
Rybury, causewayed enclosure, 89–105 *passim*, 109

St Kilda, pollen, 60
Scotstarvit, Neolithic pits, 119, 120
Seamer Moor, round barrow, 123
Selmeston, Neolithic settlement, 120
Selsey Bill, Neolithic settlement, 118, 122
Shearplace Hill, Bronze Age settlement 166
Sheepland, Beaker settlement, 131
Shetland
    Neolithic fields, 167
    Neolithic houses, 118
Shippea Hill, Neolithic settlement, 120
Silbury Hill
    turf stack, 63
    Neolithic mound, 66
Skara Brae, Neolithic houses, 115, *117*, 140, 143, 145, 146
Skendleby, long barrow, 132
Somerset Levels, trackways, 16
Sonning, Neolithic settlement, 124, *127*
South Borup, ard marks, 162
South Street
    land-snail diagram, *44–5*

South Street—*Contd.*
  long barrow, 40ff., 65, 123
  plough marks, *47*, 162, 163
  soil profile, *42*
South Sweden, rock engraving, *156*
Staines, causewayed enclosure, 89–105
  passim, 108
Stannon Down, field system, 170
Stanton Harcourt, Neolithic pits, 119
Stanydale Temple, 118
Stonehenge, Y-holes, 15
Streatley, Neolithic settlement, 123, 125
Strelice, Beaker house, 148
Sutton Courtenay, Neolithic pits, 119
Swanwick, shaft, 100
Swarkeston, Beaker house, 136, *139*, 143,
  147

Tegneby, rock engraving, 158
Tesetice, Beaker house, 148
Thames valley, crop marks, 90
The Sanctuary, timber circles, 141
The Trundle, causewayed enclosure, 89–
  105 *passim*, 108
Thickthorn Down, long barrow, 64, 68,
  123
Towednack, Bronze Age hoard, 170

Val Camonica, rock engravings, *156*, 157
Valley of Stones, field system, *176*

Vila Nova de San Pedro, Beaker houses,
  147

Walker, ard marks, 165
Walney Island, Beaker settlement, 131
Waulud's Bank, Neolithic house, *144*, 147
Wayland's Smithy, long barrow, 63
Wayland's Smithy II, chambered tomb,
  65
Welland valley, crop marks, 91
West Kennet, chambered tomb, 64, 65
Whitehawk, causewayed enclosure, 89–
  105 *passim*, 109
Whitesheet Hill, causewayed enclosure,
  89–105 *passim*, 110
Willerby Wold, long barrow, 64, 68
Willington, Beaker settlement, 140
Wilsford, shaft, 100
Windmill Hill, Hants., field system, *176*
Windmill Hill, Wilts., causewayed en-
  closure, 62, 64, 66, 89–105 *passim*, 110
Windypits, Beakers from, 132
Wingham, pollen analysis, 27, 63
Winterbourne Abbas, field system, *172*
Winterbourne Dauntsey, Neolithic pits,
  118, 119, 122, 124
Woodhead, Beaker house, 132, 136, *137*,
  143
Woodhenge, occupation debris, 143
Wykeham, Neolithic pits, 119